SCANDAL NATION

Michael Clifford is a journalist with the *Sunday Tribune*, where he writes a weekly column. He regularly contributes to a variety of programmes on Irish radio and TV. He is author of *Love You to Death: Ireland's Wife Killers Revealed* and co-author of *Bertie Ahern and the Drumcondra Mafia*.

Shane Coleman is the Political Editor of the *Sunday Tribune* and is a regular analyst of Irish politics on television and radio. He is the best-selling author of *Foot in Mouth: Famous Irish Political Gaffes, Up the Poll: Great Irish Election Stories* and co-author of *Bertie Ahern and the Drumcondra Mafia*.

SCANDAL NATION

Key Events that Shook and Shaped Us

Michael Clifford &
Shane Coleman

HACHETTE
BOOKS
IRELAND

First published in 2010 by Hachette Books Ireland

1

ISBN 978 14447 1260 5

Typeset in Sabon by Hachette Books Ireland
Printed and Bound in Great Britain by CPI Mackays, Chatham

Hachette Books Ireland policy is to use papers that are natural, renewable and
recyclable products and made from wood grown in sustainable forests. The
logging and manufacturing processes are expected to conform to the
environmental regulations of the country of origin.

Hachette Books Ireland
8 Castlecourt Centre
Castleknock
Dublin 15, Ireland
A division of Hachette UK Ltd
338 Euston Road, London NW1 3BH

www.hachette.ie

Contents

For our families

INTRODUCTION

We are where we are. It has become one of the great truisms of the economic and financial crisis that Ireland finds itself in – a catch-all shorthand for the mistakes by government, banks, regulators and property developers that landed everyone in difficulty.

There have been some efforts to explain why 'we are where we are'. There have been two banking reports examining the mistakes made by policy makers and the financial institutions. There have also been reams of analysis and opinion offered in the Dáil and through the media and a host of other fora.

But they all relate to 21st-century events. And the reality is that the seeds of the current crisis were sown over the decades that went before. It is often said that those who ignore history are condemned to repeat its mistakes. The Irish as a nation can hardly be accused of ignoring history, but are certainly guilty of disregarding its lessons.

Viewed through the lens of history, there is nothing spectacularly new about the latest crisis. Aspects of it are certainly original. Ireland has never seen its banks virtually collapse before and the property bubble was unprecedented. But a glance back at the 90 years since the foundation of the Republic confirms that there is nothing surprising about recent events. It was one giant accident waiting to happen. All roads led to this point.

Think about it. What really lies at the root of the economic and banking collapse? Greed. Poor political leadership. A lack of proper regulation and respect for the spirit, as well as the rule, of the law. Jobbery. An overly close relationship between politics and big business. An inability to hold powerful institutions to account. These are not new features in Irish society.

As we attempt to demonstrate in this book, there are copious examples over the past nine decades of such mistakes being made. An even worse indictment is that the Irish state – its legislators and institutions – failed to learn the lessons from those mistakes.

Excessive greed is nothing new. The planning system was manipulated and twisted so a small number could profit hugely. These individuals barely gave a second thought to the citizens whose lives would be adversely affected by their actions in the short term, and the whole concept of good planning over the longer term.

Political leadership has not been entirely non-existent over the lifetime of the Irish state. But for a variety of reasons – not least an electoral system where literally a handful of votes can dictate the make-up of a government – following rather than leading has been the modus operandi of successive governments.

The Irish could never be accused of being overly law abiding and there is certainly nothing new about a lack of proper regulation and of respect for the law. Over six decades, Ireland funded its health system from a sweepstake operated illegally in most of the countries in which tickets were sold and yet a blind eye was turned because it was expedient to do so.

Until the establishment in the 1990s of a tribunal of inquiry, efforts to uncover the obvious corruption in the planning system were almost laughable. And in the 1970s, some of the very people charged with the responsibility of enforcing the law were taking that law into their own hands.

Jobbery has always been rife in Ireland. Stuffing hundreds of state boards with party hacks was simply seen as the fruits of general election victory, a harmless bit of political one-upmanship. The Irish people know differently now. They should have known differently before.

The advent of social partnership in more recent decades extended the system of party patronage to share out influential and highly important positions among employer groups and trade unions. In other cases, tradition, rather than merit, became the key determinant for filling positions. When the Central Bank needed a new governor, it did not trawl the world for the best candidate, it simply gave the job to the secretary general of the Department of Finance.

The overly close relationship between politics and big business goes back to the days of Taca and indeed long before that. The dangers of such a relationship were regularly pointed out, but nothing was done about it until serious damage had been inflicted on the state. An alternative system, where the taxpayers would fund democracy, was seen as politically unpalatable.

The Irish state has proved itself incapable of holding powerful institutions to account. For many decades after independence there was virtually a parallel government, with offices in Maynooth, Drumcondra and Armagh. The Catholic Church was allowed to reign supreme in the areas of education, health and morality with, as is now apparent, disastrous consequences.

9

It is not the contention of this book that Ireland is some form of banana republic. Glance around and it is clear that Ireland is one of the more benign liberal democracies on the planet. Although some terrible things have happened in and to the Irish state, sadly examples of man's inhumanity to man are apparent in virtually every country and Ireland has experienced nothing close to that of the totalitarian regimes in mainland Europe, Asia, Central America and Africa.

What we do contend is that the roots of the current crisis in Ireland are multi-layered and complex and go back decades, even to the foundation of the state (and arguably further). It is also our view that there is nothing surprising or unexpected about what has happened.

Ireland is, after all, a country that was willing to sell its passports – the ultimate symbol of sovereignty – to the highest bidders; that continuously elected as its political leader a man about whom there were numerous ethical question marks; that ignored the common good in its planning process; that had a policy of jobs for the boys; that was willing to succumb to a virtual theocracy; that put economic and budgetary benefit before the rule of law and regulation; and that has, at times, shown blatant disregard for the health and safety of its citizens.

How did we get to where we are? We hope the next 12 chapters will, if not entirely answer that question, at least provide some insight and broaden the debate.

1

DEV'S FAILURE TO TALK THE TALK

Michael Collins had little idea of what was about to unfold. It was 20 August 1921 and he was meeting with Eamon de Valera. Relations between the two men were at that stage mixed. Both had proved they could lead, but there could be only one leader. Although de Valera was the nominal boss, a position that was soon to be ratified by the Dáil with his appointment as President of the Republic, and Collins was Finance Minister, many regarded Collins as 'the man who won the war'.

A rivalry between the two men had developed over the preceding months. De Valera had been in the United States for most of Ireland's War of Independence, which raged from January 1919 to July 1921. When he left Ireland he was the undisputed leader of the broad nationalist movement. In his absence, it had been Collins, as Director of Intelligence for the IRA, who prosecuted the war. While Dev had grappled with the machinations of Irish-American politics, Collins had stayed one bicycle ride ahead of death. It was no longer clear who the real leader was.

Following the truce in July 1921, Dev travelled to London to open negotiations with the British Prime Minister, David Lloyd

George, on the future of Ireland. The negotiations were inconclusive. Correspondence between the two men ensued and it soon became obvious that there would be a requirement for further formal negotiations involving representatives of both countries.

Plans were in train for the negotiations to take place in London. There would be a huge onus on the Irish delegation. Dev and Collins knew the limitations of what could be achieved. Both were also keenly aware that some of the extremist elements within the camp, who had been so useful in waging war, would not be accommodating of compromise.

The meeting between Dev and Collins on 20 August was also attended by Harry Boland, a long-time friend of Collins. During the War of Independence Boland had travelled to the US to assist Dev. While there, his loyalties switched from 'the Big Fella' to 'the Long Fellow'. He was now a Dev man, although Collins was not yet aware of the new alignment.

It did not take long for Dev to drop his bombshell: he would not be travelling to London as part of the delegation.

Dev knew his decision was highly controversial. He regarded himself highly as a statesman and many others agreed that he was the best thing the movement had to offer at a negotiating table. Yet, Dev felt the cause would be better served if he was to absent himself from the most crucial negotiations ever undertaken on behalf of his country.

There was worse to come for Collins. Not only would Dev be staying at home, but he would be proposing that Collins should go instead. Collins was devastated. Collins had wanted to go when Dev had travelled to London to meet Lloyd George in July, but was left at home. Dev had insisted on going alone. Now, as the smoke of war cleared and the limits of what could be achieved came into view, Dev was retreating from the trenches and putting Collins forward in his place.

A few days later Dev proposed to the seven-member ruling cabinet that he should not go to London, but instead be held in reserve to take control of the country in the event of any fallout from the negotiations. A vote followed. Dev's allies – Cathal Brugha, Austin Stack and Robert Barton – all agreed with him. Collins, W.T. Cosgrave and Arthur Griffith voted against. As President, Dev had the casting vote. He would be staying at home.

Dev's decision had long-term consequences for Ireland. The Civil War that unfolded within a year would in all likelihood have occurred anyway, but he played a major role in the renting apart of the nation. He would later found Fianna Fáil and effectively kick-start the political culture that dominated the country for the 20th century. The great dividing line in Irish politics was not based on ideology, but on the Civil War. And for a long time that came down to whether you were pro- or anti-Dev. It is reasonable to speculate that had Dev taken his courage in his hands and attended the treaty talks, Ireland's Civil War would not have been so devastating and the Irish political culture would have been shaped by policy rather than personality.

*   *   *

De Valera is the towering figure of 20th-century Ireland. Born in New York in 1882 to an Irish mother and a Spanish father, he was dispatched at the age of two to his mother's family, the Colls, in County Clare, soon after his father died. He was educated in Blackrock College, Dublin, and later became a teacher.

Dev's involvement in politics began in 1913 when he joined the Irish Volunteers, an organisation set up to counter the

Ulster Volunteers, which in turn was established to resist Home Rule. The young teacher rose quickly through the ranks, displaying ability and commitment to the cause. By Easter 1916, he was commandant of the Third Battalion of the Dublin Brigade and also a member of the Irish Republican Brotherhood (IRB), which was behind the Rising.

On Easter Monday, 24 April 1916, the Proclamation was read by Patrick Pearse outside the GPO. The Republic, which in time would become an albatross around Dev's neck, was born.

During Easter week Dev occupied Boland's Mill on Grand Canal Street. There are conflicting accounts about how he conducted himself. Supporters remember a leader with great organisational skills. Detractors claim that he suffered a nervous breakdown during the fighting. These differing versions have to be seen in the light of what he subsequently came to represent.

Following the insurgents' surrender, Dev was sentenced to death. But luck, not for the first or last time, was on his side. The logistics of the executions meant he was towards the end of the list of those to die. By the time his appointed date came around, public opinion had turned. Fifteen of the leaders had been executed over nine days. Marching out the condemned men in twos and threes to be shot was as stupid a move as the occupying power had committed in its long association with Ireland. The drawn-out nature of the executions redirected public anger from the insurgents to the British. It also formed the basis for the awakening that ultimately led to the War of Independence.

Dev's American citizenship ensured that his sentence was commuted and he was eventually released in an amnesty in June 1917.

Dev's status during the Rising, combined with his ability and force of personality, ensured that he became the major figure in the Republican movement. In June 1917 he was elected to the British parliament, and also became President of Sinn Féin. The following year Sinn Féin won a huge majority in a general election.

On 21 January 1919 the first meeting of Dáil Éireann took place in the Mansion House in Dublin. It was an Irish parliament operating despite Ireland's official status as an effective province of Great Britain. Dev had been re-arrested by then and could not attend. Others, including Collins, did not attend for fear of arrest.

On the same day, by what appears to be coincidence, two RIC constables were shot dead in Soloheadbeg, County Tipperary, by a group of Volunteers in search of arms. The shots fired that day were the first of what came to be the War of Independence and the two policemen who died were the first of its many fatalities.

In February 1919 Dev escaped from Lincoln Jail in an operation organised by Collins. The next meeting of the Dáil voted Dev as President of the assembly. In June it was agreed that the best use of Dev's status would be in the United States, where he could lobby for political and financial support of the new parliament and the wider cause of freedom.

He crossed the Atlantic that month and remained in the US until December 1920.

While there, Dev raised considerable funds – over $5 million – which were later the subject of a major dispute. Most of the money eventually found its way to Dev and was put to use in setting up the *Irish Press* some 13 years later. The newspaper became the property of the de Valera family, providing considerable wealth that was passed down through the generations.

* * *

While Dev was away, Collins prosecuted the war. His nominal role as Director of Intelligence masked the broad sweep of his influence. Collins was eight years younger than Dev and had fought in the GPO during the Rising. His experience during Easter 1916 left him nonplussed about the growing cult of Patrick Pearse, but he was impressed by James Connolly and he resolved that the next time Ireland strained against the shackles of imperialism, the combatants would not set themselves up as sitting ducks.

During Collins' year-long detention in Frongoch internment camp, he rose to prominence through his force of personality and organisational skills. He saw the necessity of using guerrilla war tactics in any forthcoming conflict in order to neutralise the far superior forces that the British would have at their disposal.

In 1919 Collins took on three separate roles that solidified his power base. He was appointed President of the IRB and Director of Intelligence of the IRA. Dev also offered him the role of Minister for Finance in the Sinn Féin government. He proved to be highly efficient in each of his posts.

As a minister, Collins set up a national bond scheme designed to raise funds for the new Republic. In the military sphere, he organised a network of flying columns that used the guerrilla warfare tactics of hitting and running. He was also responsible for the establishment of a network of spies, which gave the Irish a great advantage in the conflict. The setting up of what came to be known as 'The Squad' was another astute move. This group of young men was charged with carrying out assassinations as part of the war effort.

Through it all, Collins was on the run. In 1920 the British offered a reward of £10,000 for information leading to his capture or death. Had he been caught during the War of Independence, he would undoubtedly have been murdered or executed, most likely after suffering extreme torture. As it was, he survived the British but was killed by his own people.

When Dev returned from the US, Collins was enmeshed in a dispute with one of Dev's main allies, Cathal Brugha. It seems that Dev soon came to regard Collins as a rival.

In April 1920 the House of Commons passed the Government of Ireland Act, accommodating the partition of Ireland. With the Northern question bedded down, at least temporarily, there was now scope for the British to deal with the rest of Ireland. Intermediaries informed Collins that the British would be interested in negotiations.

The subsequent truce came into effect on 9 July 1921. Ireland celebrated. It looked to many as if a great victory had been achieved. Great Britain, with its sprawling empire, had been shot and bombed to the negotiating table by a relatively small, committed, yet inexperienced, militia. As far as some were concerned, this meant that Britain was going to concede republican status to the smaller island. In the glow of apparent victory, the capacity for delusion was limitless.

* * *

De Valera could not have been under any illusions when he travelled to London on 12 July to meet Lloyd George, just days after the truce. If he had had any notions that the British would simply roll over and hand independence to John Bull's Other Island, he would soon have been disabused of them.

17

Lloyd George was the perfect host. He knew the kind of pressures under which Dev laboured. There was never any question of Ireland being awarded the status of a republic as the implications for the empire would have been catastrophic. But he was willing to extend to his guest any courtesies he could, while at the same time keeping his eye on the negotiating ball.

When the two met at 10 Downing Street, Lloyd George brought Dev into the Imperial Room, showing him the broad sweep of His Majesty's power. He pointed to the chairs representing the various members of the Commonwealth or, as he described it, 'this great sisterhood of nations'. 'There sits India, there Africa … one chair remains vacant – waiting for Ireland.' Dev's facial features are reported to have remained inscrutable in response to this initial stab at courtship.

The two men met four times over the following week. Lloyd George was straight up about what was on the table. The Government of Ireland Act would remain in force, cementing the partition of the country. The 26 counties could have dominion status within the Commonwealth, similar to that enjoyed by Canada. The defence of the southern coastal waters would remain in British hands. The Irish would be responsible for part of the British national debt.

There was little movement between the two men. Later Lloyd George would describe negotiating with Dev as like 'sitting on a merry-go-round, trying to catch up the swing in front'. Dev was nonplussed: he had come to put flesh on the Republic declared on the steps of the GPO in 1916; dominion status would not be acceptable. His mood turned dark.

Pressure was applied from outside Number Ten. James Craig, the de facto leader of the partitioned North of Ireland, was holed up near the seat of British power. He was confident that Lloyd George would bring no pressure to bear on Unionists. While Dev was in negotiations, Craig wrote a comment piece for a London newspaper, proclaiming that Dev did not represent the whole of Ireland.

Dev was outraged. As far as he was concerned, he was there as leader of the Irish parliament, the Dáil, which had jurisdiction over the whole island. He wrote to Collins during the kerfuffle that followed Craig's comments, 'Things may burst up suddenly so be prepared.'

After venturing around in circles one time too many, Lloyd George finally laid his cards on the table, with a thump, on 19 July. Dominion status, stump up for some of the debt, partition remains, consider yourself lucky. Dev declined.

'Do you realise that this means war?' the Welsh Wizard, as he was known, told Dev. 'Do you realise the responsibility for it will rest on your shoulders alone?'

Dev answered, 'No Mr Lloyd George, if you insist on attacking us it is you, not I, who will be responsible because you will be the aggressor.'

When Lloyd George remarked, 'I could put a solider in Ireland for every man, woman and child in it.' Dev replied, 'Very well, but you would have to keep them there.'

The British proposals were put in writing and presented to de Valera the following day. Dev left without taking a copy, enraging Lloyd George as much for his lack of courtesy as anything else.

At 5.30 p.m. on 20 July Lloyd George informed his cabinet of the terms he had offered the Irishman. Nobody was too happy about the political fallout that would accrue over the effective weakening of British power to even a minor degree, but all agreed that something had to be done. If the Irish accepted the proposal, it would be a done deal.

One of Lloyd George's ministers, Hal Fisher, wrote about the briefing in his diary, noting that the Prime Minister had described Dev as 'a nice man, honest, astonishingly little vocabulary, wanted to settle but afraid of his followers'. While some of this description might well be accurate, it also illustrates the superiority complex that the British aristocrats had when dealing with upstarts with guns demanding the freedom of their country.

Back in Dublin, Dev reported to the cabinet about what had transpired. He certainly did not push the proposals, but there was some level of disagreement among his followers. In a reported exchange recorded in Tim Pat Coogan's biography of Dev (and used with artistic licence in the 1995 movie *Michael Collins*), Cathal Brugha, Minister for Defence, gave vent to the feelings of the militarists within the movement:

BRUGHA: I haven't much to add except to say how glad I am that it has been suggested we circulate these documents and consider them fully before we meet again, if for no other reason than to give you and the great masters of English you keep at your elbow an opportunity of extricating us from the morass in which ye have landed us.

DEV: We have done our best and I have never undertaken to do more than my best.

BRUGHA: We have proclaimed a Republic in arms. It has been ratified by the votes of the people, and we have sworn to defend it with our lives.

DEV: The oath never conveyed any more to me than to do my best in whatever circumstances may arise.

BRUGHA: You have accepted a position of authority and responsibility in the government of the Republic.

BRUGHA (reportedly striking the desk with his fist): And you will discharge the duties of that office as have been defined. I do not want ever again to hear anything else from you.

DEV: I think that I can promise, Cathal, that you won't have to complain again.

If accurately reported, this final response from Dev was instructive about what would unfold over the following year.

The exchange says much about the politics of the era. Brugha was a genuine hero of 1916. He still carried a limp from the horrendous injuries he suffered during Easter week. For a long time after the fighting it was thought that he would not survive his wounds. He represented the ideals of the Republic, a man for whom blood sacrifice was the highest calling. The extent of feeling within Sinn Féin at the time was such that even Brugha was a moderate compared with leading IRA figures such as Rory O'Connor.

Brugha had also developed a serious rivalry with Collins. Although Brugha was the nominal military head as the Minister of Defence, it was Collins who had led the war. Collins was thus a threat, an upstart who had barely featured in the glorious defeat of Easter 1916 but was racing ahead of everybody in the pecking order.

For his part, Dev was occupying a sticky wicket. A student of Machiavelli, he watched Collins' rising star closely. But, whatever his personal ambitions, Dev was also somebody who valued unity in the movement.

When he had returned from the US earlier that year, he expressed his dissatisfaction with the nature of the War of Independence. He felt that the use of guerrilla tactics and targeted assassinations left the movement open to accusations of being nothing more than a murder gang. He had encountered such opinions in the US. Dev was not a militarist. In May 1921, a few months after his return, the IRA departed from its usual strategy and occupied and burnt down the Custom House in Dublin, which was the centre of local government. Many believe the exercise was undertaken after pressure was applied by Dev to engage in large-scale operations. The attack was a disaster. Five volunteers were killed and over 80 were captured. Such actions were futile.

Dev surely knew that any resumption of war would have horrendous consequences not only for the IRA, but also the general population. Time would prove that he was a far more able politician than revolutionary, but in the summer of 1921 he desperately needed to keep the militarists on board.

Opinions vary on what Dev's priorities were in those months: ensuring the future of the Republic, pursuing what was best for the people of Ireland or achieving what was best for the future of Eamon de Valera. Most historians who attempt to analyse Dev's motives find that they are dealing with something beyond rational treatment. As S.M. Lawlor put it in *Britain and Ireland 1914–23*, 'it was never quite clear what De Valera stood for, or with whom he stood, at least from December 1920 to June 1922'.

In the throes of the agonising that ensued in the summer of 1921, Dev woke one morning with an epiphany called external association. It was, by the standards of the time, a sophisticated and far-reaching concept: Ireland would associate with the Commonwealth, be a part of it yet separate, autonomous yet a member of the group of nations that pledged nominal allegiance to the British monarch. It was a new way forward.

Despite his new concept, which Dev shared with many of his perplexed colleagues, there were more earthy matters at hand. Lloyd George issued an invitation to full-blown talks involving delegations from each side, 'to ascertain how the association of Ireland with the community of nations known as the British Empire can best be reconciled with Irish national aspirations'.

Here was the perfect opportunity for Dev to carry his external association idea to Downing Street and beyond, to present it to the most powerful politicians in the world, to convince them of its value and its possibilities, to press on them that it was the only way out of further conflict. He chose to do no such thing. He chose to stay at home.

* * *

After the meeting of 20 August 1921 Collins did his damnedest to get out of being sent to London. The voices in his head told him it was a fool's errand and he would be conferred with the status of scapegoat. But, eventually, he agreed. One characteristic of Collins was that once he decided on a course of action he followed through with determination. That quality was behind his success during the War of Independence.

In later years Dev claimed that his decision to stay in Dublin was not controversial, and that there was 'general agreement' that he should remain aloof from the negotiations. The records of the cabinet meeting that ratified his decision, and of the Dáil, beg to differ. On 14 September Cosgrave made a passionate plea in the Dáil for Dev to travel. As reported in the record of the private sessions of the Dáil for the day, Cosgrave said:

> [Dev] had an extraordinary experience in negotiations. He also had the advantage of being in touch already. The head of the State in England was

Mr. Lloyd George and he expected he would be one of the plenipotentiaries on the side of England ... they were sending over [a team] and they were leaving their ablest player in reserve ... The reserve would have to be used some time or other and it struck him now was the time they were required.

The record of Dev's response states:

He really believed it was vital at this stage that the symbol of the Republic should be kept untouched and that it should not be compromised in any sense by any arrangements which it might be necessary for our plenipotentiaries to make. He was sure the Dáil realised the task they were giving to them – to win for them what a mighty army and navy might not be able to win for them. It was not a shirking of duty, but he realised the position and how necessary it was to keep the Head of the State and the symbol untouched and that was why he asked to be left out.

Having fortified himself in his decision not to go, Dev then set about ensuring that Collins would travel. Notably, Dev had also offered places on the delegation to Brugha and Stack. When his cabinet allies refused to go, he did not apply any further pressure. But he was determined that Collins would travel.

Dev used his considerable persuasive skills on Collins as well as enlisting the help of others. One such man was Collins' close friend Batt O'Connor. O'Connor invited Collins to his home, where the two sat down with a bottle of whiskey to talk over the future of their country. O'Connor's daughter was 12 at the time, and years later she recalled her memories for Tim Pat Coogan:

Daddy brought out the bottle and they talked for

hours and hours. I could hear Mick's light voice arguing. Mick didn't think it was right that he should go, because he was a soldier. De Valera should go, he kept saying. It's not my place. He sounded terribly upset. But daddy kept arguing, 'You'll have to go, Mick. It's the one chance you'll get. Think of how it will look in America if you miss this opportunity. Think of what this could do for Ireland. It's your duty. It's a great opportunity. Think of what you can lose if you don't go.'

Coogan is one of the historians who believes that Dev's decision not to travel was catastrophic. As he wrote in his biography of Collins:

It was the worst single decision of de Valera's life, for himself and for Ireland. Instead of the experience and prestige of the most revered political figure on the Irish side being made available to parley against the English, De Valera's full force was ultimately to be turned against his fellow countrymen. The consequence of his decision was to drive him to an extremist position in which he helped unleash a hurricane of violence and destruction in Ireland. He knew that any agreement brought back from London would be a compromise.

Others have been less critical of Dev's decision to stay at home. The kinder interpretation is that he was principally concerned with maintaining unity and he reckoned that by staying at home he was better placed to ensure there would be no split.

Joe Lee notes in *Ireland 1912–1985* that 'Collins sensed a conspiracy against him by De Valera, Brugha and Stack.' However, Lee suggests:

His suspicions reveal something of the atmosphere in the cabinet but he was being perhaps hypersensitive. However diligently de Valera felt politicians should study Machiavelli, his real blunder was less conspiracy than miscalculation. He staked everything on preserving unity through his 'external association scheme'.

In this scenario Dev stayed at home to keep external association as a carrot for the militarists when the delegates would inevitably return with a poor result. It is a credible theory but, like many others concerning Dev's motives, we will never really know.

* * *

The talks on the future of Ireland officially began on 11 October 1921. There was an obvious imbalance in the respective delegations. The British included Prime Minister Lloyd George, the Lord Chancellor Lord Birkenhead, Secretary of State for the Colonies (and of war) Winston Churchill, Attorney General Gordon Hewart and the Lord Privy Seal Austin Chamberlain.

In contrast, the Irish included only three members of cabinet: Collins, Arthur Griffith and Robert Barton. Two other TDs, Eamonn Duggan and George Gavan Duffy, made up the rest of the delegation. The secretary to the team was Erskine Childers, a close ally of Dev, regarded by many as the Long Fellow's eyes and ears in London. There was no Dev to convey what the Irish people really wanted. There was no Brugha or Stack to represent the hardliners who would inevitably have a major say on the outcome.

Little had changed since the encounter between Dev and Lloyd George earlier that summer. Dominion status was the deal. There would have to be an oath of allegiance to the Crown. That was good enough for large countries like Canada and Australia and Ireland should not expect something more.

As little progress was made in the first weeks there was a proposal for sub-groups. On the Irish side, Collins and Griffith were the two delegates who attended these sessions every time. The British pairing rotated among their various delegates. Collins and Griffith also had a series of secret meetings with Lloyd George and Tom Jones, who was a member of the British war cabinet secretariat.

The Irish delegates had the status of plenipotentiaries, which meant they had full power to sign whatever was agreed on behalf of the Dáil. They also returned to Dublin at least twice to relay in person how the negotiations were progressing.

By all accounts, Dev sent inconsistent signals to the delegates, even in terms of their status. In *Judging Dev*, Diarmaid Ferriter touched on the problems:

> [Dev's] critics quite legitimately pointed to the inconsistency of his position; having prepared to compromise with Lloyd George, 'he had then rushed back to the rock of republicanism' and seemed to be sending conflicting messages to the Irish negotiators. Another problem was that the Dáil had granted them plenipotentiary powers but privately, they were issued with another contradictory instruction by the cabinet to the effect that before signing any agreement, they would have to refer it back to the cabinet.

Thus, Dev was prepared to bypass the will of the Dáil, but also wanted any agreement referred to the four members of cabinet who remained in Dublin. Three of those members, Dev, Brugha and Stack, had refused to go to London themselves because

MICHAEL CLIFFORD & SHANE COLEMAN

they were unwilling to brook compromise. It could well be argued that the circumstances surrounding the most important negotiations in the history of the island were a royal mess, and that the blame lay largely with one man.

In the early hours of 6 December 1921 the Irish members signed the proposed treaty. The alternative, as Lloyd George threatened, was 'immediate and terrible war'. To a certain extent they had been outfoxed by politicians with long and varied experience of negotiations. Yet it is difficult to see how anything more could have been achieved.

A scene in the *Michael Collins* movie captures the problem well. Liam Neeson's Collins gets off the boat returning to Dublin after signing the treaty to be met by his former ally, Aidan Quinn's Harry Boland. Boland is distraught at the terms of the treaty. 'How could you, Mick,' he asks. Collins replies, 'We couldn't get the Republic, it's not within their comprehension.' Never was a truer word uttered – albeit with the stamp of artistic licence on it.

Britain was just a few years out of the Great War in which it was the leading power in the defeat of the mighty German army. Its writ still ran across large swathes of the globe, effectively governing hundreds of millions of people. Yet on its doorstep, a little country that had been absorbed into a union over a century earlier was demanding a complete break of ties.

Declaring the Republic on the steps of the GPO as a preamble to a blood sacrifice was one thing. That gesture had had the desired effect and led to a quite stunning victory in terms of shooting the empire all the way to the negotiating table. But there was never a chance that it would be realised immediately.

The alternative was war, and while many in the IRA were high on the victory already achieved, few of them were aware of how depleted were the resources required to renew the conflict. Collins knew, and that knowledge perhaps reinforced his decision to sign.

* * *

When the cabinet met on 8 December 1921 the main sticking point with the treaty was the requirement for elected representatives to swear an oath of allegiance to the King. The partition of the island, which would loom large through the remainder of the century, was not the central issue at that time.

Griffith berated Dev for not getting involved in the process, sniping from the sidelines and then rejecting the outcome. The note on the meeting recorded him saying, 'We would have offered to stand out. Asked Dev to come over.' Dev responded, 'I would have gone and said, "go to the devil I will not sign".' This, of course, was a splendid proposition after the fact. Dev had been given every opportunity to go to London, both before and during the negotiations. He declined to do so.

The cabinet voted on the treaty. Dev, Brugha and Stack voted against, the other four members in favour. Dev said he could not support a treaty that was in 'violent conflict' with the wishes of the majority. It is unclear how he gleaned the wishes of the majority, but later he would claim that he had only to look into his heart to know how the Irish people felt. Within six months he would have the opportunity to test his notions, and the result would give him little comfort.

During the Dáil debate on the treaty on 14 December, Dev declared:

> ... it would be ridiculous to think that we could send five men to complete a treaty without the right of ratification by this assembly. That is the only thing that matters. Therefore it is agreed that this

Treaty is simply an agreement and that it is not binding until the Dáil ratifies it. That is what we are concerned with.

On 7 January 1922 the Dáil voted by 64 to 57 to ratify the treaty. Having lost the vote, Dev was no longer concerned with what the assembly had decided through the majority. He led a walkout of the chamber. The following week, a provisional government was established to administer the handover of the state from the British. Dev, Stack and Brugha were the only missing figures from the previous cabinet.

Over the following six months the country worked itself into a frenzy towards civil war. There are conflicting accounts of Dev's role in whipping up violent opposition to the treaty.

An election was due to be called and many saw this as the Irish people's final verdict on the treaty. Dev attempted to bring all his powers of persuasion to bear on the populace as to the rightness of his position. In one speech on St Patrick's Day in Thurles, County Tipperary, he laid out his position: 'If they accepted the treaty, and if the volunteers of the future tried to complete the work the volunteers of the last four years had been attempting, they would have to complete it, not over the bodies of foreign soldiers, but over the dead bodies of their own countrymen.'

The next day he introduced into his speech the phrase 'the people have no right to do wrong' and mentioned the prospect of 'wading through blood' to achieve the Republic. Declaring that the people had no right to be wrong was in sharp contrast to a speech he had given before the 1918 election, in which he said that Sinn Féin stood for 'the right of the people of this nation to determine freely for themselves how they shall be governed and for the right of every citizen to an equal right in the determination'.

On 20 March the *Irish Independent* reported that in a speech in Killarney, County Kerry, Dev had said that if the treaty were ratified those who opposed it would be obliged to 'march over the dead bodies of their own brothers. They will have to wade through Irish blood … the people never have a right to do wrong.' Dev took severe umbrage with the publication, but did not suggest that he had been misquoted. Although he then toned down his utterances, the damage had been done.

Despite the gathering storm, Dev and Collins attempted to sign an election pact, but it was dropped at the last minute. It would be unfair to suggest that Dev was gung ho for a return to war. Far from it. But he was not willing to accept the treaty, particularly in the context of the relentless rise of Collins' star, the trajectory of which had steepened over the previous six months. Neither could it be said that he had major influence over the militarists. But it remains the case that the anti-treatyites were able to call on the support of the leading political figure on the island.

The attraction of Dev as a political force was obvious before the events surrounding the treaty, and they would become even more obvious in the decades after. It can reasonably be speculated that that same force had a great impact on thousands of voters who may have been swaying over whether to opt for peace or war in early 1922.

When the people spoke on 18 June, the pro-treaty Sinn Féin party received 239,193 votes and Dev's faction trailed behind with 133,864. Most of the other 247,226 votes cast were for pro-treaty parties (with the exception of the Unionists). In broad terms the vote for the treaty was three times that of those opposed. The voice of the people resonated with a plea for peace. They were not going to get it.

* * *

The Civil War began in earnest on 28 June 1922 when Collins ordered the shelling of the Four Courts where an anti-treaty garrison had been established. Over the following ten months the life was almost smothered from the fledgling state. Leading figures such as Collins, Griffith, Brugha and Boland were among the 3,000 lives lost in the internal conflict. More people died violently in the Civil War than did in the War of Independence.

The Big Fella was shot dead in the early stages of the conflict on 22 August. His passing increased the bitterness between the two sides and the intensity of the engagements. A country suffering abject poverty was ripped apart as two sides went to war over whether or not to swear an oath of allegiance to a foreign monarch.

The provisional government executed 77 men for crimes against the new state. Among them was Erskine Childers, who was convicted for possession of a revolver that had been given to him a few years earlier by Collins. The executions were, by any normal standards, illegal, but the state was in a perilous condition. Over the following 50 years, '77' would become an insult, disguised as a number, to be hurled across the political divide that was forged during the conflict.

Dev had a minor role in the fighting. When hostilities broke out he signed up as a private in his old Dublin IRA brigade. He had little influence over those who were commanding operations. But just as a last-minute intervention in 1916 had ensured that he lived to lead and fight another day, fate's arrow remained true during the Civil War. Had Dev been captured with a gun in his possession during those days, it is most likely that he would, like Childers, have been put up against a wall and shot.

Some portrayals of how Dev conducted himself during the Civil War have been grossly unfair. In the *Michael Collins* movie, Alan Rickman's Dev is a snivelling wreck who visited Beal na mBlath the night before the ambush in which Collins died. There is no reason to believe that this depiction is accurate. The historical revision of Dev in recent years has to be seen in the context of the decades during which he was a powerful figure and sought to project a flattering image of his role in those heady early years. The truth, as always, lies somewhere in between hagiography and character assassination.

It is beyond dispute, however, that Dev was central to the support received by the anti-treatyites during that devastating first year in the life of the state. Why he behaved as he did has always been a matter of speculation, but most historians who examine the subject agree that his reasoning was largely governed by the pursuit of self-interest at a time when others were dying for their country.

The Civil War began to peter out through March and April 1923. Across Ireland the pro-treaty National Army gained the upper hand against the IRA. At one stage Dev appealed to the leaders of the Irregulars to call a ceasefire, but they ignored him. Then on 10 April the Chief of Staff of the IRA, Liam Lynch, was killed in an ambush in Tipperary. His successor, Frank Aiken (who later served with distinction in a number of cabinets), ordered the IRA volunteers to dump arms. This was quickly followed by a statement to the same effect from Dev.

The Long Fellow endured another spell in prison, this one lasting for about a year. On emerging, he thrust himself into politics, setting up Fianna Fáil in 1926. He won power in 1932 and led a number of governments over the following 27 years. After his retirement from the Dáil, he served two seven-year terms as President of Ireland until 1973. He died two years later.

* * *

De Valera's long political career has been dissected and revised since his death. Opinions differ as to his effectiveness and contribution to the development of the state. He unquestionably achieved much, but he also missed many opportunities.

The overriding feature of Irish politics through the first 80 years of the state's existence was the Civil War divide. It shaped the political culture, ensuring, for instance, that there was no development along traditional left and right lines. It may well have accounted for the slow progress of Ireland's development as an independent state. Not until the early 1960s, under the influence of T.K. Whitaker and Seán Lemass, the latter another Civil War veteran, did the state embark on a proper stage of economic development.

For decades after independence, political allegiance was defined by where one stood on the treaty. Floating voters were in a minority. Loyalties bordered on the fanatical. Households were firmly Fianna Fáil or Fine Gael, regardless of policy.

Although the country was haemorrhaging its young people to Britain and the US, politics in Ireland tragically failed to move beyond the tribal. If the understandable emotions triggered by the Civil War had not existed, then perhaps there would have been greater pressure on the two main political parties to address the bitter divisions and concentrate on developing policies to improve the often miserable lot of the voting public.

Perhaps Cumann na nGaedheal would have moved beyond its Commonwealth mindset in the 1920s. Perhaps Fianna Fáil would not have embarked on its disastrous economic war with

Britain in the 1930s. Perhaps successive governments would not have clung to the hugely misguided policy of protectionism until well into the 1950s for fear of being outflanked on the national question by the opposition. Perhaps these parties would not have existed at all and instead the Labour Party would have emerged as a greater force, bringing the type of radical edge to Irish politics that its counterpart in Britain brought about after World War II.

It is difficult to be definitive on these points but it is clear that for at least 30 years after independence it was not, to borrow Bill Clinton's old adage, 'the economy stupid' that mattered most. Too much energy, too many words and too much bitterness was wasted on the fallout from the tragedy that was the Civil War.

As late as 1948 the Civil War was still such a live issue that the leader of Fine Gael, Richard Mulcahy, could not lead the new five-party inter-party government because of his former role as head of the Free State Army. It would be another decade before stark warnings from senior civil servants about the viability of the state prompted the government of the day to finally focus on the issue that was most relevant to the country's citizens: the economic malaise.

Predicting how Ireland would have developed if the Civil War had not happened is a perilous business. But we can say with some confidence that, without the rawness of what happened in that tragic year when family members and former comrades became sworn enemies, it would have been better.

For all the undoubted achievements of Eamon de Valera during his long and impressive political career, his role in that conflict must always feature large in any assessment of his legacy.

2

SWEEPING DIRT UNDER THE CARPET

It was the scoop to beat all scoops. Joe MacAnthony's 7,000-word exposé on the Irish Hospitals Sweepstakes in the *Sunday Independent* was genuinely shocking to its readers in February 1973.

The 'Sweep' was an iconic Irish institution and a worldwide phenomenon. Numerous films had been based on it. It was even namechecked in Cole Porter's immortal song 'You're the Top'. It seemed like a harmless piece of fun. Thousands upon thousands of punters would buy tickets for what was in essence a lottery linked to a major horse race. If their name was drawn out, they were matched up in a separate draw with a horse running in the selected race and the outcome of the race dictated who won the most. More importantly, the Sweep had provided millions to pay for the rebuilding of the entire Irish hospital system and had employed thousands of people.

MacAnthony's investigation stripped away a myth that had existed for the previous half a century and shone a light on what was really happening. It was a devastating critique.

Irish hospitals were receiving less than 10 per cent of the value of the tickets being sold across the world; leading shareholders in the organisation were buying up ticket shares in advance of the race, thereby allowing them to win their own prizes; and the published accounts masked huge hidden expenses – something that was specifically allowed by legislation.

Even worse, the article highlighted the illegality surrounding the sale of the tickets abroad and the degree of smuggling involved; how the organisers were charging prices for tickets above the rate sanctioned by the Minister for Justice; and the covert assistance that the Department of Posts and Telegraphs was giving to the Sweep in contravention of international postal law. It revealed that Oireachtas members and civil servants were in receipt of commissions and painted a shocking picture of the Sweep's resistance to any organisation trying to muscle in on the action in North America.

It was a rap sheet as long as the Mardi Gras-style processions through Dublin that had publicised the upcoming sweepstake draw in its halcyon days.

But brilliant and all as MacAnthony's investigation was, the details can hardly have been news to those at the top of Irish society, particularly those in government. Successive governments over five decades had turned a blind eye to what the *Reader's Digest* had years earlier described as 'the greatest bleeding heart racket in the world'.

Why? Because it was deemed to be in the national interest to do so. With no money available to rebuild the crumbling hospital infrastructure, the Sweep was seen as the lesser of two evils.

* * *

Irish hospitals in the 1920s were largely run by voluntary charitable organisations, with either Catholic or Protestant management. The state involvement that is taken for granted today was virtually non-existent. Nearly all the hospitals were experiencing a huge funding crisis, some even faced closure.

The pressure to raise money to alleviate the hospitals' funding crisis was huge and sweepstake-type ventures had been very successful, as one-off projects, in the early 1920s. Many in government felt that they had no choice other than to approve a sweepstake, but they faced a very powerful opponent. Kevin O'Higgins, Minister for Justice and 'strong man' of the cabinet, was hugely opposed to legalising sweepstakes. Highly sceptical of the motives of sweepstake promoters, he told the Dáil in March 1923 that 'they were people whom I never suspected of being philanthropists' and indicated that he believed sweepstakes were associated with fraud and corruption.

The Protestant churches were also strongly opposed to them on moral grounds; the Catholic Church – traditionally more concerned with sexual vices than gambling – took a more Jesuitical approach.

The leader of the Labour Party, Thomas Johnson, was another strong opponent. He felt that the situation made a mockery of Ireland's newly won independence, exhibiting 'the sores of Ireland and the poverty of Ireland to the world and as a beggar to ask the world to come to the aid of the hospitals of this country'. Johnson advocated an additional levy of one penny per week for a year on health insurance, split between the employee and the employer, which would have raised £100,000. But there was no support for what was seen as a radical measure.

A move to legalise sweepstakes petered out in 1923, but by 1929 it was back on the agenda. Many hospitals were deeply in the red, particularly the National Maternity Hospital, which was on the brink of closure. The hospitals, understandably given their plight, were engaged in extensive lobbying of the head of government, W.T. Cosgrave.

O'Higgins had been assassinated, shot dead on his way to Mass, in July 1927. With the most powerful opponent of the sweepstake concept gone and the financial crisis worsening in the hospital sector, the momentum in favour of a sweepstake became irresistible.

New legislation was drawn up, giving significant powers to the Minister for Justice to regulate the sweepstake. Legitimate promoters' expenses (covering printing, distribution and salaries) of 30 per cent of the gross proceeds of ticket sales were allowed, along with 7 per cent for promoters' fees. The legislation also required that hospitals receive a minimum of just 20 per cent of the gross proceeds of ticket sales; pressure from Johnson to increase this to 40 per cent was resisted. The remaining 43 per cent was for prize money.

The Act was signed into law on 4 June 1930. The first legal Irish Hospitals Sweepstake was to be held on the Manchester November Handicap. It was the beginning of an extraordinary story.

*   *   *

Richard Duggan emerged as the obvious man to run the new legal enterprise. A Dublin bookmaker, Duggan had been one of the most prominent promoters of illegal sweepstakes. In 1918 he raised £1,000 for the survivors and victims' families of the mailboat *RMS Leinster*, which had been torpedoed by a German U-boat. He also ran the Mater Hospital Sweepstake in 1922, which had a prize fund of £10,000.

Duggan was prosecuted in late 1924 under the Lotteries Act 1823 and fined £50 for his involvement in Duggan's Dublin

Sweep – run on the Manchester November Handicap. He was bound over to keep the peace for 12 months and gave an undertaking not to run any more sweepstakes. However, three years later he was organising a sweepstake on the Epsom Derby from Liechtenstein. Strange as it may seem, his past record did not so much disbar his involvement as prime him for it, in an irony that would set the tone for the next 60 years.

Efforts by the Revenue Commissioners to pursue Duggan for tax on his sweepstake profits were unsuccessful. The courts found that he was exempt from income tax on sweepstakes because they were illegal and therefore should not have happened in the first place. There was no Criminal Assets Bureau in those days.

Also appointed as directors of Hospitals Trust Ltd (formerly Promotions Ltd; the name was changed in 1930 for obvious reasons) were Joe McGrath, a former government minister and lover of horse racing, and Captain Spencer Freeman, a former British Army engineer who would demonstrate a real flair for publicity. Freeman was introduced to Duggan and McGrath by his bookmaker brother, Sidney.

McGrath was a hero of 1916 and the War of Independence. He had been the right-hand man of Michael Collins and Director of Intelligence of the Free State Army. Frustrated at what he believed was the sidelining of Republican goals by the Cumann na nGaedheal government of which he was part, he resigned from the cabinet and the party in sympathy with former IRA officers involved in the so-called 'army mutiny'.

He became managing director of Hospitals Trust and quickly appointed a number of his former comrades from the War of Independence – including some who fought on the Republican side during the Civil War – to senior roles in the organisation.

When Duggan died in 1935, McGrath's control over the company strengthened and he became the Sweep's dominant figure.

* * *

The first ticket for the inaugural Irish Hospitals Sweepstake draw was bought by James MacNeill. He was the Governor General, the English monarch's representative in Ireland, a position that existed until the creation of the office of President of Ireland in 1937. The price per ticket was ten shillings or $2.50, which was not cheap in those days. Within a few years it became common for groups of people or syndicates to pool their money together to buy tickets.

The sweepstake draw took place one week before the horse race on which it was based. There were two drums: a large one with all the subscribers' counterfoils and a smaller one with the names of the horses in the race. Counterfoils that were pulled out of the larger drum were then matched with horses drawn out of the smaller one. The prizes awarded to the lucky people drawn out were based on the positioning of their horses in the actual race.

Although the sweepstake was a huge success in Ireland, with long queues to buy tickets, it was immediately apparent that the majority of tickets were being bought outside the state. This was despite efforts by the British postal authorities to intercept sweepstake mail coming into and leaving their jurisdiction. Up to 30,000 tickets were sold in the North – there were even claims that the Prime Minister of Northern Ireland, James Craig, Viscount Craigavon, had bought one.

For the first draw, a film company was hired to record the four-hour-long proceedings and a large group of English journalists was invited to Dublin to witness proceedings in the

Oak Room of the Mansion House. Loudspeakers were erected in Dublin's St Stephen's Green so people could listen in as the events unfolded.

Nurses from the participating hospitals placed the counterfoils in the drum. But, astonishingly, the draw was made by four blind boys from St Joseph's School in Drumcondra, for which each was rewarded with a large box of chocolates. Supervising it all was the Garda Commissioner, Eoin O'Duffy, who at one point assured the audience that the boys were genuinely blind – presumably to emphasise that they could not therefore rig the draw.

Despite the fact that pubic lotteries were illegal in the UK, almost 60 per cent of the prizewinners in the first Sweep came from there (that proportion would rise over the next few years). Eleven of the prizewinners were from the Irish Free State, compared with 40 English, three Scots, two Welsh and three from the North. Six Canadians won, and there were four winners each from the US and South Africa. There were also winners from exotic locations such as the Philippines, Demerara, Malay and India.

Over £666,000 was generated in ticket sales and the prizes on offer were enormous. The first prize of £202,764 – a staggering amount of money at the time – was won by an official in the Northern Ireland Ministry of Agriculture. However, he had to share the money because, having been drawn out of the drum, he had opted to hedge his bet and sell shares in his ticket to two other Belfast men and half a share to Ladbrokes in advance of the race.

The six participating hospitals also did well. Jervis Street, St Patrick Dun's and the National Maternity Hospital got just over 22 per cent each of the hospitals' allocation – an amount of almost £30,000 per hospital. The remaining one-third of the allocation was split evenly between the smaller National Children's Hospital, St Ultan's and the Dental Hospital, giving them just under £15,000 each.

Nearly £100,000, not far short of the amount allocated to the hospitals, went to pay commissions on the sale of tickets and winning-ticket-sellers' prizes. A substantial percentage of this share went to Mutual Club Ltd in Vaduz, Liechtenstein, which sold tickets outside Ireland and Britain. The promoters, Hospitals Trust, pocketed a cool £46,000. The expenses for running the sweep exceeded £71,000.

Those huge sums were soon dwarfed in size as the Sweep became the most successful lottery in the world. By the second sweepstake, organised around the 1931 Grand National, sales were up to £1.76 million. For the following year's Derby, they exceeded £4 million and the prize fund was £2.3 million (over €150 million in today's money). The proceeds did dip, however, following the UK's introduction of the Betting and Lotteries Act in 1934.

A staggering 142 million tickets were sold during the 1930s, grossing over £71 million. The majority of these tickets were sold illegally in the UK and the US, where hundreds of thousands of Irish immigrants offered a ready-made market. In her brilliantly researched book *The Irish Sweep – A History of the Irish Hospitals Sweepstake 1930–87*, Marie Coleman describes how bars, banks, cinemas and bookmakers were among the businesses offering tickets (although sales through banks were eventually clamped down on).

The success of the Sweep hit British-based illegal lotteries very hard, but even that did not foster a more benign attitude from the British authorities. Not that there was a huge amount they could do. With a common travel area between the two islands, it was not difficult to conceal sweepstake tickets in luggage. Attempts by customs officials at Holyhead to search travellers' luggage caused an outcry in the House of Commons.

Tens of millions of pounds left Britain for Ireland in contributions to the Sweep during the 1930s. The 1933 Cambridgeshire sweepstake proved so popular that, as the *Irish Times* reported, one railway company ran an extra boat to Dublin on the eve of the draw 'owing to the anticipated rush of sweepstake agents to Ireland. The number of persons travelling was 1,800, many of them carrying money and counterfoils.'

The Sweep was helped by the minimal fines handed down by the British courts to those convicted of selling tickets and the fact that a person could not be prosecuted at all for buying a ticket.

The British postal service had the legal power to open any post believed to be linked to lotteries and thousands of letters were opened prior to the first sweepstake. However, Hospitals Trust quickly came up with a way around this. It advised customers in Britain to send their subscriptions indirectly via friends in Ireland or through a bank or participating hospital.

With almost two-thirds of prizes going to Britain residents in the first 12 sweepstakes, it was clear that the British postal authorities were unable to prevent British residents from participating in the Irish Sweep. They were not alone. In those first 12 draws, prizes went to 77 different countries or territories. The Sweep's 'foreign office' – as it was known – used to handle 40 different currencies in one day.

Of the £71 million grossed during the 1930s, £45 million went on prize money, Irish hospitals got £13.5 million, while the three promoters shared an estimated profit of £1.6 million – huge riches in those days.

After an enormous first prize of £354,544 was awarded for

the 1931 Grand National sweepstake, a decision was taken to reduce the largest prize to £30,000 and greatly increase the number of prizewinners.

This change was mainly the result of pressure from the horse racing authorities in Britain, which feared that the level of money involved would induce the running of dud horses in races. As an article in the *Irish Times* put it at the time, 'the prize for a runner is so much greater than that for a non-starter, that the drawer of a horse still left in that race is in a position to offer its owner a substantial inducement to run'. The changes worked and the number of horses running in sweepstake races fell considerably.

The PR surrounding each draw was ahead of its time. The tickets were designed to look like currency. Different themes – anything from Gaelic legend to *Arabian Nights* – were chosen for each draw. Irish artists, including Seán Keating, and illustrators of the day were commissioned to provide the backdrops for the draws. The drum itself was similarly decorated. In one draw, a massive replica elephant was used. On top of the elephant was a throne and beneath it were a dozen or so ornate drums, carrying the tickets.

The theme of the 1936 draw was 'American' – no doubt because of the importance of that market for the Sweep – with staff dressed as film stars, Uncle Sam and baseball players. On an early draw, the Manhattan skyline was recreated outside the Mansion House, a stunt that was publicised all over the US.

The tickets always featured a very attractive female employee of Hospitals Trust and female employees, wearing symbolic costumes, also carried out the ticket drums ahead of the draw. With a huge degree of pomp and ceremony, the counterfoils were taken from the sweepstake offices in Dublin's

Earlsfort Terrace to the Plaza Hall on Abbey Street, under garda escort.

Counterfoils were usually transported to the Plaza Hall in a gigantic model of a black cat, Big Tom, one of the many symbols of luck utilised. In yet another a PR stunt, 3,000 black cats were brought up to Dublin to audition to be the model on which Big Tom would be based. Big Tom later went on a tour of British seaside destinations, collecting in aid of local hospitals.

A highly elaborate ticket-mixing process took place inside the Plaza Hall. The boxes containing millions of counterfoils were placed on small trucks, which were pushed along rail tracks by staff and then loaded into the mixing machines using metal scoops. Blasts of air jumbled up the counterfoils in the machines, which were then transferred to the drum for the draw.

The draw became a massive tourist attraction and photo opportunities beside the drum were the norm for visiting celebrities such as Anna May Wong and Jack Doyle. Gracie Fields famously got into the drum to examine it but, as the *Irish Times* later recalled, due to a 'workman's mistake was twirled around inside it until her screams got the drum stopped'.

Joe McGrath's old employer, the accountancy firm Craig Gardner, was the sweepstake auditor, with a company representative also supervising the draw. Marie Coleman observes how the Protestant partners of the company overcame their reluctance to be 'associated with such a major gambling enterprise', perhaps because, by the mid-1930s, sweepstake-related earnings equalled almost 30 per cent of the annual income of the firm's main Dublin office.

The biggest financial winner was, of course, McGrath

himself. Within three years of the Sweep being established, he was in a position to buy a mansion in south County Dublin. Further land accumulation meant that by the time of his death, in 1966, he owned a large part of south Dublin between Carrickmines and Foxrock. He invested heavily in bloodstock – becoming the dominant figure in Irish racing – and in indigenous Irish companies such as the Irish Glass Bottle Company, Waterford Crystal and Donegal Carpets.

Hospitals Trust became a massive business and had nine offices across Ireland by the end of 1932; it later moved to a purpose-built centralised base in Ballsbridge, Dublin, constructed between 1937 and 1939, which housed up to 4,000 staff. Despite McGrath's previous role at the Irish Transport and General Workers' Union, there was criticism of employment conditions in the company during the 1930s, particularly of the long hours worked, the seasonal nature of the employment, the relatively low wages for many of the mainly female workers and allegations of patronage during recruitment.

In a sign of the muscle that the Sweep was able to exercise – and would continue to exercise for the next 40 years – Labour's James Everett (a regular critic of the company's pay and conditions) claimed in the Dáil that the 'press were threatened by the Hospitals Commission that if these letters [of complaint by employees about their wages] were published all advertisements would be withdrawn from the daily papers'. Everett also said that while he was not suggesting 'that the Minister, or any official of his Department, or friends of the Minister, or of anybody in his Department, are receiving emoluments', he was 'suggesting that such is so in the case of Deputies of all Parties, and of Senators, and that, therefore, there is no word of protest against the treatment of the 30 shilling a week employees'.

The coming to power of Fianna Fáil in 1932 meant the issue of the fees paid to Hospitals Trust resurfaced. Not surprisingly, the question of reducing the 6 per cent promoters' fee was strongly resisted by McGrath and by many in the hospital sector who were quite content with the status quo.

In a letter to the new Minister for Justice, James Geoghegan, the chairman of the Board of Governors of the National Children's Hospital, Lord Powerscourt, argued against reducing the fee, highlighting the need to facilitate the illegal sale of tickets outside Ireland: 'Having regard to the fact that the sale of tickets and return of counterfoils is illegal in all countries outside the Free State, they have to maintain an elaborate secret network of communications at their own expense.'

As Joe MacAnthony and later Marie Coleman would point out, this was not true. In fact, the legislation establishing the Sweep specifically allowed 'the value of tickets issued free of charge by way of reward to a seller of tickets' to be excluded from the calculation of the amount of money received from the sale of tickets. This provision, Coleman notes, 'allowed the government to distance itself from the underhand activities that were necessary to secure a sizeable foreign market for tickets'.

The Sweep's promoters effectively had two sets of expenses but only one appeared in the published accounts. The actual turnover was therefore much higher than was revealed to the public. As the payments given to ticket sellers were not subject to audit, it is impossible to know how much was spent bribing police officers and customs officials.

Government departments did much more than simply turn a blind eye. There were concerns in the Department of Posts and Telegraphs about the illegality of sweepstakes in countries to which tickets and literature were posted. Article 45 of the International Postal Convention made it an offence 'to send by post ... any articles whatever of which the importation or circulation is forbidden in the country of origin or destination'. Conveniently, the Post Office decided that preventing illegal sweepstake mail from reaching Ireland was the responsibility of the country of origin and therefore was willing to deliver any mail that escaped notice and arrived unmolested in Ireland.

But the deception went much further than that. Because foreign postal authorities were obviously looking out for mail sent to Hospitals Trust, alternative postal addresses in Ireland were used. The Post Office had a list of these addresses and diverted letters sent to them to Hospitals Trust instead. Many of these names and addresses were fictitious, potentially causing problems for the Post Office with its international peers in cases where they sought proof of delivery.

Coleman uncovered a quite extraordinary situation whereby, up to 1938, sweepstake correspondence addressed to the Irish government was forwarded to Hospitals Trust. One senior civil servant in the Department of the Taoiseach questioned this practice, believing it was 'wrong that this Department should permit itself to be used as an intermediary or cover for the transmission of correspondence which, if sent through the ordinary post from these countries, would be subject to confiscation or other penal action'.

He also raised concerns about the department's liability for undelivered mail (particularly in the case of a disputed claim over ownership of a winning ticket) and about its reputation abroad, wishing to avoid 'anything which might appear to countenance an evasion of the law of other countries by their citizens'. Yet that is exactly what the Irish government was doing.

Government departments did, however, cease forwarding on any sweepstake correspondence they received; instead returning it to the sender with an explanatory note that while the sweepstakes promoted by Hospitals Trust were legal, they were not conducted by the state and government regulations did not permit departments to be used as transmitting agencies for the Sweep.

Despite these highly serious issues, there is no question that in those early days the Sweep produced enormous resources for the hospital sector and voluntary and even local authority hospitals clamoured to be included. A committee of reference was set up by the government to advise the minister as to how best to allocate the funds raised by the Sweep.

The improvements that the sweepstake funding enabled are undeniable and included new county hospitals in places such as Tralee, Cashel, Ennis and Monaghan; smaller district hospitals; fever hospitals; specialist hospitals to treat TB; and extending and improving psychiatric hospitals.

The only downside of this largesse was the growing evidence that voluntary hospitals became less concerned about cost control and budgeting and allowed spending to spiral. Between 1933 and 1939 the combined deficits of the voluntary hospitals trebled, which reduced the amount of money available from the fund for new hospital development.

* * *

The first threat to this windfall came just four years after the Sweep's establishment. The passing of the Betting and Lotteries Act in Britain in 1934 had the particular aim of clamping down on large public lotteries, with the Irish Sweep being the main target. It prohibited publication of any material associated with a lottery, thus ending the practice of British newspapers running pages of lists of sweepstake prizewinners, and also targeted ticket sellers.

The new legislation hit the Sweep hard in Britain: the percentage of total subscriptions from across the Irish Sea fell from 70 per cent to below 40 per cent. The percentage of British winners dropped to between one-quarter and one-third of prizes won.

As usual, Hospitals Trust adapted to the new legal climate. Identity numbers rather than names were used for correspondence; no addresses were printed on receipts sent back to subscribers, who were also advised to send all correspondence through intermediaries; some tickets were transmitted indirectly to Ireland via France. Most blatantly of all, Hospitals Trust promised to pay the fines imposed on anybody convicted of selling tickets. Not surprisingly, this two fingers to the British legal system led to representations to the Irish government from Britain and the circular making the promise was withdrawn.

As potential sales in Britain stalled, the US market, where the Depression had prompted huge interest in lotteries, took up much of the slack. By the 1935 Derby draw, more tickets were being sold in the US than in Britain. By 1937 over 50 per cent of tickets were being sold in the US, raking in more than £4 million a year for the Sweep.

Importing lottery material was illegal in the US and so the tickets had to be smuggled in on ships crossing the Atlantic, via England. The Canadian city of Montreal became a centre for the distribution of tickets across North America.

Presumably many palms were greased along the way, but the controversial provision in the original legislation allowing certain expenses to be undeclared means it is impossible to know how much money was involved. We do know that the going rate for smuggling tickets from Ireland to North America was £10 per 1,000 books of tickets (£5 for the leg to England and a further £5 for the onward journey to the US) and therefore it seems probable that the total bill for these under-the-counter payments ran into the hundreds of thousands.

Once the tickets arrived in the US they were distributed to the general public through agents, who were paid a commission by Hospitals Trust of ten shillings per book of 12 tickets sold. Code names were used in communications with head office in Dublin to cover the ships on which the tickets were to be smuggled and for the names of key personnel and office holders to whom bribes had to be paid – policemen, for example, were described as 'underwriters'.

The US Post Office Department initially took a tough line on newspapers carrying advertisements for lotteries and on the flow of tickets for illegal lotteries and sweepstakes. It refused to handle suspect mail to and from individuals or Irish companies – in the process disrupting the legitimate business dealings those companies had in the US. However, when President Franklin D. Roosevelt appointed Irish-American Jim Farley as Postmaster General in 1933, a much more relaxed interpretation of the law ensued.

MacAnthony wrote in 1973 that Farley was a regular visitor to Dublin, where he would meet with his friends from the Sweep. 'For what purpose was never disclosed,' he added. Farley certainly did have his photograph taken beside the sweepstake drum on a visit to Ireland in late 1936. His laissez-faire approach rather embarrassingly came to prominence when prime-time US television host Ed Sullivan announced to millions of viewers that the best place to buy a Sweep ticket was from the clerk on the counter of the Central Post Office in New York.

Of the other US agencies, the Justice Department went after sweepstake agents and the Treasury sought taxes on their undisclosed profits. The Customs Bureau meanwhile had some notable successes in intercepting tickets; on one occasion in 1938 it seized 46,000 books of tickets, valued at $2.5 million, from one boat in Philadelphia.

Two years earlier, there was a close escape when New York police raided an apartment at Central Park West, which was essentially the Sweep's New York office and the place where all its US records were stored. Thanks to a tip-off, the documents had been hidden in a linen cupboard and the police failed to find them. If they had, the Sweep would probably have been finished in the US.

The popularity of the Sweep in the US was emphasised during a trial of sweepstake agents in 1936: it took days to find 12 jurors who had never purchased an Irish Sweep ticket. This ubiquity prompted the US government, through its consul in Dublin, John Cudahy, to raise objections in 1937 with the Irish government. Though Taoiseach Eamon de Valera was sympathetic to Cudahy's representation, nothing practical came out of it.

It was a tricky issue for both governments. The Sweep was legal in Ireland, so effectively the US government would be asking the Irish government to be responsible for the enforcement of US law, which was hardly a tenable request. The Irish government, while no doubt uneasy about what was happening, depended on the largesse from the Sweep to fund the health service. Cudahy's lobbying, however, did force Hospitals Trust to tone down its activities in the US.

Not surprisingly, given McGrath's Republican background, the sweepstake organisation in the US quickly came under the control of Clan na Gael (the US equivalent of the IRB) and the

IRA. Two of the leading figures in those organisations in the US were Joseph McGarrity and Connie Neenan.

Tyrone-born McGarrity had emigrated to Philadelphia in 1892 and became a legendary figure in Republican circles as he helped to bankroll the War of Independence. Initially a close ally of de Valera – he called his son Eamon de Valera McGarrity – he did not support the founding of Fianna Fáil. He remained an unapologetic advocate of armed struggle and rejected all solutions that fell short of a 32-county Republic. His status is demonstrated by the fact that all IRA statements were signed with the moniker 'J.J. McGarrity' until the split in 1969 (while the Official IRA continued to use that name, the Provisionals opted for 'P. O'Neill'). Although he was a hugely successful businessman, McGarrity had run into financial difficulties. These were alleviated by his acquisition of a sweepstake agency that was estimated to be worth $250,000 a year to him.

Neenan, who fought in the War of Independence before emigrating to the US, distanced himself from Republicanism and became the principal agent for the Sweep in the US, filling the same role for McGrath's Waterford Crystal, until his return to Ireland in the 1970s.

Neenan and McGarrity, along with others connected to the Sweep, were indicted in New York in 1938 for 'smuggling into the US and distributing interstate commerce tickets purporting to be lottery tickets'. All of the others pleaded guilty, with a couple receiving fines and suspended sentences, but the cases against Neenan and McGarrity fell through due to a lack of evidence.

Another person on the payroll in the US, reportedly to the tune of $30,000 a year in the 1930s, was high-profile journalist Drew Pearson. Pearson had a nationally syndicated column on

Washington political life and a reputation for exposing corruption in high places.

In his *Sunday Independent* exposé, MacAnthony also revealed that Sidney Freeman, brother of sweepstake director Spencer, would travel to New York at the time of each draw, where, ensconced in a luxury hotel, he would be alerted by an encoded telegram of the result of the draw in Dublin. Aware of which ticket holders had drawn the race favourites before they were officially informed, he had a head start over his competitors in contacting those lucky people and offering to purchase shares in their tickets. The ticket holders were often glad to accept the offer as there was no guarantee the horse they had drawn would win the race, particularly in the case of the unpredictable Grand National.

In 1939 Sidney Freeman was reported to have paid over $700,000 in 200 deals, mostly in New York, with those who had drawn tickets. Nine half-shares that he bought on tickets that were matched with horses eventually placed in one of the first three positions in the race brought in $450,000 alone, suggesting a handsome profit was made. The assumption was that Freeman was acting in tandem with the senior management of Hospitals Trust. MacAnthony also claimed that the company was buying up to 60 per cent of its own winnings in Britain in this manner.

While there was plenty of positive coverage of the Irish Sweep in the US print media – and on TV and film where winning the sweepstake was a regular theme – some items were highly critical. An article in *Collier's* magazine in 1938 alleged that the number of counterfeit sweepstake tickets in circulation meant that the chances of winning a prize corresponded 'roughly to your chance of being named emperor of Japan'.

* * *

The biggest threat to the Sweep was the outbreak of World War II, which raised major questions about its survival. Given its importance to the economy in terms of employment and providing funding for hospitals, the Irish government rowed in behind the sweepstake. It amended the existing legislation to establish a reserve fund, which was separate from the Hospitals Trust fund, and basically underwrote any losses the promoters might have to endure because of the War.

The government quickly reversed this measure after the 1940 sweepstake embarrassingly saw a payment of over £61,000 go to Hospitals Trust from the reserve fund. But, even then, there was a sweetener for the promoters. To compensate for this reversal, the proportion of proceeds given to hospitals was reduced from 25 per cent to 20 per cent.

As horse races were held in Ireland during the War, the Sweep was able to continue, although takings were obviously greatly reduced. By 1946, however, proceeds were back over £1 million.

The Sweep's next major challenge emerged in the 1950s, when the presence of alternative forms of gambling, particularly the football pools, saw it decline in importance in the UK.

In 1961 gross proceeds from ticket sales peaked at £6.1 million. By 1979 sales had fallen to £1.8 million despite a rise in ticket price from £1 to £2. One of the main causes of this decline was the legalisation of state lotteries in North America, although the US and Canada remained the Sweep's two key markets throughout the 1970s.

Lobbying by Hospitals Trust in the 1960s and 1970s to persuade the Irish government to expand the number of sweepstakes, bringing it closer to a weekly lottery, was unsuccessful. There were fears in government that this would only pay its way if it was promoted in the UK, which, given that such sales would be illegal, had the potential to embarrass the government 'because of the special statutory position of the Sweeps Organisation'. Such concerns had been overcome in the past but the new hardline attitude may have been influenced by the fact that sweepstake revenues had become a much smaller part of the health budget.

The Irish media's uncritical approach to the Sweep also began to change. In 1969 RTÉ television's current affairs programme *7 Days* featured the failure of Hospitals Trust to recognise the Workers' Union of Ireland. The *Irish Times* stated afterwards that 'the picture that emerged was that of a successful company using methods illegal in other countries, yielding fat profits to a limited group of families, the whole thing stamped with the symbol of charity'.

But that picture was nothing compared with the one that emerged in 1973 in MacAnthony's brilliant investigative piece in the *Sunday Independent*. The article was so explosive that the editor scrapped plans to run it over two weeks, deciding to publish everything on the one Sunday. Although the reaction of Hospitals Trust was predictably fierce – advertising was pulled from the newspaper for the best part of two months – in the longer term the article proved a turning point in terms of public opinion.

This shift was evident in a Dáil debate three years later on amending legislation to increase Hospitals Trust's expenses ratio to 40 per cent. Whereas previously there had been a lone voice of criticism in the Dáil – normally James Everett of the Labour Party – opposition in 1976 was more widespread. Des O'Malley of Fianna Fáil was strongly critical of the high fees earned by the promoters in comparison to the small amount of money going to hospitals.

As Minister for Justice between 1970 and 1973, O'Malley had been responsible for signing an official deed on each sweepstake during that period. Unhappy at the lack of information on where the money was going, he hinted that he would withhold permission. O'Malley told an RTÉ documentary years later, 'Paddy McGrath came in to me to say that this was dreadful and ... it would lead to the immediate unemployment ... of 800 to 900 women; that I couldn't contemplate that, and that even if I could, other members of the government wouldn't contemplate it and therefore I couldn't do it.' Paddy, the son of Joe McGrath, was by then managing director of Hospitals Trust.

Responding to the criticism about the lack of accountability, the government stated that it was not realistic to impose 'public accountability over a private company'. Although the sweepstake had been established by the Dáil, its operation as a private company provided a convenient excuse over the decades to distance successive Irish governments from the illicit and embarrassing activities of the Sweep's agents.

In the same debate, Labour TD John O'Connell alleged he had been 'intimidated by people' and told he would be 'smeared' in his constituency if he voted against the legislation.

In the Seanad, John Horgan, a friend of MacAnthony, described the sweepstake operation as 'abhorrent'. Mary Robinson spoke of journalists who investigated the Sweep and who had 'not furthered their careers in doing so', a clear reference to MacAnthony, who had left Ireland for Canada.

The Sweep still retained some of its old clout. An RTÉ documentary along the lines of MacAnthony's investigation and including footage of sweepstake tickets being smuggled out of Dublin Port and revelations on kickbacks and money to hauliers was shelved in 1978 following pressure from Hospitals Trust.

Nevertheless, the Sweep was in terminal decline and was particularly damaged by the 1979 postal strike, which caused the cancellation of two draws. Irish hospitals were now predominantly funded by the state, with a negligible contribution from the Sweep – even in nominal terms the amount going to fund the hospitals was far less than in the 1930s.

The other business interests of the three sweepstake families had been centralised in a company called Avenue Investments, which also ran into difficult times and its shareholding in Waterford Crystal and other companies was sold off. The McGrath family also began to dispose of a lot of its property in south Dublin.

When the National Lottery Act was passed in 1986, clearing the way for a new licensee to run regular lottery games in Ireland, the closure of the Sweep was inevitable. The government rejected a final plea from Hospitals Trust to run fortnightly sweepstakes because of the potential for wasteful duplication.

The Sweep's last draw took place in January 1986. The remaining 150 or so staff members were laid off and later made redundant. Four days after the launch of the National Lottery in March 1987, Hospitals Trust officially went into liquidation.

A campaign by workers to secure more than the basic statutory redundancy payment lasted until 2000 when the Fianna Fáil/Progressive Democrats coalition government awarded them a lump sum of £20,000 each. Minister Mary Harney conceded the government did have some obligation to the workers because of the statutory nature of the sweepstakes (although she insisted it did not set a precedent). It was the final chapter in a remarkable relationship between the state and a private company.

To be fair to successive governments, it should be pointed out that Hospitals Trust did not always get its own way. For example, persistent efforts to get the Radio Éireann transmitter moved from Athlone to the east coast to boost the signal into Britain were rejected, despite threats from Freeman that the Sweep would remove its sponsored programmes and transfer its support to Radio Luxembourg, which ultimately happened in 1960.

And, before RTÉ television was launched, the government rejected heavy pressure from Hospitals Trust backing a proposal from a Romanian expatriate Charles Michelson to break the state's broadcasting monopoly and set up two television stations – one commercial, one public service – in Ireland. They maintained there would be no financial risk to the state in return for allowing high-powered commercial radio stations to be based in Ireland for broadcasting into Britain and Europe.

There were also some signs of concerns in the Department of Justice around the mid-1940s. It was felt that the underground activities used to sell tickets abroad were an embarrassment to Ireland. The Minister for Justice had to sanction each sweepstake and the department questioned whether it was proper for the minister to sanction a scheme 'which contains provisions designed to promote the sale of tickets in countries in which their sale is unlawful'.

But ultimately, the funds raised for hospitals, the influx of foreign currency and the employment the sweepstakes brought outweighed that concern. To some degree that position was understandable. Prior to the Sweep, Ireland's hospitals were in a terrible state – many of the county hospitals were old workhouses. There was no exchequer money available to change that. Ruth Barrington, author of *Health, Medicine and*

Politics in Ireland 1900–1970, summed it up as 'Hobson's choice', with the Sweep being the least of all evils.

The financial gain to the state is estimated at £170 million over the lifetime of the Sweep: £135 million for hospitals and another £35 million earned on stamp duty charged (amounting to billions of euro in today's terms). Not only were the voluntary hospitals saved, but an entirely new hospital infrastructure was built. Then there was the level of employment provided and the huge sums of foreign currency brought in (arguably making the Sweep one of Ireland's leading exports during that period).

With such massive funds available, however, Marie Coleman argues that there was a huge missed opportunity to build even better infrastructure due to the failure to implement a comprehensive plan to reform the state's hospital provision. She blames both the voluntary hospitals, which wanted the full benefit of the Sweep funds without any accountability to the state, and successive governments.

It is somewhat ironic that for years after independence, the Irish state was still dependent on money coming from Britain to fund services to the nation's sick. And there are obvious questions about successive governments acquiescing in a system that allowed the three promoters to build up enormous personal fortunes. However, by far the most serious issue is the state's toleration of the various illegal methods used by the Sweep to sell tickets in countries where their sale was prohibited by law.

The Irish state fundamentally 'colluded', as Coleman puts it, in these actions, doing damage to the country's reputation abroad. Coleman concludes:

The recent revelations of various judicial tribunals investigating political and corporate corruption in

Ireland reveal the sort of society in which an organisation like the Sweepstakes was allowed to flourish. If the Sweepstakes still existed there would probably be a tribunal sitting in Dublin Castle to examine it.

That is undoubtedly true. What is impossible to measure is the extent to which the state's collusion in what went on at the Irish Hospitals Sweepstake impacted on wider society.

* * *

If the state was effectively turning a blind eye to illegality, what message did that send out to the wider public? And, in this context, how can anyone be surprised about, for example, the revelations of widespread tax evasion via bogus non-resident bank accounts and Ansbacher-style schemes?

In their handling of the Sweep, successive Irish governments sent out a clear message that the rule of law is not paramount. This culture persists in Ireland and was arguably a key factor in the banking and economic crisis that came to light in the late 2000s.

Speaking in 1940, Jack O'Sheehan, Director of Publicity for the Sweep, attributed its success to its common honesty. The whole world had confidence in its direction and in its methods and nothing would ever shake that confidence, he said. How wrong he was.

Interviewed in 1962, Patrick McGrath, who would go on to become a senator and a director of Bank of Ireland, was asked about ticket sales abroad. He answered, 'The tickets leave here. Where do they go from there, I don't know. I hand them over to somebody else. That's their business.' A good example of the 'don't ask' approach that for decades was all too common in Irish life.

Back in the early days of the Sweep, the Church of Ireland Bishop of Limerick, Dr Vere White, in his role as governor of Barringtons Hospital, objected to the Board of Governors' decision to join the Sweep, warning, 'we must not do evil that good should come'. At the time this would have been seen as an overzealous warning on the dangers of gambling. In retrospect, despite the improvements to the health service, the long-term damage suggests it was a philosophy that would have served the Irish state well had it ever been adopted.

3

JOBS FOR THE BOYS

HELEN Cooke – 'Nellie' as she was affectionately known to her family – had little reason to be worried when she applied in the spring of 1950 to succeed her invalided Aunt Katie as postmaster of the sub-post office in the County Wicklow village of Baltinglass.

After all, she had to all intents and purposes been running the post office for the previous 14 years since she gave up her own post office in Rathdrum to assist her elderly aunt. And the Cookes had been managing the sub-post office since 1880 when Helen's grandfather James Cooke became postmaster. It was so strongly identified with the family locally that it was known as Cooke's post office.

Although postmaster positions were much sought after nationally, the Baltinglass sub-post office did not seem particularly lucrative. It was a commission-based post, worth about £520 a year. Even in 1950 that was not a huge amount of money when you also had to pay, feed and lodge three members of staff.

Helen Cooke was born in Glasgow but her father was from Baltinglass. She was a former nun in the Poor Clares. After leaving the convent she had also been an activist on the Republican side in the Civil War, working for an underground press that produced a Republican newspaper.

Cooke was not a universally loved figure in the village. Sharp-tongued and aloof, she apparently used to interrupt private phone calls – routed, as was the way in those days, through the local post office – to reprimand any use of bad language. 'A rip who would eat you without salt' was the description of one anonymous local, given in an RTÉ documentary some years later.

But, loved or not, Cooke was part of the fabric of Baltinglass and the assumption locally was that, given her experience in the role, the transfer from aunt to niece of the role of postmaster was a fait accompli.

The only reason the position was advertised at all was because of a change in rules, introduced by the new inter-party government – a hotch-potch coalition of Fine Gael, the Labour Party, the National Labour Party, Clann na Poblachta, Clann na Talmhan and one independent TD. The new rules confined the transfer of post office positions to direct blood relatives. But nobody locally saw this as anything other than a bureaucratic hurdle that needed to be cleared.

They were labouring under a serious misapprehension. In late November 1950 word came down from Dublin that Helen Cooke had not been selected as postmaster. The position instead went to a 27-year-old local man called Mick Farrell. Farrell's parents already owned a public house as well as a grocery and the butcher's and draper's shops in Baltinglass, all sited about 100 yards down the road from Cooke's post office.

The Farrell family was well liked in the area, particularly Mick. But, unlike Helen Cooke, Mick had absolutely no experience of running a post office.

What he did have, however, were political connections. His father, Benjamin, was a close political ally of the Minister for Posts and Telegraphs and Wicklow TD, James Everett, the man with responsibility for appointing postmasters and a politician who believed in looking after his own.

Everett was an ordinary working man who had come up through the ranks of the Labour movement. Remembered for always carrying a bag of bullseyes with him, he has been portrayed by some as being part of the 'cute hoor' wing of Irish politics.

The story goes that early in his ministerial career he responded to a public meeting of local postmen complaining about the state of the roads by unilaterally announcing there and then a national pay rise for postmen. His cabinet colleagues found out about it the next day when they read their newspapers.

But the stereotype may be unfair. Everett was one of the few politicians over a 40-year period who consistently criticised the operations of the Irish Hospitals Sweepstakes (see Chapter 2), a brave and correct stand that demonstrates there was more to him than simply being a local political fixer.

Nevertheless, he was certainly an impressive local operator, holding his seat through 16 general elections between 1922 and 1965.

Benjamin Farrell was his man in Baltinglass in the west of the constituency. Farrell was a former councillor who had also been selected for Everett's party, the National Labour Party – a group that temporarily split from the Labour Party in 1944 before the two parties reunited six years later – to run in Kildare in the 1948 general election, but his nomination was late. But with Everett running the Department of Posts and

Telegraphs, the timing was perfect for appointing Benjamin's son Michael to the sub-postmaster's job.

There was shock locally at the decision and it did not take long for the shock to turn to anger and action. After an initial meeting in the local ice-cream parlour, a public meeting was called for the town hall and attended by 500 people – some estimates put it at 700 – out of a population of just over 1,000.

The meeting unanimously adopted a resolution of protest against the proposed change. The Baltinglass Protest Committee was set up and included a number of local bigwigs – none bigger than retired British Major-General Meade Edward Dennis CBE. Dennis was a highly decorated soldier from both world wars and had been Montgomery's artillery commander at El Alamein. He was also landlord of much of the property in the town and his ancestral home was nearby. His grandfather had been instrumental in giving the original sub-postmastership to the Cooke family 80 years earlier.

The protestors also included Daphne Lalor (formerly Winters), who was a first cousin once removed of the Queen of England. A young publican, Bernie Sheridan, who proved to be a master of PR, was the key figure in setting up the committee.

A motley crew they may have been, but their campaign was about to shake a government, attract headlines all over the world and become the subject of a ballad as well as a best-selling book. The 'Battle of Baltinglass' would be the political version of the old saying that mighty oaks from little acorns grow.

The epicentre of that battle was a concrete slab outside Cooke's post office under which lay the key telephone cable that served as Baltinglass's communications link with the rest of the world. It was a piece of slab that was briefly to become as famous as the Blarney Stone.

In early December 1950 post office engineers and linesmen made three attempts to prise up the slab and disconnect the cable, only to be foiled by townspeople from the protest committee, who had begun marching up and down in front of the post office from early morning until almost midnight.

The first attempt by workers to disconnect the cable was resisted by a small group of men, who informed the workers they would not allow them to lift the slab. By the time of the second attempt, 150 locals had gathered. One woman placed a chair on the slab and proceeded to drink tea while sitting on the chair. Another woman told the *Irish Press* that a grave injustice had been done to Cooke and promised, 'We will fight to the end.'

A handwritten poster placed in front of the post office read: 'Are these the human rights that Everett spoke about at Strasbourg?' And it was this feeling that an injustice had been done that seems to have been at the root of the protest. Cooke may not have been universally loved and may not have been as popular as the Farrells, but, rightly or wrongly, many people in the area felt that she was entitled to the position, especially as she had been in situ for so long.

The *Irish Press* had already been covering the story and now, after a visit by Major-General Dennis to editor Robert Smyllie, the *Irish Times* also began to report on the case. Within days it would be making headlines across the world as British and American journalists arrived in the village to report on events (some even speculating whether a communist conspiracy was orchestrating events). At one point 26 journalists were in the village.

Although the campaigners stressed they had no personal quarrel with Farrell, it did not take long for bitterness to develop in the dispute. Farrell's mother got a letter with the words 'Death To-night' pencilled on the outside of the envelope, although there was no suggestion that anyone associated with the protest committee was responsible.

The local Labour organisation – by this point Everett's National Labour Party had folded back into Labour – rallied behind Farrell, forming the Farrell Support Committee. It organised its own protest meeting in the town hall in early December. The meeting had started with a torchlight procession along the main street, which required several gardaí to be drafted in from the surrounding areas. The local population of publicans, shopkeepers and inhabitants of Baltinglass responded by switching off their lights as a protest.

One Labour Party activist claimed at the meeting that elements of British imperialism were trying to blacken the workers and their representatives in the area. At later meetings of this group there were placards stating 'People of Baltinglass want no relations with the Queen of England', which prompted Daphne Lalor to step back from the campaign.

Most observers believe the town was split 80/20 in favour of Cooke, with Farrell's support mainly drawn from the less well-off members of the community. This divide was played up by Farrell himself, who claimed it was 'definitely the big shots against the farming and labouring classes'. Dennis – who was the direct landlord to the Farrells and the ground landlord to the old post office – was described as a 'Cromwellian rancher' by one of Farrell's supporters.

Certainly virtually all the shopkeepers outside of the Farrell family backed Cooke although it was suggested in later years that this may have been because they kept their savings in the post office and did not want a business rival knowing their affairs.

* * *

What was initially a very local dispute was by now taking on national significance.

In the Dáil on 6 December, the opposition put down questions asking if there had been any complaints during the previous 14 years about the performance of the Baltinglass post office (there had not) and asking about the cost of removing an underground cable into the post office and installing it in the proposed new premises (it turned out to be £146).

It did not take long for matters to become heated. Seán Lemass accused Everett of giving 'his pal a job', while his Fianna Fáil colleague Paddy Smith was even blunter, describing it as 'dirty, low down, mean corruption'.

When local independent TD Patrick Cogan, who was a strong backer of the Baltinglass Protest Committee, attempted to ask Everett what 'technical qualifications' the proposed new postmaster had for the position, Gerry Boland of Fianna Fáil heckled, 'He is a member of the Labour Party.'

Responding to a point from Cogan that the post office had been in the hands of the Cooke family for over 70 years, Everett infuriated Cogan and Fianna Fáil deputies by saying, 'I can assure him that 70 years ago no other Irish person got an opportunity of applying for the job.' This prompted Boland to declare that the Cookes were nationalists and always had been.

Matters became even more heated that night in the Dáil during an adjournment debate on the issue. Cogan thundered that Baltinglass raised the issue about whether public positions would be filled 'on the basis of merit alone or on the basis of political graft and corruption', adding that the appointment:

... bears on its face all the marks of the cold blooded brutality and immorality of Soviet rule ... What is Communism but a form of gangsterism which fills up appointments, not on merit, but on the basis of those who served most faithfully on the party line. The people of Baltinglass are standing firm on this issue. As I told them in Baltinglass last week, they have lighted a fire which has spread throughout the land. It is a fire which will blaze and burn until the public life of this country is finally and permanently cleansed.

Everett tried to explain away the issue by claiming that the difficulty arose because after becoming minister he had instructed officials that sub-post offices should not be transferred to relatives except in the cases of a husband, wife, son, daughter, widow or widower of the outgoing postmaster. Up until then the sub-post office could be automatically transferred to a wider range of relatives.

This prompted Smith to repeatedly accuse Everett of lying earlier in the day during question time by attributing that act to his predecessor. 'You are only a dirty low down rat,' Smith shouted, doing his best Jimmy Cagney impression.

The Dáil at this point was descending into near anarchy. Oliver J. Flanagan, then a government-supporting independent TD but a future Fine Gael minister, threatened to go across to Smith. 'If I go across you will—' his roar was drowned out by the din. According to newspaper reports, Flanagan 'at this stage rose from his seat and took two steps towards the floor but Mr Brendan Corish ... and Mr Blowick, who were sitting beside him each laid a hand on his arm. Mr Flanagan then resumed his seat, shouting: "What about the post offices at Carndonagh and Charlestown?"' These post offices were also on licensed premises, one of the key opposition criticisms of the proposed new post office in Baltinglass.

Smith was ordered out of the Dáil but responded by calling

Deputy Chairperson Patrick Hogan 'a political hack for the time you have been in that chair' and because of the 'grave disorder', the Dáil was adjourned until the following morning.

As the members were filing out, there was a shout of 'Put Everett out' from the unusually packed public gallery. The Clerk of the Dáil called to gardaí, 'Take the name of the man who shouted and hold him.' Gardaí moved in and the man, a member of the Baltinglass Protest Committee, was detained for questioning. An hour later he was released with a caution. The man had previously been a friend of Everett and had even attended his wedding.

The following day Everett defended his actions in the Dáil, stating that there was no personal objection to Cooke but he considered Farrell the better candidate.

Everett did not help matters by referring to Farrell's college education, but he was on stronger ground when he said he saw no reason why sub-postmasterships should be 'handed on by inheritance'. The advertising of the position was done as a routine matter by his department without any consultation with him, the minister said.

He did not want to cast any reflection on Cooke but the fact she was an assistant conferred no entitlement on her. While the argument had been put forward that members of her family had run the office over a long period of years, and she should therefore be automatically appointed, his inclination, frankly, was in the opposite direction. 'I consider Mr Farrell to be a better candidate. He was at least 30 years younger than the other candidate. He had a college education and he had given much voluntary service to his country.' This voluntary service included working in the Local Defence Forces (LDF) during the Emergency and he was still a member of the reserve force, the FCA.

Everett further claimed that Farrell was 'also recommended to the Department by prominent members of Fianna Fáil'. This was true up to a point. A Fianna Fáil TD later confirmed he was asked by an FCA officer to endorse another FCA officer who was seeking a job. However, he did not know Farrell or the local circumstances.

In his Dáil speech, Everett went on to argue that he could not let the cost of transferring the post office deter him from selecting the best candidate. He also claimed that many others in the Baltinglass area supported Farrell and stressed the post office would be sited in the draper's shop not in the pub. He added that the pub was not, as claimed, 'my party's HQ – all our meetings were held in the local cinema'.

* * *

The locals did not buy it, believing, as the *Irish Press* put it, that Farrell was given the job because 'his father was one of Mr Everett's political henchmen and for no other reason whatever'.

They were determined to have the decision reversed. Having successfully resisted the first attempt to disconnect the telephone wires to the sub-post office, the protest committee was honing its plans. The picket was replaced by a new system whereby one person would be on duty at all times with the responsibility of warning residents by means of a bell and also a siren erected in the town centre, if post office engineers arrived.

The local parish priest, Fr Patrick Doyle, also lent his support, appealing by letter to the Taoiseach to bring the matter to a satisfactory end. He said he could foresee 'grave moral issues coming into the question' and that he was convinced that Everett had 'done a grave injustice in appointing Mr Farrell to the position which Miss Cooke so ably filled for many years'. He asked the Taoiseach to bring a 'hasty conclusion' to 'this very unpleasant state of affairs now existing in Baltinglass,' adding, 'I am with my people in their agitation.'

Rev. J.B. Fisher, Church of Ireland rector of Kiltegan, a parish four miles from the town, also wrote to the Taoiseach voicing his 'strongest indignation at the action of the Minister for Post & Telegraphs in changing the office without any apparent reason'.

But the first real signal of the damage the affair could do to the government came when local independent TD Patrick Cogan, whose support was propping up the government, also wrote to Costello stating that until 'this wrong is righted … I will never again enter the division lobby on the government side'. He said there were bigger issues involved than the filling of a minor position:

> The civil conscience of plain people has been
> aroused by this grave injustice and the fight can go
> on till our public life and administration are purged
> of selfish greed and graft. The battle of Baltinglass
> is everybody's battle. It is a battle for clean
> administration and decent public life. It is a fight for
> justice for the weak and defenceless and in
> particular in the exercise by a minister of his
> executive functions.

Cogan concluded by asking Costello to 'right this grave wrong'.

There was also discontent locally within Fine Gael at the actions of the government. The O'Mahony – chief of all the O'Mahonys, former local Fine Gael TD and chairman of the West Wicklow district executive of the party – wrote to the Taoiseach and then sent him three telegrams urging him to take action. He later resigned from Fine Gael over the issue.

At 7.15 a.m. on 11 December the alarm bell was rung and a siren began wailing its warning – the protest committee had received a tip-off that the post office engineers were coming. By 7.30, about 100 local people had gathered. By 8.00, up to 60 gardaí, drafted in from across Wicklow, had arrived. Shortly after them came the linesmen from Carlow and Waterford, whose job it was to disconnect the cable leading into Cooke's post office and connect the new one into Farrell's.

The atmosphere was highly tense. The local curate, speaking on behalf of the parish priest, who was ill, asked the post office engineer if he would wait until Fr Doyle had received a response to his letter from the Taoiseach. The engineer replied that he would confirm his instructions from Dublin. Although he was told by Dublin to carry out his task, the engineer agreed to delay until the arrival of the next post. In that post was the letter from the Taoiseach, indicating that the minister had given the matter full consideration before reaching his decision.

In the lull before the linesmen returned, an effort was made by the committee, through Major General Dennis, to persuade Farrell to stand down but Farrell, backed up by his parents, declined.

At 1.00 p.m. the gardaí began assembling at Farrell's, so the siren was set off again. The locals, who had gone home for a belated breakfast, returned to the scene. There was some scuffling and a glowing brazier, used to keep the protestors warm, was knocked over in the kerfuffle.

Following pleading from the protest committee that there should be no violence, the gardaí moved the people away. They took possession of the slab and encircled the linesmen as they went about their work. The famous slab was lifted and while the cable was being cut there were shouts of 'Are we in Russia or the Republic?', 'Down with the Police State' and 'Are you Irishmen at all?' The shouts did not stop the new line being connected into Farrell's premises. It looked like the end of the line for the Baltinglass Protest Committee as well.

However, Cogan, who had rushed to the scene from the Tullow fair on hearing the news, addressed the crowd and declared that the Battle of Baltinglass was not over. Many had served in the LDF, he said, but they had done so to offer their lives for the country's defence not to secure jobs. As the crowd dispersed, eight women marched through the town carrying black flags of mourning. Most of the shops had drawn their blinds, as was the custom if there was a funeral.

Later in the afternoon a party of workers employed on the county council's drainage scheme nearby marched through the town carrying a tricolour, in support of Farrell. Some were in FCA uniforms. In the evening post office officials settled up accounts at Cooke's post office and postmen were ordered to report to the new postmaster. Fifteen gardaí remained in the town that night.

But there was no sign of the tensions settling down. A Labour club began a picket of the local technical school. The protestors carried placards and demanded the removal of a teacher who had backed Cooke and was on the protest committee.

In the early hours of the following day events took an even more sinister twist when four poles carrying telephone wires near the town were cut, disrupting the main trunk line between the town and Dublin and causing a two-hour delay on calls, which had to be routed through the Carlow exchange. The protest committee issued a statement disassociating itself from the action.

The new post office was open by this point but it was boycotted, a fate which in turn also befell any local shop that did not support this boycott. A rota was drawn up whereby cars and vans leaving the town took letters and parcels to post in nearby towns. Each was stamped in red ink with the words 'Baltinglass demands clean administration' – the rebel post office's stamp would later become a collector's item.

A telephone ban or day of silence was brought in. At other times the protestors deliberately rang in to jam the network.

The depth of the split in the local community was emphasised by the presence of a counter-boycott, with the local Labour organisation urging people to support only those businesses not identified with the protest committee.

When Cooke told the media she was going to have to 'sell out' and go to England with her aunt, the campaign took to the streets of Dublin. Protestors carrying sandwich boards and placards paraded through the city centre.

A small plane – flown by Norman Ashe, a glider pilot during World War II who was known to the major general – equipped with loudspeakers flew over O'Connell Street and the suburbs asking for people's support. The original plan was to drop leaflets on the Dáil but that was illegal so it opted to broadcast messages of support instead. Unfortunately the noise of traffic and the altitude meant nobody could hear them.

But the rest of the campaign was not falling on deaf ears. The controversy was proving particularly embarrassing for Clann an Poblachta, one of the government parties. It had fought the election denouncing jobbery and now it was dithering on one of its core principles.

Because of the party's inaction, the local branch of Clann na Poblachta decided to dissolve itself. Its letter to the general secretary said that although the party had campaigned that it would not stand for anything but clean government, Farrell's appointment was 'one of the many glaring cases of political jobbery that are being enacted during the inter-party government's term of office'. If the party's TDs had any respect for themselves and their followers, they would 'not stand for such corruption for the sake of their pensions' (which ministers in government would qualify for in February after three years in office). Cooke was getting no pension but a 'death sentence'.

The issue was also causing unrest in the wider party. The Westmeath county convention unanimously passed a resolution supporting the recent challenge of founder member Noel Hartnett to Everett and called for Everett's removal from office if he failed to satisfactorily address the matter.

There were more angry scenes in the Dáil as the opposition pushed for an inquiry. Cogan asserted that 'Deputy Flanagan claimed that he had got the position for Mr Farrell by threatening the Minister that he would expose two Labour scandals and also by getting the Minister for Agriculture … to squeeze the Minister for Post and Telegraphs'. Everett denied this 'emphatically'.

Cogan asked the Minister to 'state why he defied the priests and people of Baltinglass and threw an honest, faithful, Irish Catholic worker out of employment'. The independent deputy also claimed that the postmaster in Naas 'emphatically recommended' Cooke for the position.

Flanagan took the opportunity to clarify his position. He told the house that he was one of those to recommend Farrell for the position:

I was given to understand that the applicant had no job and that he had been working on his grandfather's farm until it was sold 12 months ago. I certainly made very strong recommendations to the Minister. I understand that Deputy Cogan made a statement to the House to the effect that I used threats to induce the Minster for Post and Telegraphs to make this appointment. I assure both the Chair and the House that that statement is quite untrue. I made no threats. I recommended Mr Farrell and I stand over my recommendation. I would do the same again if the opportunity occurred. If this government cannot stand over and defend its appointments then it should take up the challenge of the leader of the opposition and go to the people in a general election.

Cogan also took up the point about where the post office was situated. As Everett had said it was in the draper's shop, Cogan asked the minister whether the door leading from the new post office premises into the licensed premises has 'been effectively closed and if it will be possible in the Post office to obtain stamps and stout, groceries, sugar and shirts'.

John O'Leary of Labour asked if the minister could confirm that Cooke was born in Scotland and 'if it is the policy of Fianna Fáil and Deputy Cogan to employ foreigners rather than Irish people?' Cogan replied that Cooke was an Irish Catholic.

* * *

Back in Baltinglass, things were getting more serious. On 14 December the main telephone cable to the post office was severed at around the time that the protest committee was meeting and passing a resolution supporting gardaí and disassociating itself from line cutting. Telephone wires were again cut outside the town. The following Sunday, the parish priest Patrick Doyle issued an appeal at Masses for Catholics not to be associated with the cutting of telephone wires because the destruction of public property was morally wrong. The additional four gardaí in the town were further reinforced by three plain clothes men.

Cooke also very publicly entered the debate with a letter to the editor of the *Irish Press*. There had been claims circulating that Cooke was not Catholic and, even more outrageously, that she had been a spy for the Black and Tans during the War of Independence. Everett was never associated with these rumours, but he was accused of insinuating in the Dáil that Cooke was part of the 'Castle' tradition, meaning Dublin Castle.

In her letter to the *Irish Press*, Cooke wrote that her character had been taken away from her and that she 'never thought holy Ireland would fall so low'. She said that at the closing date for applications, Farrell had two nominations, whereas her form was signed by 90 per cent of the local shopkeepers and many other prominent citizens including the parish priest and curate. She claimed that when the two applications were examined in Dublin recently, her application had only one recommendation attached and Farrell's two had increased to 'numerous ones, including TDs' and asked who had inserted them after the closing date.

She said that she was born in Scotland, but her father was born in Baltinglass and her parents and grandparents were Catholic. Her grandfather had housed Parnell on a visit to Scotland. 'I purposely did not bring religion into this matter previously, as even if I were a non-Catholic, I am still entitled to justice.'

Cooke also cited a rule forbidding post offices to be

connected directly or indirectly with the ownership or management of a public house.

The letter served to crank up the pressure even further. There were plans by the protest group to spread the campaign into other towns and a Dublin branch of the committee was established. Across the country 35 sub-committees would be formed and over 10,000 signatures collected calling for Cooke's re-appointment – a huge number in those days of poor transport and communication links.

The Women Writers Club of Ireland lent its support to Cooke, with its chairperson, the well-known novelist Kate O'Brien, urging all members to make some protest against 'jobbery and corruption evident in Irish legislation today'.

There were also signs that the issue was causing serious difficulties for the government. The media predicted that if there was a general election it would cost the government parties seats.

An *Irish Times* editorial, describing Everett's move as a serious blunder, noted that 'for many years there has not been such a spontaneous outburst of popular indignation in Ireland and the mere fact that the immediate issue is unimportant serves only to accentuate the strength of the process'. It warned it was 'quite possible indeed that the inter-party regime might founder on the Baltinglass rock'.

One of the founders of Clann na Poblachta, Noel Hartnett, strongly criticised Everett, stating that if it emerged the minister had refused to act on the advice of his officials, then he should resign or be removed from office. The only way to remove jobbery was to remove temptation and establish an appointments commission, he said.

There was also a key intervention by Major-General Dennis. In a letter to the Taoiseach, he warned that as landlord of the Farrell property he was entitled to object to any restriction of the pub licence, which 'must, of necessity, reduce the value of my property'. Dennis repeated this concern verbally to the Farrell family, stating that while he would never evict them, he could not allow any part of the premises to be delicensed. Some observers believe this was critical in the Farrells deciding to back down.

But the Farrells must also have been feeling the pressure of local opinion. The protest committee held a referendum in the Baltinglass postal area – showing that 87 per cent backed Cooke to run the post office. Farrell disputed this result, claiming that pressure was brought on people to sign for Cooke and that he had 80 per cent support.

* * *

By 20 December, just 21 days after he was appointed sub-postmaster, Michael Farrell had had enough. He tendered his resignation to the minister personally and it was accepted.

Farrell's letter apologised to Everett that the appointment had caused him so much controversy and was used by his political opponents to launch an unwarranted attack on him. As an officer of the FCA, he expressed anxiety that the uniform he proudly wore 'should not become associated with or be in any way besmirched by the violent abuse and illegal acts for which your political opponents have been responsible following my appointment'. He was resigning in order that his and his family's name should not be used 'as a cover to launch base and undeserved attacks upon you'.

He concluded that it was 'odd' that he was eligible to 'wear the uniform of the defence forces of my country and am free to die in its service, but am denied an appointment to a small position in a country sub-post office. However, one must not expect logic when abuse and vilification have taken control of the situation.'

In his responding letter, Everett told Farrell he would be changing the long-established practice, 'inherited from our predecessors', of appointing sub-postmasters. Future candidates would be interviewed personally and any known to have sought political influence would be disqualified – the minister pointed out that Farrell's candidature had been backed by recommendations from TDs of all parties. 'I dislike intensely a system of appointment where political influence can be used in the filling of such positions and I intend at the earliest opportunity to introduce arrangements [to end this].'

There was jubilation in Baltinglass at the news.

There was also strong criticism of the 'almost complete absence of coverage' of the dispute given by Radio Éireann. The first time the story was covered properly on radio was when Everett's and Farrell's letters were read out. At the time Radio Éireann was part of a government department – the Department of Post and Telegraphs.

The protest committee decided to continue the boycott and campaign until Cooke was appointed. After what had happened with the first application process, nobody was taking that for granted. There was even speculation that Farrell might reapply for the job.

Farrell was serving his notice and, despite the boycott, he was kept busy by the large volume of telegrams and letters coming into the post office – most of which were bringing messages of support to Cooke.

Farrell's supporters had not gone away either. On 5 January 1951 a public meeting of the Labour Party was held in the town hall, attended by about 200 people. Before the meeting there was a torchlight procession through the town with people carrying such banners as 'Down with imperialism', 'Did James Connolly die for capitalists with loud speakers against Labour?'

Yet again, practically all the businesses and residences in the town were blacked out before and during the meeting, with only one shop on the main street with its lights on.

At the meeting, a resolution protesting in the strongest possible manner against the appointment 'of any non-Irish national to the position' was passed. The resolution also denounced the vile campaign of vilification and misrepresentation against Everett.

Farrell told the meeting that his supporters had gone out to the 1,600 residences in the postal area and collected 600 signatures. There were also accusations that two active members of the protest committee had approached Everett previously looking for jobs. Cooke was well-off and this was 'a fight really between the ordinary people of Ireland and the hardcore of Toryism and West Britonism which still remained in this country through the great charity of Irish revolutionaries'. This was a common theme throughout the dispute.

A thunderous editorial in the *Irish Press* accused the government-sponsored Irish News Agency, which was set up to channel Irish news worldwide, of portraying the story as 'a struggle of an Irish Catholic against the old Protestant ascendancy'. The piece from the agency had appeared in the influential *Gaelic American* newspaper.

The two-month-long Battle of Baltinglass was formally over at the end of January 1951 when a permanent selection board, which had been established to fill vacancies for postmasters, appointed Cooke to the position of sub-postmaster of the post office. She had been the only applicant.

Legend has it that the only actual punches thrown during the 'battle' were between two inebriated, and unidentified, members of the press. But there were many psychological wounds and they would take longer to heal. Indeed, the Farrells' businesses never recovered and they later left the town, settling in Rosslare, County Wexford. The post office became a tourist attraction.

Cooke retired in 1963, moving to Australia to live with her two sisters. She died in 1972. Some years after her death, it emerged that in 1933 she had given birth to a child, who was adopted by one of her sisters. Sadly, her daughter did not know that the 'aunt' she used to visit in Baltinglass was actually her mother until after Helen Cooke had died. Nobody in Baltinglass was aware of this fact either and, in the hugely conservative Ireland of the early 1950s, there is little doubt it would have impacted on the level of public support for her cause.

Helen Cooke and Michael Farrell did meet many years after the Battle of Baltinglass and shook hands.

* * *

There are conflicting views about what happened in those turbulent two months at the end of 1950 and the beginning of 1951. Paul Gorry, whose father's chemist shop was boycotted because it refused to close during one of the protest marches, described it as 'a study of mass hysteria in microcosm'.

When one TD referred to it as a 'storm in a teacup', the retort from Baltinglass was, 'It's grown into a damn big teacup and the tea is spilling out all over the country.'

It was the government that was left most dazed by the whole affair. Writer Dermot Bolger remarked in the *Irish Times* decades later that if 'Noel Browne felled the first

Interparty government (see Chapter 4), then Jim Everett's axe had already chopped its foundations away.'

The cabinet publicly backed Everett during the dispute, but there must have been severe misgivings about the damage it was doing to the government.

Ironically, the party that suffered most was not Labour or the lead coalition party Fine Gael, but Clann na Poblachta. In early February – in a huge blow to the party – the party's director of elections resigned. Noel Hartnett stated in his resignation letter that the party 'had compromised on those principles of political honesty and clean administration which we induced our supporters to believe were fundamental in our policy'. The party's amoral cynicism had expressed itself during the Baltinglass affair, according to Hartnett.

To be fair, the Clann na Poblachta leader, Seán MacBride, was horrified at both the immorality of the situation and the disastrous way it was mishandled. But, unlike Hartnett, he did not consider it an issue worth bringing down the government over. Eithne MacDermott writes in her book *Clann na Poblachta*:

> Within Clann na Poblachta, the Baltinglass scandal acted as a sort of prism focusing attention (almost by proxy) on the respective positions – principled or otherwise – held by those on the different wings of the party. Pressed by Hartnett and [Health Minister Noel] Browne to make a public protest over the Baltinglass appointment, MacBride – according to Browne – pleaded weakly that unsavoury matters are inseparable from politics.

Within weeks, Browne had resigned over the Mother and Child Scheme debacle (see Chapter 4) and the party itself was on borrowed time.

Events at Baltinglass gradually faded into the background, leaving behind a light-hearted ballad, written by Sylvester Gaffney:

The job of sub-postmaster or mistress, as might be,
Is not exactly one that leads to wealth and luxury;
But Korea was a picnic and Tobruk was just a pup
To the row the day the linesmen came to take the cable up.
[...]
Now the case has gone to UNO and we're waiting for the day
When Truman, Attlee and McBride will come along and say,
'Get back behind your parallel, drop atom bombs and gas,
And respect the bound'ries and the laws of Sov'reign Baltinglass'.

The renowned Canadian author and war journalist Lawrence Earl also wrote a book about it, called *The Battle of Baltinglass*, in a begorra and begob style not dissimilar to *The Quiet Man*.

The Battle of Baltinglass was an extraordinary example of what people power can achieve, but sadly its long-term impact was almost negligible and it was to be the exception that proved the rule. The 'jobs for the boys' ethos of successive governments was not remotely impacted by the Baltinglass scandal.

Government ministers continued to stuff various boards, bodies and the judiciary with their own people – often doing so hours before they handed over office to their political rivals in the wake of a general election. If anything, the jobbery or patronage practised in the first decades of the new state was much less significant than that after a more intimate relationship developed between business and politics (see Chapter 5). In fact, in the early years of the state, an independent Civil Service Commission and a Local Appointments Commission ensured most appointments were free from political interference.

However, many anti-treaty Republicans were excluded from public appointments until Fianna Fáil came to power in 1932. To try to balance this situation, the new government made a number of political appointments outside the framework of the two commissions and by the 1930s and 1940s state boards were highly politicised. This situation was continued by the coalition government that replaced Fianna Fáil in 1948, which, as Garret FitzGerald put it, 'saw a need to balance Fianna Fáil appointments during the preceding 16 years'.

Arguably, the practice of patronage has continued in this manner ever since. As an example of its scale, in the first two and a half years after Fianna Fáil and the Progressive Democrats took office in 1997, more than 1,000 appointments were made to the boards of state agencies.

Oliver J. Flanagan, who was drawn into the Dáil debate on Baltinglass, landed himself in hot water 18 years later in a *Late Late Show* discussion on jobbery. He told the television chat show's host, Gay Byrne:

My party does not believe in jobbery, [but] I am a firm and convinced believer in it ... I do not see anything wrong in a TD getting a job for a friend. I have found jobs over the past 25 years for numerous people from [my constituency of] Laois–Offaly and Dublin and any time I hear of Fianna Fáil ministers being criticised for putting their friends into jobs, I am angered because I am not in the same position to put my friends in jobs.

Flanagan was articulating what many politicians then (and now) would privately feel. His comments were directly in conflict with Fine Gael's stated policy that there should be an end to political appointments (a policy that was quickly ditched once the party finally got back into government five years later), but no action was taken against him. On the contrary, at a party meeting, his party leader criticised two Fine Gael councillors who had publicly taken exception to Flanagan's comments.

Donogh O'Malley of Fianna Fáil caused a stir around the same time when he said that all things being equal a job would go to a party member. Liam Cosgrave, leader of Fine Gael, said much the same thing.

Fianna Fáil politicians, having been in power far longer than those of any other party, were and are the past masters in the 'jobs for the boys' league. In the early 1980s, in the interim period after Charles Haughey's governments lost two elections and before the new government came in, the board of the planning appeals body, An Bord Pleanála, had a majority of places filled with two sets of friends of Ray Burke, the since disgraced cabinet minister who was later found to be corrupt in relation to planning matters (see Chapter 6).

'As a result, in early 1983, Dick Spring as Minister for local government had to abolish that board and reconstitute it with directors chosen from lists drawn up by different outside groups, so as to protect this hugely sensitive body from any further political manipulation,' Garret FitzGerald later recalled.

When the story first broke in 2006 about former Taoiseach Bertie Ahern receiving financial 'dig-outs', as he famously described them to RTÉ's Bryan Dobson, Ahern claimed that he had appointed people to state positions not because of anything they had given him, but 'because they were friends'.

Virtually all of Ahern's main supporters, known as the 'Drumcondra Mafia', have been appointed to public boards, including to some of the leading semi-state companies. In a letter to a supporter in the early 1990s, Ahern assured the person that he had and would continue 'to assist my better friends in obtaining employment'.

Such comments do not make Ahern unique or imply that he has done anything wrong. The reality is that many, perhaps most, TDs succeed in looking after their own. It is part of the Irish political culture.

The same culture dictated that (until the appointment of Patrick Honohan in 2009 during the banking crisis) the Governor of the Central Bank had to come from the Department of Finance. The same culture ensured that the board of the national training and employment authority, FÁS, was filled with appointments from the social partnership process. The same culture resulted in a board at Irish Shipping in the 1970s being filled with political appointees. Many of these appointments had disastrous consequences.

And if the first criteria for appointments to key state positions is party affiliation, no one should be surprised if Ireland does not always get the right people filling those positions. Nor should we be surprised by the consequences of such appointments.

* * *

So what made Baltinglass different? Why in a culture of jobbery was there such an outcry over what happened to Helen Cooke? The most likely answer is that there was a human face to what happened. It was not the typical case of a state board being filled by a party apparatchik with little direct impact on any specific individuals. In Baltinglass, a local woman's livelihood was being taken away and that stirred people into action.

There is more than a little irony about the fact that while giving the position to Michael Farrell smacked of jobbery, the counter argument that Cooke had an automatic right to the position because she and her family had filled it for decades was itself far from ideal. If Cooke had passed away or voluntarily given up the position of postmaster, would people have objected to Michael Farrell getting the job, even if it was not the result of an open and fair process? It is impossible to know for certain, but the best guess would be that they would not. And that would also explain why the Battle of Baltinglass, although successful in reinstating Cooke and shaking a government to its core, ultimately changed nothing in Irish political culture.

Sixty years later, there are finally moves by the Green Party in government to introduce legislation to eradicate political patronage in appointments to state boards in Ireland. If what lay at the heart of the struggle in Baltinglass, and its success in tapping into the public mood nationally, was really about establishing a genuine meritocracy for state appointments, then it surely would not have taken so long for such proposals to be made.

4

IN A STATE OF DISGRACE

THE telephone rang in the office of the Minister for Health, Noel Browne. It was 10 October 1950. On the line was the secretary to John Charles McQuaid, Archbishop of Dublin and arguably the dominant church figure in Ireland in the twentieth century. It was a short conversation. Browne was ordered to the archbishop's palace to attend, alone, a meeting the following day to discuss the Mother and Child Scheme. The scheme proposed the then radical idea of providing free medical care for expectant mothers and children up to the age of 16 years without a means test.

Browne, although something of a political innocent, not unreasonably was stunned at the diktat. He could not understand why the meeting was not taking place in his office in the Department of Health, as would be the norm with other citizens, regardless of rank or station. He took the summons by a private citizen as an affront to his office and to the people who had elected him.

In reality, however, it was the practice under Irish government protocol for a minister to attend, when told to do so, a meeting at the archbishop's palace. When Browne raised the matter with his cabinet colleagues, they could not comprehend his difficulty with this arrangement.

The meeting the following day began in a small anteroom in somewhat bizarre circumstances. Browne was greeted with a warm smile by McQuaid and would later claim the archbishop opened the conversation by discussing child prostitution and informing Browne that 'the little child prostitutes charge sixpence a time'. After this 'strange interlude', Browne was invited to a larger room, where the Bishop of Ferns, Dr James Staunton, and Bishop of Galway, Michael Browne, awaited.

A letter to the Taoiseach from the hierarchy was read to Browne by McQuaid. The letter said that while the minister's plans were 'motivated by a sincere desire to improve public health', the powers taken by the state in the proposed Mother and Child Scheme were 'in direct opposition to the rights of the family and of the individual, are liable to very great abuse … If adopted in law they would constitute a readymade instrument for future totalitarian aggression. The right to provide for the health of children belongs only to parents, not to the state. The state has the right to intervene only in a subsidiary capacity, to supplement, not to supplant.' Demonstrating exactly where the hierarchy's priorities and sympathies lay, the letter continued:

It may help indigent or neglectful parents. It may not deprive 90% of parents of their rights because of 10% necessitous or negligent parents. It is not sound social policy to impose a state medical service on the whole community on the pretext of relieving the necessitous 10% from the so-called indignity of the means test …

And getting to the heart of the matter, the letter warned:

Education in regard to motherhood includes instruction in regard to sex relations, chastity and marriage. The State has no competence to give instruction in such matters [unlike, presumably, a celibate clergy]. We regard with the greatest apprehension the proposal to give to local medical officers the right to tell Catholic girls and women how they should behave in regard to this sphere of conduct at once so delicate and sacred.

Gynaecological care may be, and in some other countries is, interpreted to include provision for birth limitation and abortion. We have no guarantee that state officials will respect Catholic principles in regard to these matters.

And in what would prove to be the ultimate irony given the secrecy the church later attempted to maintain with regard to abusive priests, the letter argued:

The proposed service also destroys the confidential relations between doctor and patient and regards all cases of illnesses as matter for public records and research without regard to the individual's right to privacy.

The elimination of private medical practitioners by a State paid service has not been shown to be necessary or even advantageous to the patient, the public in general or the medical profession.

The letter tellingly concluded:

The Bishops desire that your government should give careful consideration to the dangers inherent in the present proposals ...

End of lecture. The bishops assumed the interview was over.

But Browne was no shrinking violet and he took issue with some of their points. There was no question, he said, of compulsion for either patient or doctor. The figure for the poor involved was 30 per cent, not 10 per cent, and the comment 'represented a strange attitude from a powerful prelate of a Christian church towards the life and death of the "necessitous poor" and their children'. As a doctor, he argued that a free health service was an essential prerequisite to an effective and just health service. He described the necessitous poor as his 'special responsibility'.

Bishop Browne countered that it was unfair to tax the rest of the community to 'give the poor a free health service'. Minister Browne replied that tax was not a matter of morality but an issue for the government.

By this point a distinct cooling in the previously warm manner of the archbishop had occurred. McQuaid postulated the inevitability of contraception and abortion. Browne replied that 95 per cent of doctors, nurses and patients were Catholic and later said that he had asked McQuaid, 'Could he not depend on his flock to obey the teachings of their church?'

The minister signalled that he was amenable to compromise, particularly on 'the education of mothers', which he offered to reconsider and submit to the hierarchy or alternatively the hierarchy could consider the offending clauses and submit them to his department for improvement. If an agreement was not possible, since the provisions were not the most important section of the scheme, the minister 'would agree, regretfully, to withdraw the section completely'. This claim is backed up by Bishop Browne, who said the minister had stated it was not his intention that there would be antenatal clinics teaching birth control or abortion.

There are conflicting claims about how the meeting ended. McQuaid says Browne walked out slamming the door. Browne's version, to some degree supported by Bishop Browne's account, was that he was escorted to the front door by McQuaid, who was chatting along the way and bade him farewell at the door of the palace.

Farewell certainly, but as events would show, not goodbye.

* * *

Even at the peak of its powers in the newly independent state, the Catholic Church had no privileged legal status other than a rather vague reference accorded to it by Article 44 of the Constitution. That article, later abolished following a referendum in 1972, simply recognised the special position of the Catholic Church as the 'guardian of the faith professed by the great majority of its citizens'.

But while it may not have been written down in black and white, there is no disputing the iron grip the Catholic church held on public life after the foundation of the state in 1922. It utterly dominated primary (through the parish priest who was the de facto school manager) and second-level education, with dioceses or religious orders owning (and in many cases staffing) the vast majority of schools. Even at third level, the church had considerable influence through the National University of Ireland.

In social services, church orders ran hospitals, orphanages, reformatories and other welfare institutions, with the aid of grants from the government.

The Constitution of 1937 was not effectively drafted by the Catholic church as has often been suggested – in fact it disappointed conservative Catholics, but it certainly reflects church teachings on family, marriage and social issues. One of the key advisers to Eamon de Valera in drawing up the Constitution was a young President of Blackrock College, Fr John Charles McQuaid.

The church ostensibly stayed out of politics as long as

politics did not infringe on what it regarded as church teaching – an extremely broad area including education and health. With the Mother and Child Scheme, the state was – in the church's eyes – about to trod all over its patch. And that simply could not be tolerated.

* * *

In the late 1940s radical changes were taking place in health care across the Irish Sea. While Britain embraced the utopian vision of the National Health Service (NHS), with its commitment to universal service, health care remained pretty basic in Ireland. The country had a high death rate due to TB. Infant mortality rates also remained high. An independent Department of Health was not established until 1947. Ireland's slow progress was perhaps because health was seen as the church's sphere of influence and governments feared political reprisals if it strayed into that territory.

But there were tentative signs of change. Fianna Fáil TD Dr F.C. Ward had in 1944 been given responsibility for public health matters within the Department of Local Government and Public Health. Around the same time, Dr James Deeny, a GP and reputable scholar with (because of his practice in County Armagh) experience of the North's health service, was appointed Chief Medical Officer. Deeny firmly believed in the benefits of a strong public health policy and would prove very influential in shaping health legislation in Ireland.

In 1946 Taoiseach Eamon de Valera announced the intention to establish separate Departments of Health and Social Welfare. Ward, who had brought forward a Public Health Bill, was forced to resign on an unrelated issue. The hugely experienced Jim Ryan – a doctor by profession who had served in the GPO in the 1916 Rising as medical officer and would eventually chalk up nearly 30 years at the cabinet table – became Ireland's first Minister for Health. The wily Padraig Ó Cinnéide was appointed as Secretary. These choices suggest that de Valera knew some delicate handling would be required.

Ryan introduced a new Health Bill, which retained much of what Ward had proposed. It gave the state power to compel children to submit themselves for medical examination in school. It also provided a free medical service, without a means test, for mothers and children up to the age of 16.

While the measures seem wholly uncontentious by today's standards, they represented at least as radical a change as the health reforms introduced in the United States by President Barack Obama in March 2010. They put a lot of noses out of joint.

The church hierarchy did not like them at all, believing that the state was muscling in on their territory. They protested privately to de Valera in September 1947, arguing that the Act 'was directly and entirely contrary to Catholic social teaching, the rights of the family, the rights of the Church in education, and the rights of the medical profession, and of voluntary institutions'.

The main opposition party, Fine Gael, also opposed the Bill; as, unsurprisingly, did the Irish Medical Association, which was clearly worried about the financial implications for its members of a move it was quick to dub the 'socialisation of medicine'. James Dillon, then an independent TD but later leader of Fine Gael, was opposed to the compulsory inspection of school children and initiated a court action to test whether it was 'repugnant to the Constitution'.

But with Fianna Fáil losing power after the 1948 general election (for the first time in 16 years) the controversy did not come to a head. The battle was deferred and the problem passed on to a new government – a new government that was hugely ill-equipped to deal with it.

* * *

After the February general election, the first inter-party government, an 'ABFF' (anybody but Fianna Fáil) coalition, was surprisingly cobbled together from five political parties and independents. The cabinet contained some impressive talents and taking over the health portfolio was a 32-year-old newly elected doctor: Noel Browne.

Browne represented Clann na Poblachta, a new party led by former IRA leader Seán MacBride, which stood on a platform of social radicalism and had grandiose (and misplaced) ambitions of usurping Fianna Fáil. Tragedy had struck Browne early in life when he lost both his parents (his father had been an officer of the National Society for the Prevention of Cruelty to Children) and two sisters to TB. Due to the generosity of a well-off Irish Catholic family with English connections, he was able to avail of an expensive education at the English Jesuit public school Beaumont College – dubbed the 'Catholic Eton' – and then at Trinity College, Dublin.

A political novice, Browne was a surprise choice for minister. One of the reasons he was picked was that, unlike some of his colleagues in Clann na Poblachta, he did not have a controversial political past. This apparent virtue would soon become his party's, and the government's, biggest problem. 'That is one of my troubles,' he would confide to a senior public servant during a meeting, 'I don't know a lot about politics.' It was an assessment that would be proved uncannily accurate.

Despite (or perhaps because of) his inexperience, the new minister brought enormous enthusiasm and a crusading zeal to the campaign against TB, helped no doubt by the personal stake he had in the battle against the disease. Although his arrival coincided with the emergence of new drugs and much of the campaign's preparatory work had already been initiated, Browne's energy greatly speeded up the process, creating 2,000 emergency beds for TB patients in just over two years. As the death rate from TB tumbled, almost halving in the four years between 1947 and 1951, Browne quickly developed a public image as a highly efficient and competent minister.

As well as tackling TB, the other major issue on Browne's desk surrounded the 1947 Health Act introduced by Fianna Fáil. Although Browne was blissfully unaware of what had gone on behind the scenes between the Catholic hierarchy and the previous government, he decided to make changes to the legislation to ensure that he had cabinet support.

The government, with minimal fuss, made a decision to amend the sections on compulsory inspection of school children to ensure they would not infringe parental rights, thus addressing the concerns of James Dillon, who had also become a minister in the inter-party government.

Another matter to be addressed was whether the Mother and Child Scheme should be free for all, as Fianna Fáil had intended, or means tested. Although this would become a major sticking point for him, Browne does not appear to have felt that strongly about the issue initially. He raised it at cabinet in 1948, pointing out that a means test might mollify the medical profession, but the government decided to stick with the original proposal.

With those two points of principle clarified at cabinet, Browne was free to plan for the service that the 1947 Act had authorised. The framing process took considerable time and it was not until June 1950 that the draft was completed.

The proposals involved free medical care for women before, during and after childbirth and for all children under 16 years, without a means test. This care would be provided by salaried dispensary doctors and there would also be free midwife visits to the home.

There was much in the scheme that was obviously highly desirable, even for deeply conservative champions of Catholic social teaching, but it was by no means beyond criticism.

The absence of a means test, it could legitimately be argued, meant resources were spread more thinly than was necessary and it might have made more sense to target them at the poorer sections of society. There were also question marks over whether the facilities existed to provide this service. But such problems were just the tip of the iceberg that the government was about to sail into.

* * *

In his first couple of years as Health Minister, Browne had a series of run-ins with the church over the building of St Vincent's Hospital and a number of other relatively trivial issues. Nevertheless, they were small-scale differences and he anticipated that the main opposition to the Mother and Child Scheme would come from the medical profession. He was half-right.

Browne's view on the means test had hardened in the two years since he had brought the matter to cabinet and it became the one point of the scheme that was not open to negotiation. Speaking in the Dáil, he described the means test as 'an unforgivable degradation and an interference with the privacy of the individual'.

The medical profession, with whom Browne was having an increasingly difficult relationship, strongly disagreed. Doctors viewed the proposals as the first step in the gradual erosion of private practice at the expense of a salaried state service.

It did not help matters that Browne became very bitter towards the Irish Medical Association (IMA). Indeed, one cabinet colleague later recalled that Browne appeared to develop a 'pathological hatred' of doctors. As the stand-off with the doctors began to deepen at the end of 1950, a document was circulated in Clann an Poblachta branches – which Browne was suspected of writing – insinuating that the real objection to the scheme was that doctors might lose money.

The church's real concern was that Catholic mothers might be exposed to instruction on gynaecological matters, infant care, etc. from non-Catholic doctors. But, like the IMA, it was on the absence of a means test that the bishops chose to take a stand. Browne was about to embark on a war with two fronts.

There was a distinct edge of elitism to the arguments of both the church and the medical profession. The key church figure in the affair, Archbishop McQuaid of Dublin, was, as historian Joe Lee points out, a 'doctor's son with an exalted sense of the dignity of the professions'. Bishop Browne of Galway, another highly influential critic of the scheme, had previously demonstrated a 'reverential attitude' towards the professions and medical doctors in particular.

The Catholic hierarchy met in October 1950 on the issue and agreed to write a letter of protest to Taoiseach John A. Costello and to meet Browne to inform him of this as a matter of courtesy. That meeting, outlined at the beginning of this chapter, marked, as Lee put it, the beginning of 'a series of misunderstandings that would have been farcical were not the consequences so tragic'.

Despite the extraordinary events of that meeting, Browne

appeared to believe that any issues with the church could be relatively easily overcome. He was not entirely complacent in his approach to the church, but at that time it did appear that the dispute with the IMA would be the most urgent issue.

Browne and his most senior civil servant prepared a memorandum for submission to the Catholic hierarchy. It stressed that in introducing the scheme, the government was simply giving effect to what had been passed by the Oireachtas in 1947 and that the scheme was 'in no sense compulsory' and that 'whatever guarantees the hierarchy wish' in the matter of 'instruction of mothers' would be unreservedly given. The minister also 'respectfully' asked whether the hierarchy considered the scheme 'to be contrary to Catholic moral teaching'.

The memo was then sent to the Taoiseach (because protocol meant that a 'mere' cabinet minister had no direct access to an archbishop's office) to be forwarded to the bishops. Strangely, that handover did not happen until the end of March 1951, even though Costello was in constant verbal contact with McQuaid during this period.

By the beginning of 1951 a number of Browne's cabinet colleagues were becoming uneasy at what they saw as his obdurate handling of the issue. The situation worsened considerably in March when Browne – frustrated at the antics of the doctors – announced that the IMA was engaging in delaying tactics and he was going ahead with the scheme without further negotiation. Critically, he made this announcement without consulting his cabinet colleagues.

Relations between Browne and MacBride had also reached breaking point, largely over disagreements on Clann na Poblachta matters. Browne had endured a stormy special meeting of the party executive during which he was accused of disloyalty, incompetence and picking a row with the church for personal advancement. He pre-empted a vote of no confidence, but it was clear that the party was not big enough for both Browne and MacBride.

Alienated from his party and colleagues in cabinet, it was no surprise that government support for Browne's position and the scheme fell away and Costello began to take a tougher attitude towards him.

On 9 March Browne got a letter from the bishops in which he was bluntly told that they were still intent on preventing the implementation of the scheme and, as Browne would later put it, sought his 'unconditional surrender'.

Perhaps preoccupied with his spat with the doctors, Browne seemed to disregard the importance of this letter and continued to do so despite concerns raised by his cabinet colleagues. He insisted that a member of the hierarchy had assured him that they had no objection to the scheme on grounds of faith and morals. Sadly, faith and morals would have little relevance to this whole affair.

Two weeks later Browne, perhaps under pressure from Costello, sought a further meeting with McQuaid. The meeting took place on Holy Thursday. At this point, the extent of church opposition to his proposal must finally have become clear.

According to McQuaid's account of what happened, Browne made the case that he had already satisfied the hierarchy's concerns but was shocked when McQuaid went through the details of their meeting of the previous October and stated that their objections remained as strong as ever. Browne asked for a decision from the entire hierarchy on the scheme and, according to McQuaid, gave an undertaking that he would abide by their decision.

A meeting of the hierarchy was set for 4 April and before that Browne called upon a number of bishops to lobby for support. When he visited Dr Michael Browne he was offered handmade cigarettes from Bond Street and champagne. The minister claimed that the meeting barely mentioned the details of the scheme and was solely focused on its cost and the bishop's fear of an increase in the burden of rates and taxes.

He also met with the Bishop of Ferns, Dr Staunton, and Cardinal Dalton of Armagh. In a generally banal meeting with the latter, Browne made the point that Catholics in Dalton's diocese were using the NHS. Dalton's reply should have been a wake-up call, if one was still needed, for Browne. 'We are prepared neither to apologise nor to explain,' Dalton said. It is a line that continues to resonate.

Browne would later describe these meetings as a waste of time. He saw himself as a 'mendicant government minister uselessly pleading for the underprivileged of the Republic with the princes of their church'. A more skilled politician would have adapted to the environment, however trying.

Cabinet colleagues urged him to accept the hierarchy's ruling with the basic argument that 'you cannot afford to fight the church' and you must 'satisfy the Bishops'. In response, Browne argued that he had not made the law – the Oireachtas had done so in 1947 when it voted for the free and no-means-test conditions under which the scheme was to be implemented.

Browne also drew up a memo for the Taoiseach, which was forwarded to the hierarchy (notably without any word of support from Costello), arguing that the state was not taking away parents' rights and that the education aspect was restricted to issues of hygiene and diet.

To ensure that there was nothing of an objectionable nature

or that did not tally with Catholic teaching on sexuality, Browne said he would submit the regulations for approval to the hierarchy. The memo also said there was nothing new in the keeping of public records of illnesses and that he was willing to amend the scheme to include private practitioners. He also made the point that a number of social services – including children's allowance and the infectious disease service – were provided without a means test.

The memo concluded by asking whether, given these observations, the hierarchy could consider the scheme to be 'contrary to Catholic moral teaching'. Browne had already been advised by an eminent theologian that it could not be so considered and believed this was key because the church's moral teaching was binding on a conscientious Catholic under pain of sin. But this focus missed the central point that the church simply was not going to accept his scheme.

When the bishops met to give their verdict, they were careful not to pronounce on the morality of the scheme and instead unanimously denounced it as conflicting with Catholic social teaching.

The bishops claimed that the state was attempting to exercise control over education in very intimate matters and taking over functions that the vast majority of citizens could fulfil on their own. The hierarchy also claimed that the level of taxation required to fund the scheme would morally compel citizens to use the services. It would damage the self-reliance of parents whose income could cover the medical treatment of their children.

This response was full of holes. It failed to deal with a number of the points raised by Browne in his memo and, by getting into the taxation arena, also surely overstepped the hierarchy's legitimate concerns.

The church effectively took sides in a political dispute between a government minister, the medical profession and other members of the cabinet. 'They seem to have placed less emphasis on the moral dangers and more on the social consequences of the scheme,' Ruth Barrington would later argue in *Health, Medicine and Politics in Ireland 1900–1970.*

Browne, like a fire engine going to the wrong fire, seized on the fact that the response had said it was contrary to Catholic social teaching not moral teaching and went to the GPO to defend the scheme on Radio Éireann. He was appealing to the wrong audience. The people he really needed to be persuading were his ministerial colleagues. On coming out of the GPO he was summoned to an emergency cabinet meeting at which the hierarchy's letter was the only issue on the agenda.

The atmosphere was 'tense and awkward'. Costello read out the letter from the hierarchy, looked at Browne and said, 'This must mean the end of the Mother and Child scheme.' Browne recalls that 'all heads around the table began to nod, like those strange toy Buddhas'. Browne asked each minister if they accepted this. They all did, with only one Labour minister meekly demurring, 'They shouldn't be allowed to do this.'

Browne pleaded for patience, pointing out the letter had referred only to social teaching and not moral teaching, which allowed a conscientious Catholic to implement the scheme as agreed by the cabinet. The theological nuance fell on deaf ears. The bishops had spoken. There was nothing left to discuss.

It did not help Browne's cause that ministers, even those who were sympathetic to the scheme, were fed up with him. Seán Lemass later surmised that Costello and MacBride greeted the affair as a God-given – or at least bishop-given – opportunity to dispense with a colleague who they found extremely difficult to work with.

Browne left the cabinet room after making a remark about considering his future action. In his absence, the cabinet quickly agreed that the scheme should be abandoned and replaced with a less controversial proposal (i.e. one aimed at the less well-off and in keeping with Catholic social teaching). The cabinet also committed to consider whether any amendments to the 1947 Health Act were 'necessary or desirable'.

Just three days later, Costello wrote to McQuaid informing him of these decisions. In his reply, McQuaid expressed his 'deep appreciation of the generous loyalty shown by you and your colleagues'.

Meanwhile, the internal tensions in Clann na Poblachta erupted at a second highly charged meeting of the party's national executive. One of the charges levelled at Browne in a subsequent meeting of the executive was that he had been photographed shaking hands with a Protestant archbishop, which he had done at the laying of a foundation stone for a new development at the Rotunda hospital.

Clearly some senior figures in the party felt Browne was being deliberately provocative to the Catholic hierarchy, but the charge also reveals the constraints that were placed on politicians (a point never better illustrated than on the death of former President Douglas Hyde the previous year, when the cabinet and senior opposition figures waited outside the Anglican funeral service at St Patrick's Cathedral because of a prohibition on Catholics attending a Protestant service).

After what was a fierce meeting – Browne would later describe it as his trial – all but three members of the party executive voted to support MacBride's condemnation of the Minister for Health for disloyalty to his party leader and for mishandling the Mother and Child Scheme negotiations.

One resolution specifically gave MacBride the endorsement to remove Browne from government if he deemed it necessary. The whole thing may well have been stage-managed, but the lack of support for Browne suggests there was some truth to the argument that he had lost the confidence of the great majority of the party's membership.

There was a last-minute intervention by the trade union movement to try to broker a compromise. It proposed the mother would pay a nominal ten shilling fee for the service but, although this was agreeable to Browne, it never got off the ground. Indeed, it served to make matters worse. The fact that the newspapers were reporting that Browne was reconsidering his resignation at the request of the Irish Trade Union Congress proved the final tipping point. Ministers were furious at what they saw as Browne's undermining of the cabinet.

On 10 April MacBride personally delivered a letter calling on Browne to resign from his position as Minister for Health. Browne complied the following day. Costello backed MacBride's action, saying that if the Clann na Poblachta leader had not done so, he would have called for Browne's resignation himself.

* * *

Many historians have correctly argued that it is an oversimplification to present the controversy surrounding the Mother and Child Scheme as a straight church versus state battle: it was considerably more complicated than that. Desmond Williams described it as an improbable series of coincidences:

> The conditions of coalition government, the tactics
> of the most successful trade union of all, the Irish
> Medical   Association,   Dr   Browne's   own

misinterpretation of episcopal negotiation, the
minister's own peculiar relationship with the leader
of his party, Seán MacBride and the special
phraseology of Archbishop McQuaid – all these
gave this particular political crisis a character which
it would have lacked under different circumstances
and with different personalities involved.

Certainly Browne, a tense and highly strung individual, and for
many something of a tortured soul, could have handled
matters a lot better. Rather than seeking to secure a
compromise solution, he opened up four different fronts of
conflict: the bishops, the doctors, his cabinet colleagues and his
party leader.

Those who worked with Browne were not sparing in their
criticism. Costello said Browne was 'not competent or capable'
of fulfilling his duties at the Department of Health. He was
'incapable of negotiation; he was obstinate at times and
vacillating at other times'.

Con Lehane TD of Clann na Poblachta said Browne was
'constitutionally incapable of listening to criticism' and that he
had seen him, over a period of a year or more, walk out from
five or six different committee meetings.

James Deeny, the state's brilliant Chief Medical Officer,
despite always retaining a fondness for Browne, eventually
found him impossible to work with.

But the complexities of what occurred and Browne's
mishandling of the situation notwithstanding, the affair did
serve to demonstrate with shuddering force the Catholic
hierarchy's political power. They were not to be messed with.

Browne argued in his autobiography, *Against the Tide*, that
it 'is now widely acknowledged that the condemnation by the
bishops of the health scheme was crudely political.

Unashamedly the church was "playing politics" even to the point of bringing down a properly elected representative government on the issue.'

And it was not just a case of politicians being unwilling, for pragmatic political reasons, to alienate the church. For many of them, the church's position was instinctively their own position as well.

After the Mother and Child Scheme controversy, Costello told the Dáil that he accepted 'without qualification in all respects the social teaching of the Church as interpreted by the Roman Catholic hierarchy of Ireland'. This was a reflection of Costello's genuine piety and faith, but it was still an extraordinary statement by a leader of a democratic republic.

The state's subservience to the church is all the more remarkable considering the presence of Clann na Poblachta in government. But despite its radical reputation, MacBride opted not to bring down the government on this issue; if he had, his party might have survived.

For all the justified criticism of Browne, it is hard to disagree with his description of the Irish government process as 'an elaborate sham'. He wrote, 'In spite of their best efforts to conceal this fraudulent reality of mock power, the cabinet's influence and submission to Rome was proven without doubt by cabinet ministers themselves in their own correspondence, behaviour and speeches.' Home Rule was Rome Rule, after all.

Browne took the decision to publish the confidential state correspondence between himself, Costello and the bishops, knowing it would end his ministerial prospects:

I was pilloried for my failure to respect cabinet and church confidentiality. But the pretence of a cabinet to be the supreme instrument and authority in the state, when in fact it was subject to an outside non-

elected pressure group, was to me the supreme
deception. Mine, easily, was the lesser breach of
trust. In fact had I suppressed that revelation about
the reality of government in the Republic I would
have become a guilty partner in the deceit.

Browne took a stand on two issues: the fundamental rights of
the electorate and the right of the public to a proper health
service. He believed that the government should not, under any
circumstances, 'concede to the bishops the right to set aside a
law already passed by the Oireachtas'. 'The hierarchy,' he
wrote in *Against the Tide*, 'had become the factual instrument
of government on all important social and economic policies in
the Republic'. The Mother and Child Scheme was no longer
the most important issue: 'The real challenge being mounted
by the hierarchy was their implicit claim to be the effective
government,' with the Dáil playing a 'subsidiary role'.

＊　＊　＊

The state's first inter-party government did not fall directly
because of the Mother and Child Scheme. A dispute over the
price of milk ('cows', not mothers', as Lee later put it) lost it
the support of three rural deputies and precipitated the general
election of June 1951. But it was never going to recover from
the Mother and Child controversy.

In the general election, Clann na Poblachta lost eight of its
ten seats, with MacBride just scraping in. Browne romped back
to the Dáil as an independent TD, along with three other
supporters, and voted for de Valera as Taoiseach, helping him
to return as leader of a minority government.

Dev had kept his head down during the controversy, but
once back in government he faced the same difficulties in
dealing with the church. With Ryan reappointed as Minister for

Health, a new Health Act was introduced in 1953, proposing improved services and increasing the numbers entitled to either free, or reduced rate, hospital treatment from 30 per cent to 85 per cent of the population. It was originally intended in Ryan's White Paper as 'no means test at all' but once again there was enormous opposition from both the church and the medical profession.

The church hierarchy drew up a public letter outlining their (predictable) objections. They said that the new Health Bill was opposed to Catholic thinking on the ground that too much power was transferred to the state, thereby lowering people's sense of responsibility and weakening their moral fibre. Its other criticisms centred on claims that it extended the scope of state-controlled medical services (in the process undermining voluntary hospitals) and that there were no safeguards to protect patients from having to be treated by practitioners who 'advocate practices contrary to natural law'.

Bar the one about extending state-controlled medical services, most of these arguments were groundless. For example, the Bill did not guarantee mothers a free choice of doctor. But instead of taking on the church and exposing the weakness of their arguments, de Valera opted for compromise. He intervened at the last minute and the publication of the letter never happened, thus heading off another public wrangle between politicians and the church.

After consultations between the hierarchy and the government, further concessions were introduced, including greater choice of doctor and hospital and safeguards on treatments being in line with a patient's religious principles. The bishops then, very grudgingly, removed their objections to it.

De Valera did not agree with the Costello doctrine, summed up by Lee as 'the Taoiseach disposes as the Hierarchy proposes'. But even he, with a united cabinet behind him, was unwilling to go head to head with the church, despite the weaknesses of the hierarchy's arguments. By instinct, the prospect did not appeal to him and he saw the dangers for his government.

In pure political terms, Dev and Fianna Fáil proved cannier and ultimately delivered their programme largely intact. The basic principles of the legislation survived: free maternity services to all (albeit with the top 15 per cent of earners now included only on payment of a very small insurance contribution) and free or heavily subsidised hospital services to 85 per cent of the population.

It was seen in many quarters as a victory for Fianna Fáil over the hierarchy. In many ways it was. Given the climate of the day, which was such that the bishops were by no means the most extreme in their views, it was a notable achievement.

This had been evident when the Minister for Social Welfare and Labour Party leader, William Norton, proposed in a White Paper at the end of 1949 to unify the three distinct social insurance schemes (unemployment, sickness, and widows' and orphans' pensions). Benefits were low and Norton also proposed simplifying the regulations, extending the benefits and adding further benefits such as a contributory old age pension.

Although hardly radical, and obviously desirable, the proposals attracted what John H Whyte described as a 'barrage of criticism from exponents of Catholic social teaching'. At the time, it seemed as if it, and not the Mother and Child Scheme, would become the main divisive issue between church and state. Again, the concern was about the increase in state control, with the argument that social security should as far as possible be run by vocational groups.

Norton, who was despised by Browne as 'a man of many talents, all dedicated exclusively to his own betterment in society', played the much smarter game and ensured that he kept the support of his ministerial colleagues. He also, as the *Irish Times* pointed out at the time, made sure 'he was not without friends in ecclesiastical quarters'.

Norton cleverly argued that 'as a Christian nation we must give practical expression to our Christianity. Surely it would not be suggested that it is a Christian attitude to pay such low rates of benefit as bear no relation to the requirements of the time.' He also cited papal encyclicals to back up the scheme. The inter-party government fell before Norton's measure became law, but the process showed the climate of opinion in which even the canniest of ministers had to operate.

The influence of the church was also extremely marked in the delay in introducing legal adoption, which had been common in other countries for many years. The Attorney General, Charles Casey, defending the decision not to legislate, arguing that as Ireland was a predominantly Catholic country, the parliament cannot 'surely be asked to introduce legislation contrary to the teaching of that great Church'.

Bearing in mind that 'membership of the Church is the best means of saving one's soul', he asked, 'How can any Catholic logically demand or permit any legislation which would endanger the soul of a single child?' With legal adoption, a child is gone forever from his or her biological mother's control. In the case of an unmarried Catholic girl who hands her child over to kindly people not of her faith, when that mother has 'rehabilitated herself', she will know that she 'has done wrong according to the belief of her faith, yet she is powerless to bring her child up in what she knows is the true faith ... Legislation has denied her the opportunity to discharge the rights and duties of the natural mother imposed on her by the law of God.'

As John H. Whyte would write years later in his definitive work *Church and State in Modern Ireland*, this argument is remarkable on two main grounds: 'Its detailed recital of the Catholic Church's teaching on the conditions for salvation and its explicit statement that the state should harmonise its legislation with this teaching.' Of course, harmonising legislation with church teaching was exactly what had happened since independence.

The Catholic church's role as quasi-legal and moral guardians was also driven home in a statement that the bishops issued in June 1950 in relation to agitation to allow pubs to open on a Sunday:

From the earliest times the Church has prohibited on Sunday public trading, markets and other forms of public buying and selling ... There is no doubt whatever that the opening of public houses for the sales of intoxicating drink comes under this prohibition; and to introduce the practice would be a grave violation of the law of the church. In fact, the opening of public houses, by reason of the drunkenness and other sins and temporal evils to which it is calculated to lead would be particularly repugnant to the sanctity of the Lord's Day. Accordingly, where there has been no existing and longstanding custom, to open public houses on Sunday even for a few hours would be a serious violation of this ecclesiastical law. So as this ecclesiastical law remains, it would be sinful to agitate for their opening.

The message was clear: not only would any legislation be wrong but it was sinful even to look for such legislation. It worked. The agitation for a change in the Sunday opening was killed off and it would be several years before it was raised again.

Despite the 'integralism' of this period, whereby various groups and individuals were working to make Ireland more totally Catholic, Whyte argues it would be wrong to say this was all-pervasive. 'Counter currents,' as Whyte describes them, 'were detectable as well'.

Norton did not, after all, abandon the social insurance plan because it was opposed by the Catholic social movement; the Adoption Society continued its campaign for legal adoption; and the agitation for Sunday opening was later revived. The moral and social consensus of the early post-independence years was breaking down.

Nevertheless, the power exerted by the church in that era had far-reaching consequences. For starters, there is the impact on the church itself.

*   *   *

The old adage that 'power corrupts, absolute power corrupts absolutely' seems highly relevant here. To have successive governments falling over themselves to placate and indulge the hierarchy was neither good for society nor healthy for the church. Every institution needs to know there are checks and balances.

At the same time as these battles were being contested, 6,378 children were in industrial schools managed by religious orders but funded by the state and (in theory) subject to state approval and inspection. We now know, from investigative documentaries such as *Dear Daughter* and *States of Fear* and from the *Report of the Commission to Inquire into Child Abuse*, about the savage cruelty and abuse inflicted in these institutions, which were reminiscent, as one newspaper editorial in 2009 pointed out, of 'authoritarian regimes'.

Officialdom knew of the abuse of children in industrial schools but complaints fell on deaf ears in a climate of deference and submissiveness to the religious orders. That deference and submissiveness was there before the row over the Mother and Child Scheme and would have continued if that row had never happened. But given the chastening experience of Browne, is it any surprise that it took several decades before the state tackled the wrongs carried out by church figures in industrial schools and in parishes?

The suggestion has been made that perhaps instinctively rather than as part of a fully thought-out strategy, Browne wanted to bring about a clash between the state and powerful vested interests in the knowledge that even if he lost, it would ultimately bring about the radical change to society that he was committed to achieving.

Whyte argues that Browne's actions had a very 'extensive effect'. Before this episode, church–state relations were little discussed and there was 'a widespread feeling that it was somehow disedifying for the role of the church to be examined in public'. He highlights Costello's speech in the debate on Browne's resignation, in which the Taoiseach stated:

All of this matter was intended to be private and to be adjusted behind closed doors and was never intended to be the subject of public controversy, as it has been made by the former Minister for Health now, and it would have been dealt with in that way had there been any reasonable person, other than the former Minister for Health engaged in the negotiations at that time … The public never ought to have become aware of the matter.

Whyte observes:

> The fact that Mr Costello could unselfconsciously
> utter such words in 1951 is a sign of his confidence
> that Irish public opinion would generally agree with
> him. If Church State relations are now a topic of
> rational discussion in Ireland, this is in part due to
> Dr Browne's courage, or rashness, in bringing them
> into the open ... Dr Browne has enlarged the area of
> political discourse in Ireland.

But there is surely an equally compelling contrary view that the
controversy surrounding the Mother and Child Scheme
confirmed the church's absolute authority and ensured that it
would remain untouchable and unchallenged for decades to
come.

On the morning after Browne's resignation, an *Irish Times*
editorial concluded that the 'Roman Catholic Church would
seem to be the effective government of this country'. Was
Ireland a theocratic state, where the power of the Catholic
hierarchy was decisive in any matter in which it chose to
intervene? Comments from the leading politicians of the time
would suggest it was.

In his letter to McQuaid informing him that the Mother
and Child Scheme was being withdrawn, Costello said that 'the
decision expresses the complete willingness of the government
to defer to the judgment so given by the hierarchy that the
particular scheme in question is opposed to Catholic social
teaching'. And in the Dáil debate, the Taoiseach said, 'I, as a
Catholic, obey my Church authorities and will continue to do
so, in spite of the *Irish Times* or anything else.'

Norton echoed this stance when he said in the same debate
that there would not be an issue where the bishops and the
government were on opposite sides. 'This government will not

travel that road ... There will be no flouting of the authority of the bishops in the matter of Catholic social or Catholic moral teaching.'

MacBride, leader of the supposedly radical Clann na Poblachta, said that politicians who are Catholics 'are of course bound to give obedience to the rulings of our church and of our hierarchy'.

The Finance Minister, Patrick McGilligan, told a party meeting that he would not break the moral law and if he was not sure what the moral law was he would resort to the bishops.

Browne himself, do not forget, asked the hierarchy for a ruling. And in his resignation speech he said, 'I as a Catholic accept unequivocally and unreservedly the views of the hierarchy on this matter.'

In the subsequent election campaign, Browne rounded on his former cabinet colleagues but did not criticise the bishops, describing suggestions that he had opposed the hierarchy as 'malicious'.

Obviously it did not make electoral sense for a politician to be seen to be in conflict with the church.

There is also a view that some members of the cabinet were not keen on the Mother and Child Scheme in the first place, regardless of the church's concerns, and were only too happy to see it fail. There is even a view that, far from accepting the bishops as the real rulers of the country, politicians used them to get rid of a difficult colleague.

Numerous historians have argued that, however critical its intervention may ultimately have been, the church was just one of the many forces opposed to Browne's measure. Whyte suggests:

Whether the hierarchy's ruling would have been so

decisive without these other factors – whether
indeed a ruling would have been made in such
confident terms – seems uncertain. The mother and
child scheme crisis shows that the Catholic
hierarchy wielded great influence in Ireland but the
exact nature and extent of that influence cannot
fairly be deduced from a single episode as this.

Perhaps, but in politics perception is often more important
than reality and there can be no doubting that the perception
existed that Browne and his Mother and Child Scheme were
victims of a church that no government could afford to cross.

Commenting afterwards on the private nature of the
church's lobbying, which became clear when Browne published
all his correspondence on the issue, independent TD Peadar
Cowan said, 'As a Catholic, I protest against this secretive,
occult and objectionable practice. As a Dáil deputy I am
entitled to know all the factors that enter into the
consideration of legislation.'

Cowan also said that while the hierarchy were entitled to
express their views on all matters of public welfare, they must
do so in public, otherwise 'our democracy is a fraud, our
Constitution a sham, and our general elections humbug,
pretence and swindle'.

Of course, many other bodies engaged in private lobbying,
but, as the writer Seán O'Faoláin points out, none of those
institutions held 'the weapon of the sacraments', a weapon
'whose touch means death'.

Whyte concludes that Ireland was not a theocratic state,
pointing to the genuine relaxation of the church's influence
from the late 1950s on, the change in the adoption laws, the
introduction of multi-denominational schools and the
availability of contraception. Lee argues that it was more the

cabinet's handling of the Mother and Child Scheme than the bishops' attitude that determined the outcome. They may be correct but so was O'Faoláin when he said of the hierarchy: 'the lightest word from this quarter is tantamount to the raising of the sword'.

It was a sword of Damocles that would hang over Irish governments and society for decades to come, with disastrous consequences. Ireland, unlike many Western democracies in the 20th century, did not succumb to totalitarianism but the shocking revelations about what went on in church-run institutions demonstrate that the new state was far from being free of repression.

The Irish people, wrote Paul Blanshard in his bitingly critical 1955 book *The Irish and Catholic Power*, permitted 'ecclesiastical dictatorship and political democracy to live side by side without any sense of incongruity'.

5

A DONATION ONCE AGAIN

NEIL Blaney stood on the podium, the perspiration glistening on his face. A senior government minister of Blaney's standing addressing his party's annual conference would normally be akin to a victorious general rousing his battle troops. But the January 1969 Fianna Fáil ard fheis was different. Things were getting hot and heavy. The troops were not just restless, they were almost in revolt.

Just a couple of months earlier Fianna Fáil's second effort to abolish the proportional representation voting system had been resoundingly defeated in a referendum. It was the first time that Fianna Fáil had failed to secure 40 per cent of the vote in any electoral contest since it took power in 1932. The result had led to much soul searching and prompted questions about Jack Lynch's leadership of the party.

Party members laid the blame firmly at the door of Taca, the Fianna Fáil fundraising organisation set up a couple of years earlier to tap the business community. Fianna Fáil, traditionally the party of the small man, now looked like the representative of big business. Under pressure after the referendum fiasco, Lynch had moved to reform Taca, making it more accessible and transparent. But speaker after speaker at the ard fheis was adamant that this was not enough. They wanted Taca gone and they looked set to deliver a bloody nose to the leadership in the process.

Until, that is, Blaney took the microphone. The Donegal man had little time for Lynch but Fianna Fáil needed him. He paused briefly to mop each of the corners of his face with a handkerchief. He stuck out his chin and then launched into a stirring defence of Taca, the sweat 'running in thin rivulets down his active jaws' – as the *Irish Times* reported at the time – as he belted home his point.

It was almost the 1970s. You needed money to compete with the well-heeled gentlemen of the Labour Party and Fine Gael. The Taca men had been there for the party over many years in every election and by-election. Many of them hadn't a seat in their pants when Fianna Fáil had started out. Now Fianna Fáil had brought prosperity to the country, they were giving something back.

Blaney sat back down to a standing ovation and thunderous applause. The entire ard fheis was in the palm of his hand. In the ensuing vote, only a dozen hands were raised in opposition to the new Taca. It was, however, only a temporary respite for the fundraising body. Within a year it would be gone.

Despite the attempts to reform the organisation, Taca was effectively ended by the 1968 referendum result, which was somehow fitting because it had begun with another electoral embarrassment.

* * *

The 1966 presidential election was far too close for comfort for Fianna Fáil. It was a David and Goliath contest. Eamon de Valera, legend of the Republican movement, Taoiseach for two decades and President for the previous seven years, was up against the relatively inexperienced Tom O'Higgins, a Fine Gael TD. Yet, when the votes were counted, O'Higgins had come within half a percentage point of beating 'the Chief' and had come out well ahead in Dublin. Yes, it was all far too close for comfort.

De Valera was 83 years old and had not campaigned at all so the result should not have been a surprise. But it was. It caused consternation within Fianna Fáil, with the view forming, rightly or wrongly, among party figures that it simply could not match Fine Gael's financial muscle.

Fianna Fáil activists had always liked to present the party as being for the 'have nots', rather than the 'haves', in stark contrast to what they saw as the pro-Establishment, senior-counsel-populated Fine Gael.

One of the main aims of Fianna Fáil's constitution was 'to make the resources and wealth of Ireland subservient to the needs and welfare of all the people of Ireland'. But the party was nothing if not pragmatic and had been accepting donations from business for decades. Albeit in an ad hoc kind of way.

In the early 1930s Joe McGrath, the hugely wealthy boss of the Irish Hospitals Sweepstakes (see Chapter 2), gave a subscription of £500 – a huge sum in those days – without warning. McGrath, a 1916 Rising and War of Independence veteran, had previously been a Cumann na nGaedheal minister. Because of this and the fact that the donation ran contrary to the party ethos, the general secretary asked the advice of Minister Gerry Boland.

Boland was one of the party's founders and its joint honorary secretary. 'Send it back to him, of course,' was Boland's response. The donation was sent back with a polite explanation that it was party policy not to accept subscriptions of this nature.

But not everybody in Fianna Fáil agreed. Future Taoiseach Seán Lemass was the other joint honorary secretary and he raised the matter at a subsequent party meeting. There was a discussion and a decision was taken to accept the subscription.

'It is at least an arguable proposition that this decision contained within it the seeds of the parasitic growth which eroded the FF ethos,' Kevin Boland later wrote. Kevin was Gerry Boland's son. Something of a purist – principled if perhaps unrealistic and overly dogmatic – he succeeded his father at cabinet before resigning from the party.

It may have been un-republican to accept donations but with precious little money coming from the state to fund political parties and the church gate collection only going so far, the costly business of getting hold of and keeping power needed to be funded.

Fianna Fáil set up an election finance committee, run by businesspeople, to collect money from associates in the business world. They came together at election time and collected subscriptions. The strategy was that money collected at one election would be kept in reserve for the next. The various cumann still had to raise money locally.

In the 1950s, during a rare spell in opposition, a group called Comh-Comhairle Átha Cliath was set up by Fianna Fáil to finance a reorganisation drive. While each constituency in Dublin would nominate members, the general membership was to consist of people who for various reasons had not joined Fianna Fáil. Members would pay an annual subscription of £10 – described by Kevin Boland as 'an undreamt of amount in those days'.

According to Boland, apart from financing the reorganisation drive, the members of the new group would constitute an audience who would be invited to hear ministers or front benchers making important statements and they could also provide a forum for discussion based on talks or lectures given by experts in different fields. The first meeting of the Comh-Comhairle heard an important statement from Lemass about how the economy could establish 100,000 new jobs.

There were objections to this 'Top Hat organisation', which many party traditionalists saw as being beyond the scope of ordinary Fianna Fáilers and as downgrading the traditional party organisation and the cumann structures. The leadership responded that this was certainly not the case and in fact it was not actually part of the Fianna Fáil organisation at all.

But by the mid-1960s, and particularly after de Valera's close call against O'Higgins, an idea formed that the election finance committee be given some formal standing and kept on a permanent basis.

Enter Joe Malone, later director-general of Bord Fáilte, but who had then just sold his major car rental business. Malone was involved in a committee helping out Charles Haughey in his capacity as the party's national director of elections. The finance committee was having problems and Malone was asked along to a meeting.

'Two of us who attended afterwards went to dinner that night and we came up with a very good idea to raise funds for the Fianna Fáil party which ultimately resulted in Taca being formed,' Malone recounted some years later, adding, 'Unfortunately, the initial idea and what subsequently resulted wasn't what we had in mind.'

Taca is Irish for 'support'. And Malone maintains that the idea originally was to get young people who were interested in the community and interested in being involved to form an organisation, irrespective of what their political affiliations were. They would be given an opportunity three or four times a year of having a seminar with government ministers, who would talk to them on whatever was the most controversial topic at that time or whatever was of most interest to the businesspeople involved.

'Our idea was that they would do it in an impartial way, not as a pressure group but to let the Minister have a feedback as to how the business community was thinking.' It would be a type of focus group, years before anybody had heard of the concept.

Malone said it was originally decided to launch Taca at a press reception in the Hibernian Hotel. He had been out of the country and when he returned he was horrified to find that there would not be a public launch. '[T]hey felt they should play it low-key. I strongly disagreed with that because there was nothing secretive, there was nothing to hide.' Those at or near the top of Fianna Fáil preferred a different approach.

Haughey is the person most associated in the public mind with Taca. It was Haughey who apparently drew up the blueprint for the organisation.

The idea was that a total of 500 people would be invited to join a new group (although it is thought that 200 letters were sent out originally). Taca would be a separate legal entity to Fianna Fáil and its function would be solely to provide election finance for the party. The members would pay £100 a year, which would be lodged in a special account. The interest earned on this deposit would be used by Taca to finance a small number of private dinners where members would be addressed by ministers on specific and current national problems.

At the end of the year the principal of £50,000 would be

lodged into a Fianna Fáil election account. The election account would be under the control of three people: Taoiseach Jack Lynch, Neil Blaney and Kevin Boland. Two out of these three signatures would be needed to withdraw the money.

In reality it is believed Taca raised a net of €10,000 to €20,000 a year – not inconsiderable money at the time. Kevin Boland claimed that, when he resigned from Fianna Fáil, Taca had £60,000 in cash.

The chairman of Taca was Desmond McGreevy, a leading quantity surveyor in Dublin. Handsome, clever and urbane, the Jaguar-driving McGreevy had unsuccessfully sought a seat in the Seanad and was also chairman of the National Building Agency. Other Taca directors included Ken O'Reilly-Hyland, a successful businessman who would chair Fianna Fáil's fundraising committee in the 1970s and 1980s; John Reihill, head of Tedcastle McCormick; Ireland's first 'starchitect', Sam Stephenson; Eoin Kenny, head of J.A. Kenny & Partners; Dillon Digby of the First National Building Society; Noel Griffin of Waterford Crystal; Denis McCarthy, head of Odearest; and solicitor Liam McGonagle.

Harry Boland, Haughey's school friend and business partner in the Haughey Boland accountancy practice, was Taca's secretary and treasurer.

The first Taca function was a formal dinner at the Gresham Hotel in Dublin, which was attended by most, if not all, of the members of the government. The media was specifically excluded.

Kevin Boland's recollection of that first event is most revealing: 'We were all organised by Haughey and sent to different tables around the room. The extraordinary thing about my table was that everybody at it was in some way or other connected with the construction industry.' Boland was Minister for Local Government.

* * *

Despite the low-key approach, Taca soon became a household name. In March 1967 Labour TD Frank Cluskey, a no-nonsense Dubliner who would go on to lead his party, raised the Gresham Hotel event in the Dáil. In the first of hundreds of such suggestions from the opposition over the following 18 months, he said there was 'a rumour abroad to the effect that people who are members of this Fianna Fáil association of businessmen, known as Taca, will receive preference with regard to the distribution of grants from public funds'.

Cluskey said that people thought, and he could see why they thought, that these gatherings of businesspeople 'addressed in great secrecy by senior ministers' could be a direct tie-up between special grants and grants for extending business premises and grants in various other forms. Cluskey added that it was important to reassure the people that the privileges these businesspeople would undoubtedly expect would not involve grants from public funds.

It was George Colley, the member of the cabinet who would be most critical about Taca, who happened to take this question in his capacity as Industry and Commerce Minister. Colley accused Cluskey of throwing mud and asked if he had any evidence to support his allegations. 'Was the deputy suggesting that any administration under my department is paying grants because of money paid to Fianna Fáil?'

Cluskey ended up being ejected from the chamber for persisting with his questioning. It was not long before others joined him in the fray.

Fine Gael's Gerry L'Estrange described Taca people – or

'Tacateers', as they became known – as 'fast buck operators' and said they would always be considered more equal than others. Invoking *Animal Farm*, James Dillon said you could not get 'a fair deal from our own government unless you became a member of Taca'.

Labour's Michael O'Leary called it 'Tammany Hall tactics' – a reference to the Democratic political machine that controlled New York politics and helped Irish immigrants to rise up the ladder for well over a century – and likened Taca to a 'new Masonic order at the service of Fianna Fáil'.

Labour's Seán Dunne went even further, likening Taca to the Mafia:

The government, whether they wish it or not, are being used by this clique, and I am going to designate them. There has been a lot of talk about them. The name hitherto given to them was Taca. That is the wrong name. Taca is the Irish name for it. I am going to designate them for what they are: 'Cosa Nostra'. And here are the similarities: the family blood ties are there, are they not? As in the Mafia, the idea is to remain secret, is it not, as it was in the Gresham when some of the waiters were paid to keep out the cameramen and the reporters ... I was supplied with a list of the Capo Mafiosi – is that what one would call them, the captains of the Mafia? Whom do we find as the principal one, no less a person than the Minister for Finance [Haughey].

Evoking W.B. Yeats, he asked, 'was it for this the wild geese spread their grey wings on every tide' before concluding his remarks 'on the Cosa Nostra by saying that the name of the head of the Mafia in the US is Charlie Lucky. There you have the complete parallel.'

Mairin de Burca of Sinn Féin also went for an historical analogy, claiming that 'the selfless idealism of Easter Week has become the self-seeking degeneracy of Taca'.

As did Fine Gael leader Liam Cosgrave, who departed from script at his party's ard fheis to say, 'Freedom was not won, liberty was not secured, our forebears did not die, so this country could be handed over to political palm greasers for the purpose of political exploitation.'

Fianna Fáil strongly resisted the claims of the opposition, but in politics, as the adage goes, once you're explaining, you're losing. Brian Lenihan 'explained' that the costs of electioneering had gone up enormously and the party needed more financial support than was provided by the national collection, which did not yield enough for the needs of the time.

To cheers in the Dáil, Haughey said the men who contributed to Taca, 'expected nothing, nothing except good government from a great party. They believed in Fianna Fáil and wanted to see Fianna Fáil continue in office.' Haughey later described Taca as a 'fairly innocent concept' intended 'to make the party independent of big business' and claimed that some individuals would have previously contributed far more money to the party than the cost of Taca membership.

This view was echoed years later by Kevin Boland, who said all the members of Taca 'had for some years been subscribing at election time substantially more than the total of their between election Taca subscriptions even if elections were to come only at the full five year intervals'.

So it was clear where the brash, buccaneering young guns of

the cabinet stood on Taca, but what did the man whom they regarded as only a caretaker leader think of it?

Labour's Barry Desmond noted that no word of public support for Taca had come from Lynch and called for the two main political parties to agree to public disclosure of all donations to political parties. The Fianna Fáil response was that Labour spelled Taca quite differently: I-T-G-W-U, a pointed reference to the annual subsidy the party received from the trade unions.

Although the suggestion that Lynch distanced himself from Taca persists, some claim that the whole concept was born in November 1966 after Lynch succeeded Lemass as party leader and Taoiseach. In his first ard fheis address as leader, Lynch said that he had some thoughts on how to streamline the party and make it more efficient. A largely ignored press release was issued to say that a new fundraising organisation called Taca had been set up.

And, as T. Ryle Dwyer points out in his *Nice Fellow* biography of Lynch, the then Taoiseach certainly defended Taca from the outset. 'In order to maintain our system of democracy, we have to have political parties,' Lynch said. 'Political parties can't run without funds and these funds can only be provided voluntarily.' With the increasing costs of running elections, maintaining headquarters and offering additional services, 'the existing means of collecting funds have not been sufficient, even though we have been stepping up our national collection'.

Lynch insisted that any Taca members who had joined expecting 'some favour from government' would be 'gravely disappointed'. Unfortunately for him and his party, that was not the perception across the country.

The opposition naturally played to the gallery, raising questions about the selection of property rented by government departments and agencies. There was a bit of a furore in the Dáil when a Taca subscriber and a Fianna Fáil fundraiser was given a senior posting at a state agency. And there were allegations that a semi-state body had invested substantially in the firm of a well-known Fianna Fáil supporter.

Kevin Boland insisted that he 'never did a thing' within his department for any member of Taca, but he admitted that other ministers might have been susceptible.

The opposition continued the pressure on Taca into 1968, with Labour's Michael O'Leary claiming that a meeting of Taca, held in Leinster House, had decided to create an £80,000 to £100,000 war chest to finance the government's campaign to abolish the PR electoral system in a referendum.

Attacks on Taca featured strongly in the campaign leading up to the October referendum. Political commentators argued that changing the electoral system would guarantee Fianna Fáil a landslide victory at the next election. The party's opponents claimed that with a new electoral system, this new alliance of Fianna Fáil and commercial interests would be able to rule indefinitely.

There was also evidence that many Fianna Fáil TDs did not campaign in the referendum and some of those were lukewarm about the ending of PR. They feared that the 'young thrusting Taca types would replace old traditionalists' in the new system of single-member constituencies.

This opinion was echoed in an *Irish Times* editorial, which speculated that if Fianna Fáil won the referendum 'a few Taca subscribers will, no doubt, find their way into safe, single seat constituencies'.

After the referendum there was a revolt within Fianna Fáil against Taca. A general election was likely to be held the following summer and Taca was dragging the party into the mud. One anonymous party TD described it in the media as 'that sinister organisation that has destroyed the image of Fianna Fáil as the party of the small man, the small farmer and the workers in the towns'.

There was nothing wrong with raising funds, the problem was the secrecy surrounding the organisation and the 'terrible rule' whereby it was confined to businesspeople paying £100 a year.

Worries were expressed that 'Tacateers' were 'directing policy' and there were also misgivings over the ruthless attitude of some personalities in cabinet (presumably Blaney, Haughey and Boland, the three ministers most associated with Taca in the public mind).

Lynch, given his shaky position, could not afford to ignore such concerns. In the postmortem period after the referendum setback, he told the parliamentary party that the whole question of Taca was under review. A special committee was appointed to study the appropriateness of Taca, its form, its organisation, its name and its function and to see if its work could be performed by any other body.

The result was a new and improved Taca, more in keeping with the Fianna Fáil ethos. There was a reduced minimum membership fee of £5 (members could still pay up to £100 if they wished but the level of fee paid was kept secret) and all dinners, functions and meetings would be held in public with the press present. A press officer would be appointed to ensure maximum publicity.

The new Taca would act as an auxiliary to the Comh-Comhairle, contributing ideas as well as cash. Its objectives would be to raise funds and hold seminars to encourage interest in political matters.

Taca would also be brought within the Fianna Fáil organisation. Members of the new Taca executive would be nominated by the party leader and three of them would be members of the Fianna Fáil party executive. These changes were being made, Fianna Fáil said, to 'refute the scandalous and false allegations being made by the opposition'.

Just before these proposals were put to the party for approval, Colley delivered a speech in which he said 'under no circumstances can we allow big business to dominate or appear to dominate the party'. The speech was widely seen as Colley demanding an end to Taca and was also seen in some quarters (probably incorrectly) as a challenge to Lynch. If Colley meant what he said, a newspaper editorial declared the following day, then the 'days of the Mercedes set's undue influence on Fianna Fáil are numbered'.

Lynch, who possessed a steely resolve underneath his gentlemanly demeanour, responded decisively, insisting that 'no member of Taca had benefited from his membership. Nor do I believe any member ever expected to so benefit.' Colley moved quickly back in step with his leader, giving his unequivocal support for the reformed Taca.

But many of the party's grass roots wanted Taca shelved rather than reformed – a point highlighted by numerous speakers at the January 1969 ard fheis before Neil Blaney's dramatic intervention.

* * *

Despite Blaney's tour de force, Taca was abolished within one year. Lynch realised no reform could change the public's perception. Taca was scrapped because, as political journalist Dick Walsh said, it 'combined fund raising with ostentation'.

In its place came the Fianna Fáil general election fundraising committee, which was run by its secretary Des Hanafin, a young party activist and businessman, from room 547 of the Burlington Hotel.

Hanafin, with the approval of Lynch, stopped the dinners and the public interaction between ministers and businesspeople, but of course the corporate sector was still tapped for party funds.

Questions remain over whether Taca was really scrapped or whether it just went underground for a decade. In a piece written in the *Irish Times* in 1997, as the McCracken Tribunal revelations into Haughey were emerging, then political editor Geraldine Kennedy noted the number of original Taca members who stayed on with the new fundraising committee: O'Reilly-Hyland, McGonagle, Reihill and McCarthy.

The party argued that it made sense not to dispose of their experience, but that Taca, as the public understood it, was certainly gone. Back on the ard fheis podium a year after his passionate defence of the fundraising body, Blaney was referring to 'an organisation formerly known as Taca'.

Under the new Hanafin regime, there was a tradition of segregation, with the names of donors not being revealed to Lynch. When Haughey took over the leadership in 1979, he immediately set about getting control of the operation.

Hanafin was in the Colley/Des O'Malley wing of Fianna Fáil and he distrusted Haughey's intentions. He bravely refused to hand over what was known as 'The Black Book' containing the names of the secret subscribers to the party. There was a stand-off until 1982 when Haughey fired Hanafin, though the latter disputed his right to do so because technically the committee did not come under the control of the party leader.

The other members of the committee were called in by Haughey and asked to agree to sign over the confidential files to party headquarters. The committee was then disbanded, effectively legitimising Hanafin's sacking. Haughey now had complete control of fundraising, something he would use to his advantage (see Chapter 9).

During the leadership of Albert Reynolds and the early years of Bertie Ahern's tenure, another Des – Des Richardson, an integral member of Ahern's 'Drumcondra Mafia' – was the party fundraiser. Operating from a suite in the Berkeley Court Hotel, Richardson made serious inroads into the party's debt, holding a number of private dinners for wealthy businesspeople, which were attended by senior Fianna Fáil politicians. Richardson helped raise an estimated £2.5 million in funds in the few years of his tenure.

* * *

It would be wholly misleading to suggest that Fianna Fáil was the only party soliciting business interests for donations. In the early years of Fianna Fáil, it had been a proud party boast that it won elections at a fraction of the cost at which Fine Gael and the Labour Party lost them. Whether or not that was true, Fine Gael was just as active over the years in trying to secure money from business interests.

The development of the Fianna Fáil general election fundraising committee – or the organisation formerly known as Taca to use Blaney's description – certainly gave Fianna Fáil an edge in terms of financial muscle in the late 1960s and 1970s. But by the three general elections of 1981/82, Fine Gael was back on a level playing field.

As with Fianna Fáil under Lynch, Fine Gael insisted that any fundraising was done at arm's length from the party leader, who was unaware of who was making donations. However, in May 1997 the *Sunday Tribune* disclosed letters written by three previous Fine Gael leaders to a major beef industry figure to solicit donations.

One such letter was written in December 1987 by then party leader Alan Dukes. Dukes wrote that he would be 'glad to have your advice on issues which you believe to be important. To that end, I should be more than happy to ensure that you have access to me and my front bench.' There was a follow-up letter in 1988, thanking the businessman for his 'commitment to a very substantial level of support' and adding, 'I am confident that you will find your generosity in this regard well placed.'

In 1991 the new Fine Gael leader John Bruton wrote to the same businessman, saying he was approaching 'a few people in the business world' to help tackle the party's financial problems.

The *Sunday Tribune* also revealed that in 1987 Fine Gael had drawn up a list of hundreds of top businesspeople to solicit contributions from for the party. It read like a who's who of Irish business. During the period from 1994 to 1997, when Fine Gael was in government, the party's huge debt was wiped out as it attracted an estimated £4 million or more in donations.

When Michael Noonan became leader of Fine Gael, he took the decision to stop taking corporate donations. This position was quickly reversed by his successor Enda Kenny. Stopping corporate donations was a noble decision, but in reality it put the party at a serious competitive disadvantage to Fianna Fáil.

In the 1960s the Labour Party, despite its objective of a socialist state, was also sending out letters to businesspeople looking for support. Then, of course, there is that party's continuing financial support from the trade union movement. Union subsidies may be less politically contentious than donations from big business, but there is no question that both represent funding from vested interests. Ideally, in a republic, that scenario should not arise.

Meanwhile, Sinn Féin was at one point raising so much money in the United States that politicians from other parties warned about its unfair financial advantage.

The effectiveness of the Progressive Democrats at raising money from the corporate sector was inadvertently revealed in 1997 when highly sensitive financial documents (detailing dozens upon dozens of donors to the party from the mid-1980s to 1992) were discovered in a skip and passed to a Sunday newspaper.

The list of PD donors featured most of that period's top Irish business leaders, including the Smurfit Group, Larry Goodman, Irish Distillers, Sisk, Mark Kavanagh of the Custom House Docks Development Company, Tony Ryan of Guinness Peat Aviation, Neil McCann of Fyffes and Tim O'Mahony of Toyota.

The documents also included a 1992 letter from party fundraiser Paul Smithwick to party leader and Minister for Industry and Commerce, Des O'Malley, which referred to a 'confidential meeting' between Michael Smurfit and O'Malley in January of that year. Enclosed with the letter was a copy of a cheque donation of £30,000 to the party from the Jefferson Smurfit Group. 'Michael will prove to be an extremely good supporter of our party and I cannot tell you how appreciative he was for our confidential meeting in January,' Smithwick wrote.

The PDs subsequently issued a statement in which it said that it was 'normal and proper' for the Minister for Industry and Commerce to meet with Smurfit and that O'Malley had met 'with many other industrialists' during his time in office.

Smurfit also met John Bruton at the K Club within days of Bruton becoming Taoiseach at the end of 1994. Five years earlier Smurfit had made a £60,000 donation to Fianna Fáil, which Haughey as party leader used for himself.

It is important to stress that Smurfit had not done anything wrong in making a political donation and is by no means alone among business figures in giving money to various political parties – Ben Dunne, for example, gave money to Fine Gael as well as giving over £1 million to Haughey – and there is no suggestion of any impropriety on their part.

The reality is that political parties had little option but to seek such fundraising opportunities because, until recently, the amount of state funding for political parties was extremely low by European standards. Fianna Fáil, Fine Gael and Labour all had chronic debt problems in the 1980s. They were spending money they did not have. Between 1981 and 1992 the parties had to fund six extremely expensive general election campaigns.

The whole system was entirely unregulated. Political parties in Ireland were not recognised formally until 1963, which seems to have been a reflection of the state's founding fathers' utopian – and of course highly unrealistic – belief that party politics could be avoided.

Prior to the Electoral Act 1963 candidates stood (in theory) as individuals and party labels were not included on ballot papers. And there were no limits on election spending until the late 1990s. And until that same point all political fundraising was essentially done in secret.

It was inevitable, given this lack of regulation, that lines would be blurred about how politicians used the 'political donations' they received. And, as the McCracken, Moriarty and Flood/Mahon Tribunals have since uncovered, those lines were certainly crossed by many politicians at both national and local levels (see Chapters 6, 9 and 11).

Matters came to a head in 1997 with revelations of payments to politicians, in particular to Haughey. This information helped the passage of the Electoral Act 1997, which increased the levels of public funding available to parties, as well as bringing some transparency to the sources of all funding and some accountability to how money was spent, including time limitations, at election time.

Under the 1997 Act, general funding was given to any party that received over 2 per cent of the vote at the previous general election. This funding comprised an annual contribution towards running costs and a reimbursement of election expenses.

The legislation was amended in 2001. By 2002 almost €13 million in state funding was going to the political parties (from €4.67 million to Fianna Fáil and €3.5 million to Fine Gael, all the way down to €62,000 for the Socialist Party). The figure in 2009 was €13.6 million. This compares with far less than half a million in 1989 – the year of a general election some believe was called because of the opportunity it offered Haughey to tap the business community for money.

While there were still major donations made to political parties after the 1997 Act, they were at least made public. The 2001 Act set a limit on anonymous donations, at €126.97, and required candidates to declare all donations above €634.87 (or £500 as it was before the introduction of the euro).

Parties were also obliged to declare all donations in excess of €5,078.95 and donations from individuals were restricted to €6,348.69 in a single year. Candidates were prevented from accepting donations from any one individual in a single year exceeding €2,539.48.

And no candidate or party could accept donations from outside the state, unless they came from Irish citizens – a move that targeted Sinn Féin and its extremely successful fundraising activities in the US.

Restrictions were also introduced on how much candidates could spend in a general election campaign. For example, candidates in a five-seat constituency were limited to €38,092. In the 2002 general election, candidates spent just over €7 million, but only Fianna Fáil and the PDs came close to spending their full allowance, reaching 87 per cent of what was allowed.

The new rules are not perfect. Although major donations from top businesspeople have largely disappeared, parties have tended to favour big draws, golf outings or fundraising dinners with individual amounts donated coming under the limit required for disclosure.

For example, a table of eight at a dinner might be sold at €1,800, meaning that under the ethics legislation the average contribution per guest is below the legal limit for disclosure. Technically, a politician could raise well over €100,000 from a dinner of 200 people without having to declare who had bought tickets.

In 2009, the most recent year for which figures are available from the Standards in Public Office Commission (SIPO), just €76,617.05 in disclosed donations were given to political parties – the lowest amount since the introduction of the rules requiring disclosure in 1997. And, despite local elections, European elections and the second Lisbon referendum taking place in that year, the three main parties (Fianna Fáil, Fine Gael and Labour) had no disclosed donations whatsoever.

Little wonder SIPO stated that there is 'a strong case to be made for a new approach to the general funding of political parties, for increased transparency in such funding and for greater scrutiny of political party expenditure'.

As journalist Fintan O'Toole put it in the days following SIPO's release of the 2009 figures:

> You don't have to be Sherlock Holmes to work out what's going on. The limit below which donations do not have to be declared is €5,078.95. I'll take a wild guess and say that there are an awful lot of individuals and companies who find that they can just about afford €5,078.94 to support our precious democratic system.

Nevertheless, the situation, although imperfect, has greatly improved.

* * *

The financial support to political parties comes at a cost to the state but, given what we now know about the old system, it is hard to argue that this is not a price worth paying.

Taca, like the Fianna Fáil tent at the Galway Races in the 1990s and the early 2000s, came to represent the overly close links between business and politics that many blame for Ireland's current malaise.

Yet Taca was arguably less objectionable than the fund-raising that went on before and after. At least Taca was in the public domain. The same holds for the tent at the Galway

Races, which was accessible to the media and which raised a relatively small amount of money.

Although the media and the general public became very exercised by such fundraising activities, the secretive donations that went on for decades – and still go on – rarely became an issue.

Kevin Boland's take on Taca is worth considering:

> Certainly Taca was a development of great significance in regard to the character of Fianna Fáil but it had nothing to do with corruption. Its significance was that it unmistakeably marked the accelerating change from the small man's party, priding itself on its total dependence on the small subscriptions collected once a year in every parish in the 26 counties, to a party still using the same type of election worker but now financially patronised by the bosses ...

> What Taca established was that the financial support of the entrepreneurial class was very substantial and had become vital and this was a very serious development indeed. The danger seen by a few in the early 1930s had materialised and it seemed to be only a matter of time until this financial dependence would manifest itself in the matter of policy to such an extent that the people would realise there had been a definite shift to the right in [Fianna Fáil's] political position.

T. Ryle Dwyer puts it more succinctly in his biography of Lynch: contacts made through Taca 'gave rise to suspicions of corruption within Fianna Fáil that were not eradicated during Lynch's lifetime'. According to the party's opponents, they still have not been eradicated.

While some have argued that having a system that is entirely state funded would prevent a new political party (like the PDs in 1985) from getting off the ground, it should be possible to come up with innovative solutions to get around this problem.

It is hard to disagree with the 2010 assessment of the Director of Public Prosecutions, James Hamilton, that 'as long as you allow political parties to receive donations from individuals without any presumption that there is some impropriety, then you are wide open, I think, to a form of corruption.'

The Fianna Fáil/Green Party coalition elected in 2007 committed to end corporate donations to political parties entirely. Some commentators have questioned the constitutionality of such a measure and it remains to be seen whether this commitment translates into action. Only when that happens can we definitively say that, more than 40 years after its demise, the lessons from Taca have been fully absorbed.

6

PLANNING FOR THE PAY DAY

Ray Burke was bang to rights. The *Sunday Independent* had investigated the planning process and how some councillors were using it to enrich themselves. The article claimed that Councillor Burke, who was also a newly elected TD, had engineered the rezoning of land of which he was a beneficiary. It was June 1974, a time of great innocence in the world of planning.

Burke, as a member of Dublin County Council, had seconded a motion to rezone lands at Mountgarry, near Swords, from agricultural to industrial use. The lands increased in value by around £400,000 as a result of the rezoning. According to a document published by the newspaper, Burke had received £15,000 when the land was sold on. This figure was the equivalent of 5.85 per cent of the total value of the land.

Crucially, the professional planners were totally opposed to the rezoning. There were problems with drainage, access and proximity to the flight paths near Dublin Airport. No matter. The councillors went ahead. There was progress to be made. As Burke told a local newspaper about the rezoning, 'I would be delighted to see as many jobs coming to the north county area as possible.'

Until the *Sunday Independent*'s Joe MacAnthony pieced together the full story, few were aware that Burke was also in line for a major payday. MacAnthony had located documents in the Companies Registration Office linking Burke to the payment from a company owned by two builders, Tom Brennan and Joe McGowan. The annual returns for a Brennan and McGowan vehicle, Dublin Airport Industrial Estates Ltd, included a payment of £15,000 to Raphael Burke under the heading 'Planning'.

Responding to the story, Burke claimed that he had not had any financial interest in the lands at the time of the rezoning. He had since had a relationship with McGowan and Brennan through his auctioneering business. Nothing to see here, folks, move along. But, for those with an intimate knowledge of planning, Burke was at the centre of a system that stank to high heaven.

The story hit the front page on 23 June with the opening line: 'After months of investigation, the *Sunday Independent* now believes there are grounds for a public inquiry into whether local authority representatives should declare their financial interests in matters coming before the councils on which they sit.'

There was an immediate furore. Taoiseach Jack Lynch assigned his newly appointed press officer – a young eager beaver by the name of Frank Dunlop – to deal with the matter. This was to be Dunlop's first involvement in planning in the Dublin area. In time, planning in Dublin would garner him a fortune and then lead to his imprisonment.

Throughout the controversy in 1974, Burke retained the confidence of his party leader. The imperative for Lynch appears to have been to put out the fires of scandal rather than to find out whether anything really lay behind the story. It would not be the last time that Burke would be able to call on his party leader for support.

Burke had a perfect explanation for the entry in the books. When he was not tending to the constituents of north Dublin as a local TD, he was operating as an auctioneer. He had a professional relationship with Brennan and McGowan, and the payment was in respect of fees that were due to him.

The defence offered by Burke – and accepted in the political arena – demonstrated the potential that existed for corruption. Nobody thought it unusual that a man filling the roles of councillor and TD could also operate as an auctioneer.

Even if this excuse for the £15,000 was accepted, it effectively meant Burke could vote for the rezoning of land as a councillor and then make money out of selling the houses constructed on the rezoned land as an auctioneer. This glaring conflict of interest was not given a second thought.

The uproar over MacAnthony's story required that the matter be properly investigated. There would, however, be no public inquiry. That would have to wait another 23 years, and would take place in a different Ireland, when the smell of corruption just would not go away.

Instead, a garda probe was initiated. MacAnthony was one of the first to be interviewed. Years later he would recall that the detective who visited him said that he did not have any confidence that anything would result from the investigation. He was right about that. It concluded without any recommendation of a prosecution.

Burke resumed the upward trajectory of his political career, unstained by what was filed away as a baseless allegation. Just for good measure, the company records showing the offending payment were later altered, the payment deleted.

The fortunes of the reporter who broke the story went in

the opposite direction. Following his Burke story, and another which demonstrated how the Irish Hospitals Sweepstakes (see Chapter 2) had been manipulated to benefit a few individuals, MacAnthony was forced to emigrate to Canada. Ireland was not ready to look in the mirror and admit that corruption was indeed a fact of public life.

The scandal of Burke's £15,000 payment from a construction company thus ran into the sand. It would be over two decades before MacAnthony was completely vindicated and Burke was exposed as a deeply corrupt politician and eventually jailed for tax evasion.

In the intervening years Burke became one of Ireland's leading politicians. Planning corruption became endemic and was largely regarded as an activity that could be undertaken with impunity. All may have been so much different if the organs of state and society had the capacity and willingness to follow up on MacAnthony's 1974 story in the *Sunday Independent*.

* * *

The potential for planning corruption in the Republic of Ireland was greatly enhanced, oddly enough, by the law. The cornerstone planning law for the state was enacted in 1963 and decreed planning to be undertaken for the 'common good'. It also, however, bestowed on county and city councillors the power to designate land as suitable for a particular use. For instance, the most common redesignation is for agricultural land to be rezoned for residential or industrial use.

Ideally, rezoned land would meet the proper planning guidelines. But, if councillors deemed it appropriate to rezone, then those vital issues become irrelevant. It did not matter that such land might not be suitably serviced for a new use. There may not be road access or an adequate sewage system in place. Nor did it matter that there may not be any discernible requirement to rezone a piece of land to facilitate ordered development.

Land could be rezoned for housing, even though population or residential trends suggested there was no need for it. Thus, rezoning, instead of acting as a tool to facilitate the development of the state, was often used as nothing more than a means of enrichment for landowners.

Councillors had the power to make overnight millionaires of landowners, turning muck into gold at the stroke of a pen. In such a system, corruption lurked in the shadows, waiting to pounce at the right opportunity.

By the late 1960s the flaws in the system were becoming obvious. Landowners naturally lobbied to receive favourable rezoning in development plans. When their interests were deemed by officials not to coincide with the common good, they lobbied politicians for change. Very often, this lobbying was successful.

Thus, planning was not done on the basis of the professional interpretation of the common good, but on the political interpretation of it. The vulnerability of politicians in this type of relationship is obvious.

A landowner would apply to have a plot rezoned under a development plan. Thereafter it would be perfectly legitimate to lobby county councillors as to the validity of the application. For those in the know, there was another route: identify a councillor who was willing to take money and get him or her onside with a brown envelope. More often than not, more than one envelope was required.

Sometimes the envelope was a political donation and treated as such by the councillor. There was, however, little regulation of this area and one person's political donation might be another's annual family holiday. And for some, the size of the donation was on a different scale from any legitimate political expenses that accrued.

In 1971 the government commissioned a report to look into the method of rezoning land, and particularly how it might be better achieved for the common good. The Committee on the Price of Building Land was chaired by Judge John Kenny of the High Court. It reported in 1974. One of its major recommendations was that rezoned land should be valued at the agricultural price plus 25 per cent. This, it was felt, would dampen down the frenzy for land speculation and lead to a greater incentive to proper planning.

As with so many other reports, the fate of the Kenny report rested on the political will to implement it. In 1974 a coalition government of Fine Gael and the Labour Party was in situ, led by Fine Gael's Liam Cosgrave.

According to one account of what transpired at cabinet, the Kenny report was presented by the Minister for Local Government, Jim Tully, who was a member of the minority coalition partner, Labour. Cosgrave and the Minister for Finance, Richie Ryan, were reported as saying that they opposed the implementation of Kenny. None of the other voices around the table, including Tully as the report's sponsor, made any serious case for implementing the report. Noted socialists such as Labour Party leader Brendan Corish and Justin Keating remained silent. As did self-proclaimed social democrats such as Conor Cruise O'Brien and Garret FitzGerald.

In an interview with the *Sunday Tribune* in 2006, FitzGerald could not put his finger on why the Kenny report was not implemented. 'I'm still not clear in recollection as to why it wasn't tackled when we were in,' he said. 'I remember some discussion as to the arguments but I can't recall the outcome.'

With no serious advocate for the report, it was shelved, then buried. With it died any prospect of reshaping the planning process in a progressive way. As long as rezoning had the potential to yield massive profits, then rezoning would remain the focus of the process for all the interested players, including the politicians.

It could well be that the cabinet members did not realise the chance that was being offered by Kenny. Far more likely is that they simply did not have the stomach to take on powerful interests such as landowners and developers.

* * *

Ray Burke was elected to Dublin County Council for the first time in 1967. He was just 24. A few months later he set up his auctioneering business. His father, Paddy, who was the sitting TD, helped him out with the business.

The two jobs complemented each other. In his public role, Burke was one of the most flagrant rezoners of land on the council. In his private role, after the land was rezoned, he often sold the house built thereon. It was a perfect racket.

Burke was first elected to the Dáil in 1973. He topped the poll with 10,652 first preference votes, which he acknowledged was largely down to his father's reputation. Paddy Burke had held the seat for 29 years.

On 10 October 1973 Burke and his family moved into a substantial new house in Swords, in the heart of his constituency. The house had been built by a Brennan and McGowan company, Oakpark. The firm's business was constructing housing estates, but for Burke the two men were willing to do a one-off house.

There is no record of any money ever being paid for the house, Briargate, or the land on which it was built. One solicitor associated with the transaction would give evidence some 26 years later that he had been asked to 'bury or lose' the conveyancing file. So by the time of the MacAnthony story, Burke was already a bought man.

Once Burke saw that he could act with impunity, it was open season. Over the following 20 years planning corruption would become endemic in developing the greater Dublin conurbation. Burke would be a central character, but far from the only one.

Records show that Burke's auctioneering firm was paid £1,000 a month from April 1975 to August 1982 by a Brennan and McGowan vehicle. This was at a time when Brennan and McGowan were the biggest house builders in the Dublin area.

Burke's annual income from the builders was twice that of his Dáil salary of less than £6,000 in 1975. Nearly all the money was channelled through the auctioneering firm for Burke's personal use. There is no record of any work being done for the money. Quite obviously, neither party had any fears that their arrangement would be discovered, or even if it was, that it would amount to a hill of beans, following the shutting down of media inquiries in 1974.

Fianna Fáil returned to power in 1977 and the vote-getting ability of Burke was rewarded with a junior ministry. He said that he was giving up the auctioneering business, but his two house-building pals continued making payments.

He resigned his council seat in 1978 in deference to his elevation on the national stage. But he remained a highly influential figure with his party colleagues on the local authority. Through these years, the pace of questionable rezoning quickened.

A coterie of councillors from Fianna Fáil and Fine Gael proposed and seconded most applications. In such a milieu, senior and domineering politicians like Burke had great influence over some of their colleagues. If Burke was in favour of something, he could be guaranteed to influence a clutch of councillors.

Those who benefited included party supporters, party financers and quite often relatives of the councillors.

There were persistent rumours that money was being paid for votes, but nothing was provable. After all, a garda investigation following the MacAnthony story demonstrated that there was nothing untoward afoot.

Through that period there were many controversial decisions to rezone, but only one major decision was reversed. In April 1981 a decision to rezone 150 acres in Lucan in the west of the city came before the council. One of the councillors, Fianna Fáil's Liam Lawlor, left the meeting before the vote was due to take place. He did not, however, say that he had any beneficial interest in the land. Later, it emerged that he was the owner and stood to gain over £300,000.

The news caused a major public outcry. Taoiseach Charles Haughey called in the Fianna Fáil councillors and told them to reverse the decision. The irony of Haughey being outraged at a politician attempting to snaffle a fortune on the back of his public office would not become fully apparent until nearly two decades later. In any event, Lawlor failed to get that particular windfall. The decision was reversed.

Rezoning activity was getting out of hand. In October 1980 Haughey had appointed Burke as Minister for the Environment. The following year Minister Burke complained of the 'highly objectionable' activity of some councillors in their overzealous approach to rezoning.

By then he had opened offshore accounts to accept payments from his old pals, Brennan and McGowan. On 21 December 1982 a deposit of £50,000 sterling was made to a Burke account in the Isle of Man. On 18 April 1984 a sum of £35,000 sterling was deposited to the account of another off-shore vehicle, the aptly named Caviar. On 21 November 1984 £60,000 sterling was deposited in the same account.

The Planning Tribunal would eventually find as a fact that all of these payments were corrupt, although it was unable to establish exactly what favours were supplied in return. Through all this time, Burke must have had few concerns that his acceptance of large sums of money from the house builders would ever be discovered.

The offshore accounts put the money beyond the reach of the Revenue Commissioners and, if the worst came to the worst, past experience armed him with the knowledge that any garda inquiry would run into the sand. He knew that planning corruption operated within a culture of impunity. He had nothing to worry about.

Fianna Fáil was sent into the wilderness of opposition in 1983. Two years later, Burke returned to the council. He was elected as chairman of Dublin County Council and remained in the position for two years. His tenure was marked by a firm hand on the party whip, ensuring that all the party members voted as he decreed. On the issue of rezoning, this was, strictly speaking, illegal.

Each elected member is charged with a quasi-judicial function when undertaking rezoning decisions. This means that each is obliged to vote according to his or her own judgment on the merit of the decision. A feature of rezoning in

Dublin throughout the 1980s and 1990s was that nearly all members of the two main parties voted under the whip.

In 1987 Fianna Fáil returned to power under a government led by Haughey. Burke was appointed Minister for Energy, and later Minister for Industry and Commerce.

In February 1989, another Garda inquiry was launched.

The central plank of this inquiry was a complaint from a builder, Peter Loughran, that he had been approached for money by a member of An Bord Pleanála. He was developing a hotel in Sligo at the time. Loughran agreed to testify and was granted immunity.

Charges were brought against an official of An Bord Pleanála, William Tobin. At the trial, Loughran gave evidence, but the prosecution case ran into major difficulties as there was little substantial evidence beyond the claims of the chief prosecution witness. Tobin was acquitted.

The garda inquiry also took into account a number of other allegations made about planning in Dublin around the same time. All were investigated over the course of 15 months, but came to nothing.

Detective Superintendent Brendan Burns, who led the investigation, remarked at one stage, 'What we're dealing with here is not just a few backhanders. What we're dealing with is a nest of vipers.' Yet it was not possible to amass enough evidence to bring a prosecution.

Unable to discover any hard evidence, the garda report of the investigation concluded, 'Newspaper articles suggested that bribery and corruption were endemic in the planning process. Whilst my inquiries were largely confined to the city and county of Dublin, I found this not to be the case.'

Burns and his team kept coming up against a brick wall. The allegations that payments were routinely being made were based on rumours and hearsay. Any politician under suspicion could deny it as an outrageous claim and explain away any of his or her decisions as being one of 'pro-development'.

Of course, neither the givers nor the receivers of these monies were ever going to admit to the activity, so unless somebody saw a transfer of money and recorded the parties agreeing that it was for a planning favour, there was little in the way of evidence.

Crucially, the garda inquiry did not have access to bank accounts, which might have left a trail between the parties, and could circumstantially be linked to specific decisions. That level of investigation would have to await the establishment of a tribunal.

In May 1989 Haughey decided to call an election, in search of a more secure mandate. Burke received three large payments over the following weeks, all of which he claims were political donations. He got at least £40,000 to organise the rezoning of land; £35,000 from Oliver Barry, a director of Ireland's first independent radio station, Century; and £30,000 from a signage company, Rennicks, which was owned by a company controlled by Tony O'Reilly, a businessman with vast media interests in Ireland. A tribunal would eventually rule that the first two of these were corrupt payments. While initial investigations were made into the Rennicks payment, nothing conclusive ever arose from it.

The payment of the £40,000 was a prime example of planning corruption and would be the starting point for the Planning Tribunal, which was still a long way off.

* * *

In June 1989 Burke was preparing for the general election. In the unregulated climate of political donations, it was a bright and shiny time for any politician who wanted to hoover up as much money as possible.

Meanwhile, an old friend of Burke's was involved in another venture at the time. Michael Bailey was a co-director with his brother Tom of house-building firm Bovale Developments. In some ways, the Bailey brothers had taken up where Brennan and McGowan left off: they were from the west of Ireland, they ran one of the biggest house-building firms in Dublin and they were close to Burke, the local bigwig.

Another builder with extensive interests in north Dublin was Joseph Murphy, a Kerryman who had made his fortune in London. Since the 1960s Murphy had been acquiring land where he thought there might be development potential. In 1989 he sold one lot of this land, at Forest Road in Swords, to Bailey for £1.45 million. He still had around 700 acres and was of a mind to sell up and get out. Murphy held these lands through a company called Joseph Murphy Structural Engineers (JMSE).

Bailey was interested in buying the lands for sale, but he also had another proposal that might interest Murphy's company. In a letter dated 8 June 1989, he wrote to JMSE executive James Gogarty and proposed that he could either buy the lands outright or, through his contacts, ensure that planning permission would be obtained for the lands, which would hugely boost their value. Bailey inferred that he would be able to obtain the planning permission through his political contacts.

Gogarty consulted with his boss, Murphy, Murphy's son Joe Junior and other JMSE executives. A decision was made to go along with Bailey's proposal to obtain planning permission.

Gogarty says that on the appointed day, he showed up at the office of JMSE and was told there was a sum of £30,000 in cash that was to be given to Burke. He was told that another £10,000 was required and Gogarty signed a company cheque for that amount. Gogarty was given to believe that Bailey would provide matching funding for the bribe.

A few days later Bailey collected Gogarty and drove to Briargate to meet Burke. There is a dispute over whether Joe Junior accompanied them to meet the politician. During the journey Gogarty addressed Bailey on the accounting procedure for the money they were about to hand over.

'Will we get a receipt?' Gogarty asked.

'Will we fuck,' Bailey replied.

At the house, Burke invited them in. He was up the walls with the election and not in the mood for a long chat. Gogarty handed over the bulging envelope. Gogarty claims that Bailey handed over another envelope containing £40,000 in cash. Burke thanked them and put the money in a drawer. He saw them out and got back to pursuing the ideals of democracy in the forthcoming election.

The lands in question were not rezoned. Murphy sold them later that year, and everybody presumably put the bribe down to a bad debt. But the incident demonstrated once more the impunity with which people like Burke believed they could act.

None of this information would have come to light if Gogarty had not developed serious animosity towards Murphy over the latter's failure to pay him a proper pension. In the heat of his hostility, he answered an advertisement in 1995 about planning corruption, which eventually led to the establishment of the Planning Tribunal.

Back in 1989 the rumours continued to swirl around Burke. In that year he had received at least £105,000 in large payments, which was nearly three times his ministerial salary. Still, he remained untouchable.

Burke was a deeply corrupt individual, whose position and morals allowed him to reap vast sums, but he was not operating in a vacuum. There were many others charged with operating in the public interest who saw planning as a route to easy bucks.

*   *   *

In the early 1990s a new development plan for the greater Dublin area was formulated. In terms of rezoning, this was like hitting the jackpot for dozens of landowners who had the potential to become overnight millionaires.

The plan was the source of much dispute in the early 1990s and many of the rezoning decisions taken were highly controversial. Through it all, vast fortunes were made and at the centre of the whole affair was a player par excellence when it came to swaying the decisions of councillors.

Frank Dunlop knew his way around politics. In 1974 he had been appointed to the new role of government press secretary. He was just 26 and had worked in RTÉ for the previous two years. One of his first tasks in the new job was to deal with the fallout from the Joe MacAnthony story. Thus, Dunlop began a career of spinning.

For the following 12 years he worked in government. After Lynch resigned in 1979, his services were retained by the new leader, Haughey. Then, when Fine Gael assumed power, FitzGerald also kept him on.

By 1986 he had a powerful insight into how government worked and he had amassed a bulging contacts book of politicians and party supporters from both Fianna Fáil and Fine Gael. It was time to put his experience to lucrative use in the private sector.

He joined leading Dublin public relations firm, Murray

Consultants, but within a few years he had set up his own PR

Consultants, but within a few years he had set up his own PR and lobbying firm, Frank Dunlop and Associates. It was the 1990s and the economy was emerging from years of recession. A development plan for Dublin city and county was in gestation. It was a good time to be a lobbyist of Dunlop's calibre.

Dunlop has admitted that he was involved in extensive bribery in the formulation of the county development plan in the early 1990s. He was retained in a professional capacity by landowners in relation to 18 different amendments to the plan, proposing rezoning. He says he kept a large stash of cash with which to bribe councillors for their votes. He made a distinction between bribes (paid in cash) and so-called legitimate political donations (paid by cheque).

'It wasn't rocket science,' Dunlop told the Planning Tribunal in 2005. 'Some [councillors] proffered their support for signing motions [to rezone] in return for cash. The motion was the ticket to the ball. If you weren't at the ball you couldn't dance.'

Dunlop always maintained that the system of bribes was in place before he entered the business. He said that his friend Liam Lawlor informed him early on that he would have to 'pay to play'.

All of the councillors who were named by Dunlop as being in receipt of bribes have denied it. Two are deceased.

As of June 2010 the Planning Tribunal had not yet ruled on Dunlop's evidence, but the picture he paints is one of widespread corruption in the planning process, in which he was a middleman and a beneficiary. He was jailed for 18 months in 2009 after pleading guilty to corruption charges.

Some of his projects were of enormous size. For instance, a plan to rezone 107 acres in Carrickmines in south County

Dublin. The lands were bought by a shadowy outfit called Jackson Way, which had links to Lawlor. Dunlop was retained to lobby, and in doing so he claims to have issued a number of bribes to various councillors.

Just 17 acres were eventually rezoned but that move increased the value of the lands from £.6.3 million to £48 million. Dunlop asked the developers for £50,000 as his cut for getting councillors on side by any means necessary. In the end, he settled for half that amount.

The Criminal Assets Bureau became involved over a decade later and froze the assets. But the example shows the fortunes that were to be made with the agreement of sitting councillors.

In July 1993 the rezoning frenzy had reached fever pitch and was the subject of persistent rumours. The *Irish Times* ran a series of articles that detailed how unnamed developers had handed over large sums of cash for votes. The series, written by Frank McDonald and Mark Brennock, relied on extensive interviews with a range of people involved in planning.

The first article began: 'Landowners and developers have offered and in some cases paid sums of money to Dublin county councillors who supported controversial land rezoning schemes in Co Dublin, a property developer, a developer's agent, a councillor and a former councillor have confirmed to the *Irish Times*.' Inside the paper, the reports gave a flavour of what was afoot:

A property developer was on the phone to a Dublin county councillor lobbying him about a particular scheme. The councillor wandered off the subject on a number of occasions and began to drone on about his car and how old and decrepit it was. The developer was left with the clear impression that the councillor was asking for his car to be replaced, in exchange for his vote.

Agents, or intermediaries between developers and councillors, were also canvassed. The report went on:

'One developer's agent said the system operated on basis of "straight cash in brown paper bags".' The agent revealed, 'There is a certain number of people in that council chamber who put a value on their votes. They are the power brokers who can bring five votes with you, or five votes against you, depending on how they're looked after.'

The reporters were at pains to point out that the majority of politicians were not involved in the bribery. 'Even councillors and developers who say that such bribery takes place – and there are many – believe very few individuals are involved, and that the vast majority of councillors are decent, honest public representatives.'

Following the series, another garda investigation was launched. It too came to naught. The difficultly was once again no access to bank accounts, which would have provided supporting evidence of corruption. Impunity in planning, it appeared, was here to stay. In time the substance of the *Irish Times* articles was seen to be entirely on the button.

In the aftermath of the reports, the Minister for the Environment, Michael Smith, made a speech decrying what appeared to be afoot. 'The stage has now been reached where zoning has become a debased currency in the County Dublin area, where even desirable changes in zoning are being tarred with the same brush as those which arise on the promptings of landowners or developers.'

It was as if the national politicians were declaring themselves helpless in preventing their local colleagues from corrupting the planning system. It was the same line that had been repeated over the previous 20 years. Despite the smell of something rotten, the government was unwilling to overhaul the system.

Two years later a pair of environmental activists, Michael Smith and Colm MacEochaidh, undertook a project that would finally blow the lid on planning corruption in Ireland.

They organised for an advertisement to be placed in the *Irish Times* under the heading, '£10,000 Reward Fund'. The advert offered the money for 'information leading to the conviction on indictment of a person or persons for offences relating to land rezoning in the Republic of Ireland'.

Smith and MacEochaidh are barristers and perfectly literate on the law in the Republic, but such were the tentacles of corruption that they placed the offer through a firm of solicitors in Northern Ireland. The advert attracted 52 allegations, most of which were subsequently investigated by the Planning Tribunal.

One of those who responded to the advert was James Gogarty, the executive with JMSE who had since fallen out bitterly with his employer over a pension. Gogarty met the two barristers and detailed the payment to Burke in 1989. They introduced Gogarty to journalist Frank Connolly.

In early 1996 Connolly reported in the *Sunday Business Post* that a 'senior Fianna Fáil politician' had received a large sum of money for a planning favour. On the face of it, this was one more rumour, one more unnamed case, no different from all the others that had popped up over the decades. But Connolly kept digging and stories kept appearing.

The crucial difference this time was that there was a changing atmosphere in public life. In November 1996 government minister Michael Lowry was forced to resign after it was revealed that an extension to his County Tipperary home was paid for by retail magnate, Ben Dunne.

Within months it emerged that Dunne had given £1 million to Haughey. The rumours about Haughey that had circulated for the previous 20 years were suddenly given flesh. A tribunal of inquiry was established under Justice Brian McCracken to investigate Haughey and Lowry. The culture of impunity for senior politicians was beginning to show cracks.

In June 1997 Fianna Fáil returned to power under Bertie Ahern. Despite a healthy economy, the outgoing coalition of Fine Gael, the Labour Party and Democratic Left could not match the guile and charm of Ahern and his team at the polls. Fianna Fáil would be the major party in the new government, in coalition with the Progressive Democrats and supported by four independent TDs.

The campaign had been punctuated with questions about Burke. Ahern resolved to find out whether there was any truth to the rumours.

When asked about the issue in August, Ahern claimed that he 'had been up every tree in north Dublin' and could not find anything untoward. By then, he had appointed his old pal Burke as Minister for Foreign Affairs, despite the misgivings of his coalition partner, Mary Harney.

Harney had her own information, independent of that appearing in the newspapers. A party activist whose spouse worked for JMSE had told her that Burke had got £60,000 from the company. Ahern assured his Tánaiste that everything was 'just oxo' with Ray. After all, he was the 'Teflon man'. They had been coming after him since 1974 and nothing ever stuck.

When the Dáil resumed after its summer break the pressure had been ramped up to the level where it was incumbent on Burke to make a public statement. He chose to do so in the Dáil, applying the weight of solemnity accompanying the spoken word in a democratic chamber. As it was to turn out, he issued a litany of self-serving lies and showed utter contempt for the House.

On 10 September he delivered his speech, characterising it as a 'line in the sand' that would bring closure:

> The facts of the matter are that during the 1989 general election campaign I was visited in my home by Mr. Michael Bailey of Bovale Developments Ltd., and a Mr. James Gogarty. Mr. Bailey was well known to me as he was a resident of north County Dublin and a long-time supporter of Fianna Fáil. I had not met Mr. Gogarty previously but he was introduced by Mr. Bailey as an executive of Joseph Murphy Structural Engineers – JMSE. Mr. Gogarty told me JMSE wished to make a political contribution to me and I received from him in good faith a sum of £30,000 as a totally unsolicited political contribution. At no time during our meeting were any favours sought or given. I did not do any favours for, or make any representations to, anyone on behalf of JMSE, Mr. Michael Bailey, Bovale Developments Limited or Mr. James Gogarty either before or since 1989.
>
> [...]
>
> If Mr. Gogarty is the source of these allegations, then he is the author of a campaign of lies against me. I have also been the recipient of a number of anonymous threatening letters relating to these allegations. I have turned this correspondence over to the Garda.
>
> [...]
>
> I am taking the opportunity to state unequivocally that I have done nothing illegal, unethical or

improper. I find myself the victim of a campaign of calumny and abuse. It is totally unacceptable that this matter should be allowed to continue to fulfil an agenda which has nothing to do with election contributions or any other aspect of reasonable or reasoned political debate in public life. If any further untruths are published about me, I will take all necessary steps to vindicate my good name and reputation.

A few weeks later *Magill* magazine published the 1989 letter from Bailey to JMSE, promising to 'procure' planning permission for lands in north Dublin.

By then, Harney was pushing Ahern for a public inquiry. Ahern insisted that Burke's name not be used in the terms of reference.

The establishment of a tribunal to examine planning matters was announced in the Dáil. Burke was to stay on as minister during the inquiry, which Ahern suggested should complete its work by Christmas.

A few weeks later the weight of controversy had become too much for Burke. A story was published in the *Irish Times* linking him to a passports for sale scandal (see Chapter 12). On 7 October he resigned.

That afternoon, Ahern spoke movingly in the Dáil about the political demise of his friend at the hands of assorted oppressors:

Those who choose politics as a profession know from the outset that they are putting their lives on the line in their determination to serve the public. They have to accept the criticism which attends their decisions and their every action. Their families too learn to take the brunt of stinging remarks which often overstep the boundaries of civility and courtesy. In the case of Ray Burke, I see a much more sinister development, the persistent hounding of an honourable man to resign his important position on the basis of innuendo and unproven allegations. Some who would class themselves as protectors of basic civil rights have harried and hounded this man without according him the basic right of due process which deems us innocent unless proven guilty. The according of due process is not just a basic right but the very essence of common decency.

While Ahern most likely had no idea what his friend had been involved in over the previous 30 years, his words would later apply to his own predicament. When the Planning Tribunal began investigating Ahern's finances, he saw himself as another innocent man being hounded.

The tribunal was established on 4 November 1997, under the chairmanship of High Court Judge Feargus Flood. Following initial inquiries, and further allegations from the public, the terms of reference were broadened in 1998 to allow the inquiry to investigate:

... any acts associated with the planning process which may in its opinion amount to corruption, or which involve attempts to influence by threats or deception or inducement or otherwise to com-promise the disinterested performance of public duties, it shall report on such acts and should in particular make recommendations as to the effectiveness and improvement of existing legislation governing corruption in the light of its inquiries.

Three garda investigations had failed to uncover any real

corruption in the planning process. For 25 years newspaper articles had appeared alleging such corruption, but always the substance of the allegations was constrained by the libel laws. Now there was to be a judicial inquiry. Could this be any different?

*   *   *

The Flood Tribunal began hearings in Dublin Castle in 1998. For the first year the main witness was Gogarty, then over 80 years of age. He proved to be a feisty adversary for the lawyers representing Burke, the Murphy interests and Bailey.

Flood gave him plenty of leeway. This was partly due to Gogarty's age, but also because his evidence was all that the tribunal had. Despite what had transpired in planning over the previous 30 years, the only person who could be found to give evidence was a pensioner who harboured extreme bitterness towards his former employer.

Within months of its establishment the terms of reference were broadened to include other aspects of Burke's finances. The procurement of his home, Briargate, was investigated. So too was money he received from interests in Century radio.

Gogarty was the main witness regarding the handover of money to Burke in 1989, but much of the other matters involved following a money trail. This led to Burke's offshore accounts and to Brennan and McGowan, and others associated with them.

Along the way the trawl caught other fish. In April 2000 Dunlop was invited by the tribunal to account for large sums of money. The inquiry had found a hidden account that had contained up to £250,000. Withdrawals from the account coincided with major rezoning votes. Could he explain these things?

Dunlop explained by admitting that he had been involved in extensive bribery of councillors. His evidence was sensational. Anybody who had flagged the carry-on in Dublin County Council down through the decades finally felt vindicated.

Fianna Fáil and Fine Gael immediately set up internal inquiries, ostensibly to find out who had been getting money. In time both inquiries would be shown to have been little more than public relations exercises.

For the general public, Dunlop's confession brought the extent of the corruption into the light for the first time. What had long been suspected was finally being admitted to.

* * *

The Flood Tribunal became an excavation of corruption going back nearly 30 years. In 2002 Flood reported that the 1989 payment to Burke at Briargate had been corrupt. He ruled that the acquisition of Briargate from the builders Brennan and McGowan also amounted to a corrupt payment.

Another witness stepped forward. Tom Gilmartin was a native of Sligo who had emigrated to the UK in the 1950s. When he returned to Ireland in the late 1980s he was intent on bringing home the expertise in development that he had garnered on the far side of the Irish Sea.

His experience in attempting to develop sites in Dublin city centre and in the west of the conurbation was, by his account, horrifying. Every juncture was manned by 'roadblocks' where somebody was extending a hand, looking for money.

Gilmartin made a series of allegations against a wide range of politicians and businesspeople. Some of his allegations were reinforced by testimony from others and financial records; others were shown to be fanciful. Overall, his entry into the inquiry provided another window into how planning was undertaken while impunity ruled.

The tribunal also uncovered serious tax evasion by a number of people in both politics and business. In 2005 Burke was jailed for six months for tax evasion. The following year the Bailey brothers made a settlement of €22 million with the Revenue Commissioners.

Lawlor was jailed three times by the High Court for contempt over his failure to co-operate with the inquiry. In 2005 he was still involved with the tribunal when he was killed in a car crash in Moscow.

In 2008 Dunlop became the first person to be jailed for corruption arising from evidence first adduced at the tribunal. The former Dublin City and County Manager George Redmond had also been jailed after being convicted of corruption, but this conviction was overturned on appeal.

Dunlop pleaded guilty to sample charges of paying councillors bribes in the early 1990s. All of the councillors concerned denied they had received bribes, although some admitted accepting 'political donations' from the lobbyist.

The political system was also obliged to act on what was unfolding at the tribunal. New laws on political donations were enacted, although with enough loopholes to ensure that transparency in political funding remains a long way off.

Despite all its exposure of corruption, the tribunal itself became a matter of serious public concern. The tribunal model is designed to investigate a matter of 'urgent public interest'. The Planning Tribunal entered the record books by persisting for over 13 years. Whatever urgency there was in 1997 soon disappeared.

The broad remit of the terms of reference led to further controversy. When Gilmartin made allegations against Ahern, the Taoiseach was forced to account for major inflows of money into his bank accounts. While there was no direct evidence connecting Ahern to planning controversies, his bizarre explanations for the receipt of over £200,000 ultimately led to his resignation from office.

In 2010 the tribunal endured further controversy when the Supreme Court expressed 'serious concerns' about how it had conducted itself with its main witness, James Gogarty.

Another serious concern for the public was the cost of a tribunal that paid barristers over €2,500 for a day's work. The final bill for the inquiry will not be known for many years, but it is safe to say it will run into hundreds of millions of euro.

Without the tribunal, however, it is unlikely that the Irish public would ever have discovered what went on in the world of planning. Everything would have been put down to vicious rumour and begrudgery.

There might never have been a need for a public inquiry if things had been different in 1974 when Joe MacAnthony's story was published. If the state had had the capacity and willingness to properly investigate what was afoot then, the history of planning in Ireland in the late 20th century could have been entirely different.

How different, for instance, might the government have treated the Kenny report if Burke had been exposed as corrupt and the flaws and dangers of the planning system as it existed had been fully explored?

MacAnthony is in no doubt as to what flowed from his exposé. In 2008 he gave an interview to the mediabite website in which he highlighted the impunity that ruled at the time:

What puzzled me about the Burke case was that I
had found the document in the Company's office
that damned him. And still nothing was done. Just

173

as the detective who came to interview me predicted.

Certainly, if I had stayed with the *Sunday Independent*, I would have stayed on his tail, and on those who made contributions to his phantom political fund.

I put down the welter of corruption in Irish politics to Burke's escape from retribution after that exposure in 1974. It gave everybody in the game a licence to steal.

MacAnthony's is an analysis with which it is difficult to find fault. He was a man before his time. The state as it was then run preferred to wallow in denial than to face up to some uncomfortable realities about how powerful elements conducted themselves.

7

THE BENT ARM OF THE LAW

Gardaí came looking for Nicky Kelly five days after the robbery. It was around 7.00 a.m. on Monday 5 April 1976, when they raided his flat in Dublin's north inner city. Kelly was not there, but his girlfriend, Nuala Dillon, was. She told them that Nicky had gone home to Arklow for the weekend.

The flat filled up with four detectives, led by Inspector Ned Ryan, who was something of a legend in the force. They searched the premises and then waited for Kelly to show up. When he had not arrived by 9.15 a.m. they decided to leave, but they were not going empty handed. They told Dillon she would have to come with them. She was brought to Dublin Castle to await the arrival of her boyfriend, who was suspected of involvement in what was Ireland's 'great train robbery'.

Within an hour Kelly was located at a friend's house in Arklow. He was told he was being arrested under section 30 of the Offences Against the State Act. Section 30 enabled an officer who harboured a suspicion that a person was involved in a crime to detain that suspect for up to 48 hours.

Kelly was one of nearly two dozen people arrested in the week after the robbery. On the night of 30 March the Dublin

Cork Travelling Post Office had been stopped by armed and masked men outside Sallins in County Kildare. The amount taken was then unknown, but was later estimated to be £300,000. This made it the most lucrative train robbery in the history of the state.

Nearly all those arrested were associated with the Irish Republican Socialist Party (IRSP), which had formed a few years earlier following a break from Official Sinn Féin. The IRSP, through its armed wing, the Irish National Liberation Army (INLA), was under suspicion for a few relatively small robberies from trains over the previous year. The Sallins job had the IRSP's fingerprints all over it.

Gardaí immediately began rounding up suspects, many of whom they 'section thirtied'. In the case of most of the arrests, a senior detective would ultimately tell a court that the suspects were arrested following the receipt of 'confidential information'. Naturally, the detective was not in a position to say what the information was, as to do so might identify the informant.

An Garda Síochána was under severe pressure. In 1976 the security imperative for the Fine Gael-led government was to ensure that the Troubles in Northern Ireland did not spill across the border. A number of incidents over the previous five years – including the Dublin and Monaghan bombings in 1974, prison escapes and frequent robberies to fundraise for arms – had resulted in a state of paranoia in some quarters.

If things were not kept under control, the killing, which had become a daily feature in Northern Ireland, might begin in earnest in the Republic.

Sallins was a major robbery and the fear was that it could be used to fund serious arms purchases. It would have to be stopped.

One of the first people visited by gardaí in the hours after the robbery was Tony Gregory, a young socialist activist who was loosely linked to the IRSP. Gardaí woke him up, checked to see whether the engine on his car was hot and then left. Gregory heard about the robbery a few hours later on the morning news. In 1982 he was elected to the Dáil as an independent TD and remained there for 27 years until his death in 2009.

Others were not so swiftly eliminated from inquiries, but it would be five days before some suspects were taken in and ultimately charged. At the time of his arrest, Kelly was 25 years of age, unemployed and active in the IRSP. He was arrested in Arklow at 9.55 a.m. that morning and later taken to Dublin's Bridewell Garda Station. Five other men were detained over the following 48 hours. They were Osgur Breathnach, Brian McNally, Mick Plunkett, Michael Barrett and John Fitzpatrick.

In the course of their detention, all except Barrett signed statements admitting to a role in the robbery. Details contained in the confessions bore remarkable similarities. The men claimed that they had not dictated the confessions, but that they had signed their names to pieces of paper after being repeatedly beaten. The gardaí involved denied any ill-treatment.

The claims of ill-treatment included a variety of assaults. Kelly, for instance, said that his head was slammed against a locker and that he was spreadeagled against a wall next to a door, having the feet kicked from under him, and then somebody opened the door, ramming it into his face.

He claimed that when lying on the floor, two legs of a chair were put on his open palms, a garda sat on the chair and spat at him.

He said he was punched repeatedly in the upper arm and pushed from one detective to another.

He said he was put sitting in a chair, questioned by one detective while another stood behind him. When he gave an unsatisfactory answer, the detective behind slapped both his ears.

The other men related similar claims of brutality. The gardaí denied categorically that any of the allegations were true.

Kelly, McNally, Fitzpatrick and Plunkett were all medically examined when they were ultimately remanded to Mountjoy Prison. They presented with injuries and bruising in various areas including the buttocks, swelling and discolouring of the eye and abrasions of the ear.

The men had sustained obvious injuries, but that was just one of a number of disturbing aspects to their detention and what flowed from it.

Following their detention, they were not taken to the District Court on the morning they were due to be charged. If they had been charged in open court, it would have been necessary to parade them before a large gathering of the public and members of the media. Any injuries that they had sustained to their faces, for instance, would have been obvious, as would their general condition.

Instead, they were charged later that evening at a special sitting of the court, at which the only attendees were the judge, court officials, gardaí and a single reporter.

The men were then remanded back to garda custody following the initial charges. This was highly irregular, but perfectly legal. Again, if they had been immediately sent to prison, a doctor would have examined them and documented their condition.

Back in custody, the six men were put in pairs into three separate cells, against garda regulations. Afterwards, it would be claimed that the suspects had inflicted their injuries on each other during this period in a conspiracy to claim that they had been assaulted by gardaí.

In any event, it looked like the cops had caught the robbers. Hadn't the men all made confessions, admitting to a role in the robbery? What more was needed? All that was then required was to bring the case before the Special Criminal Court, which had an unusually high conviction rate.

The case was eventually brought to court some two and a half years later. Kelly was asked how he was pleading to the charges. 'Not guilty, framed by the Heavy Gang,' he replied. Breathnach replied to the charges, 'We have been the victims of a state conspiracy. Framed. Not guilty.' Plunkett's response was, 'Ned Ryan's Heavy Gang are guilty. I'm not guilty.'

Ned Ryan was a detective inspector at the time and was involved in the interrogation of the Sallins suspects. He had an excellent reputation in the force. His name cropped up in a number of allegations of garda brutality, but he always denied ever being involved in ill-treatment. The allegations against him never led to charges.

The 'Heavy Gang' was a phrase well known to the general public. To some it was a byword for police brutality, referring to a group of gardaí who frequently used violence to extract confessions from suspects.

Others believed that it was an invention of Republicans and their fellow travellers, no more than propaganda intended to blacken the name of the An Garda Síochána. These Republicans were intent on overthrowing the state and had no compunction in using violence through their armed wings, so how could they be believed when they claimed that upstanding officers were beating the daylights out of suspects behind closed doors?

The Kelly case would go on to make history in the Irish criminal justice system. It would also come to be regarded as the most notorious case involving the Heavy Gang although no charges were ever brought against the officers involved. Serious questions were asked about how suspects were treated and processed, but they would never be adequately answered.

Men who were ultimately declared innocent were jailed. And just as damning as the cloud left over the force was the response of the government and the judiciary, for the one overriding feature of the scandal of the Heavy Gang was that whatever they may have done, they knew they could act with impunity.

* * *

The issue of police brutality began to surface around 1975. There were a few constants in the allegations: the use of sleep deprivation, threats of violence, assaults that were relatively minor. There was also plenty of talk about punching to the stomach and the genitals. Some of those making allegations maintained that the officers involved made an effort to minimise bruising and therefore any evidence of assault. A number of people recorded these allegations with their solicitors.

The object in each case was to obtain a confession. Often, one was forthcoming. Often, the confession was a genuine one, albeit made under onerous and illegal circumstances. But inevitably, if the allegations are accepted, there were cases where suspects were willing to say anything to stop the beating.

The names of a small number of gardaí often came up in the allegations. These were the men known as the 'Heavy

Gang'. There is no dispute that there did exist within the force a loose alliance of officers who might be described as members of the Heavy Gang. None of them was ever charged on foot of the allegations made against them.

The core of the gang was drawn from a specific unit, the investigation section of the Technical Bureau. The bureau, as its name suggests, was primarily concerned with technical or scientific investigation. This included mapping, fingerprinting, forensic investigators and crime scene investigation. One section of the bureau had no scientific expertise. The investigation section was peopled by detectives trained in interrogation techniques.

Throughout the 1960s the bureau was known as the murder squad. Ireland experienced little serious crime and the only time the bureau was sent for was when a murder had been committed. That situation changed when the North exploded in violence in the late 1960s. The emergence of the Provisional IRA and a whole raft of splinter groups ensured that there was plenty of serious crime to be investigated into the 1970s and beyond.

The officers in the investigation section travelled wherever their work brought them and interacted with many local detective units across Ireland. After a while they became aware which colleagues would be useful in lending a hand with specific investigations. The loose grouping that emerged from these contacts formed the Heavy Gang.

In February 1977 the Heavy Gang was introduced to the wider public through the pages of the *Irish Times*. An investigation by the paper led to a series of articles that made numerous allegations of police brutality. The first piece, published on the front page on 14 February, began:

Brutal interrogation methods are being used by a

181

special group of gardaí, as a routine practice in the questioning of suspects about serious crimes.

This group uses physical beatings and psychological techniques similar to some used in Northern Ireland, to obtain information and secure incriminating statements.

Republican suspects were involved in most, but not all, of the cases. The paper's reporters had spoken to a number of people who claimed to have been assaulted in custody. The same named gardaí kept cropping up in these stories.

Most of the violence was alleged to have occurred in the course of interviews in garda stations, but in a few cases, it was more open. There was the case of Mrs D, a young mother from Northern Ireland living in north Dublin. Her version of what happened to her was drawn from a statement submitted to her solicitor.

In April 1976 five plain-clothes gardaí called to her high-rise flat with an arrest warrant for a young man who was staying there. Mrs D was four months pregnant and she also had a son living in the flat. The gardaí left with the man. There was no disturbance.

Soon after, she heard a loud crash and looked out to see broken glass on the roof of the garda car. She presumed somebody had thrown something at the car. She returned to making her son's breakfast. Five minutes later, there was a knock on the door.

On opening the door, no words were spoken, one garda, wearing a brown jacket dragged me by the hair, swung me round the hall and punched me several times. Two other gardaí grabbed both my arms pinning them to my sides and one kneed me on the lower parts of my body. They then bent me

forward and several times punched me round the
back of the head. One garda shouted into my face
that I had thrown a milk bottle out of the window.
He spat in my face.

There were many other cases instanced, not least the
interrogation of the Sallins train robbery suspects.

The articles, written in an authoritative and informed
manner, were shocking in their implications. Certain gardaí
were systematically beating up and intimidating suspects in
order to secure convictions for criminal offences.

The authorities rubbished the investigation. The Garda
Press Office issued a statement saying that there was no section
or unit in the force:

> ... which as a matter of practice or policy inflicts
> physical violence on persons in custody ... Brutal
> interrogation methods are not a routine practice at
> the moment, they never have been. Such practices
> are not condoned by our present commissioner, Mr
> Garvey, nor have they ever been encouraged or
> condoned by any previous commissioner of the
> force.

This statement was entirely accurate. The Heavy Gang was not
a specific unit, and An Garda Síochána did not have an official
policy of beating up suspects. The response, however, failed to
address the meat of the allegations.

There was no internal investigation ordered. There was no
outside body, such as an ombudsman, who could investigate
gardaí. If the top brass in the force said these things did not
happen, then that was it. Unless, of course, their political
masters felt that the allegations merited some further probing.

Their political masters were of no such mind. Following the
publication of the *Irish Times* series, the Minister for Justice,

Paddy Cooney, denied that there was any such entity as the Heavy Gang. And that was it. Even though the Attorney General had called earlier that month for the prosecution of British soldiers who abused suspects in custody in Northern Ireland.

The opposition took the allegations more seriously. Fianna Fáil's justice spokesman Gerry Collins resolved to get to the bottom of the matter once his party was in government. 'The Minister for Justice has a very grave responsibility to immediately set up a judicial inquiry into the allegations made,' he said. 'The rights of the individual must be protected at all times and when we are protecting the individual we must also protect our guards.'

Collins was destined to get the chance to set up his judicial inquiry four months later, when he was appointed Minister for Justice following a general election. In the great tradition of opposition bluster, he immediately changed his tune once his legs were under a ministerial desk. No inquiry was set up. No investigation was launched. The matter was conveniently swept under the carpet.

Collins and Fianna Fáil were not unique in this respect. The allegations of police brutality had been consistently ignored by the Fine Gael-led coalition that governed between 1973 and 1977.

Following the brief furore caused by the *Irish Times* articles, two serving gardaí went to Garret FitzGerald, then the Minister for Foreign Affairs, and told of their concern. These two officers were reflecting an unease that was felt in sections of An Garda Síochána. The Heavy Gang and the allegations surrounding them were undermining good policing and the integrity of the force, it was felt.

FitzGerald, who revealed the approach two decades later,

dithered, and ultimately did nothing with the information. In his autobiography, *All in a Life*, he admits that he had heard rumours about the Heavy Gang the previous summer:

> I was distressed by these reports, which appeared to me to warrant investigation. Several of my colleagues shared my anxiety. Having reflected on the matter during our holiday in France in August, I decided to raise it in the Government and, if necessary, to force the issue to a conclusion by threatening resignation. In the event I was deflected from my purpose by a consensus in the government that we would be sending very conflicting signals to public opinion if at the same time as enacting legislation that, among other things, extended to seven days the maximum period for which suspects could be held under the Offences Against the State (Amendment) Act, we instituted an inquiry into the interrogation of suspects being held by the Gardaí. I allowed myself to be persuaded to leave this sensitive issue for several months, and my recollection is that I raised it again in November and/or January, but to no effect; I have no record of this, however.

Hindsight has afforded FitzGerald a view that was not evident in his actions at the time. If he was so moved by the allegations that he contemplated resignation, then he was certainly out of step with many of his colleagues.

One cabinet minister had even more reason to suspect that systemic abuse was afoot in garda stations. Conor Cruise O'Brien was the Minister for Posts and Telegraphs and one of the Labour Party members at cabinet. In *Memoir: My Life and*

Themes, he recalled a conversation with a detective about the 1975 kidnapping of businessman Tiede Herrema.

Herrema was a Dutch national who ran a factory in Limerick. He was kidnapped by Republican elements, but rescued some 60 days later after a siege at a house in County Kildare.

O'Brien wrote that the detective with whom he spoke had told him how gardaí had arrested a suspect they believed knew where Herrema was being held:

> The escort started asking him questions and when at first he refused to answer, they beat the shit out of him. Then he told them where Herrema was.
>
> I refrained from telling this story to Garret [FitzGerald] or Justin [Keating, another cabinet minister] because I thought it would worry them. It didn't worry me.

This was the atmosphere in which the Heavy Gang operated. Despite repeated allegations, expressions of concern from fellow officers and physical evidence, politicians did not want to know. In such an environment, errant gardaí could behave as they pleased, secure in the knowledge that they would not be called to account for their actions.

* * *

The first trial of the Sallins train robbery suspects took place in January 1978, 21 months after the robbery. By then, the cases against two of the six (Barrett and Fitzpatrick) had been dropped. No reason was ever forwarded for the dropping of charges against them.

The trial took place in Green Street courthouse, where the non-jury Special Criminal Court sat. As already outlined, the only evidence was the confessions, which the men claimed were beaten out of them. The major feature of this trial was therefore a trial within a trial to determine whether the confessions were admissible.

Eventually, the trial was aborted because one of the three judges died. In the months prior to his death, and during the trial, Judge John O'Connor was suffering from a condition, of which he was unaware, that caused him to fall asleep, and this occurred for periods when he was on the bench.

Within the court, it was perfectly obvious that all was not as it should be. Reporting for the *Hibernia* magazine shortly after the trial began, Niall Kiely noted:

Judge John O'Connor seemed to fall asleep on Wednesday last; the courtroom is high ceilinged but the well of the court is packed and very stuffy by mid-afternoon.

At 2.42 his head was only inches above the bench but three minutes later he sat up and began to write; at 3.10pm his head seems to be actually resting on the bench but two minutes later he again sits up.

Various methods were attempted to politely waken the judge. Books were slammed down hard. At one stage defence lawyer Patrick McEntee requested a brief adjournment to visit the toilet. One of the defendants, Mick Plunkett, stood up and said that maybe his lawyer could not say it but the adjournment had nothing to do with nature's call. It was to give the judge the opportunity to wake up. He was told to sit down.

Eventually, on day 50 of the trial, defence lawyers applied to have the court discharged on the grounds that Judge O'Connor appeared to frequently lapse into sleep. The three judges adjourned to discuss the matter. They decided that the application had no merit and they would continue.

The defence lawyers applied to the High Court to have the

court discharged on the basis of the sleeping judge. The High Court denied the application.

There followed an appeal to the Supreme Court. The appeal was denied. Chief Justice Tom O'Higgins ruled that the Special Criminal Court had found as a fact that Judge O'Connor had performed his duty. In other words, he was awake for the entirety of the proceedings. Yet everyone in the court had seen the man constantly fall asleep.

The trial resumed. On day 65, Judge O'Connor did not show up. Word came through that he had dropped dead while preparing to come to court. The trial was aborted and a new one ordered.

* * *

The second trial opened on 10 October 1978. On the second day, the case against Plunkett collapsed and he was released. The confessions of the other three were ultimately deemed admissible in evidence. This effectively sealed their fate.

It meant that the judges did not believe they were assaulted in custody or forced to sign confessions. It meant that the judges did not consider that gardaí had inflicted the injuries on the men recorded in Mountjoy. It meant the judges did not connect the unusual manner in which the men were charged, and then returned to police custody, with the allegations of abuse.

Kelly, fully aware that he was facing a long term in prison for a crime he did not commit, scampered before the verdict was returned. He was sentenced to 12 years in prison.

In May 1980 Breathnach and McNally were released by the Court of Criminal Appeal on a technicality that had nothing to do with their allegations of ill-treatment.

That left Kelly, who was on the run in the United States.

Following the acquittal of his co-accused, he returned home on 4 June 1980 and was arrested by the Special Branch at Shannon. His appeal was unsuccessful and he was dispatched to serve his 12-year prison term.

Kelly became something of a cause célèbre, but it took another four years, involving a high-profile campaign and a hunger strike, before he was released. He was about to embark on his second hunger strike when on 17 July 1984, the Minister for Justice, Michael Noonan, announced that Kelly was to be freed on humanitarian grounds.

If a second hunger strike had gone ahead, the government would not have wanted to be seen to give in. The prospect of Kelly dying in prison was clearly too much for the government to contemplate.

The Kelly case showed up the worst of the state. At its root was the allegations of assault by the Heavy Gang. In today's world, the confessions that were allegedly made would never be admitted to court. But back then, the word of a garda was not questioned.

Just as troubling was the reaction of the government and the judiciary. The former could not involve itself in the case, but it ran a mile from ever investigating the recurring allegations of abuse in custody. The admission of the confessions on the part of the judiciary, and the apparent refusal to admit that one of its number was falling asleep on the job, beggars belief.

The overarching message conveyed by the result was simple: whatever the evidence to the contrary, the forces of government will not contemplate taking action against gardaí accused of abusing people in custody. It was a message that was to resonate down through the following two decades, much to the cost of the force and many innocent victims caught up in the culture of impunity.

* * *

By the late 1970s things had settled down in Northern Ireland to what came to be cynically known as 'an acceptable level of violence'. In the Republic this translated as the passing of any threat that the bloodshed might spill across the border.

In such circumstances, the Heavy Gang began to dissipate. The loose grouping of officers that constituted the gang had less and less reason to find themselves together investigating the Republican threat. Many of them were promoted by Gerry Collins, the Minister for Justice who had been so appalled by the allegations of ill-treatment when he was in opposition.

Life moved on, but within the force old habits persisted. While the majority of gardaí went about their investigations with integrity and professionalism, the germ that inveigled itself into the force at the height of the 1970s paranoia was still active.

Throughout the 1980s a number of cases popped up in which suspects of all manner of alleged crimes ended up confessing in unusual circumstances. The most bizarre of these cases involved a settled Traveller, Michael Ward.

Ward was arrested for driving offences in Naas, County Kildare, on 5 June 1983. During his detention he signed statements admitting to a number of robberies, including stealing £150 from an address in Saggart on 25 April.

Gardaí said that Ward accompanied them around Naas in a squad car, pointing out other houses that he had burgled over the previous few months.

Ward was very specific about his crimes. In an estate called The Paddocks, he pointed out a house where he had stolen a video and jewellery valued at £3,000. A second house in the same estate had yielded jewellery and coins worth £1,186. Both those robberies took place on 16 April, some three weeks before his arrest.

As far as Ward's conviction on these offences was concerned, it looked like an open and shut case. The gardaí maintained that in a fit of guilt he had decided to confess to his crimes.

Ward alleged that he had been beaten and abused in custody and had merely signed his name to a piece of paper to stop the hurt. It was his word against that of a number of respected guardians of the peace.

Case closed except that Ward could not have committed the burglaries to which he had confessed. On the dates that he was supposed to have been busy robbing in Naas, Ward was a prisoner in Mountjoy, where he had been detained between 9 and 29 April. Unless he had escaped, found his way down to Kildare, done a few jobs and returned to his cell in time for lock-up, he was not guilty.

When the case came up in Kildare Circuit Criminal Court, the state withdrew the charges. Ward's solicitor, Dermot Morris, objected to the withdrawal, claiming that it was done to protect the gardaí involved from criminal charges. The judge rejected Morris's objection. He said he would not allow his court to be used for issuing such wild allegations.

Once again, a member of the judiciary could not contemplate that a suspect may have been abused in custody. Once again, the judge in question was not curious about the supporting evidence that might suggest it had occurred.

The following year brought another major controversy for An Garda Síochána. This time, it would ultimately lead to questions that were not so easily swept under the carpet. This time, an open judicial inquiry would be held to determine what went on.

* * *

On the evening of Saturday 18 April 1984 a farmer from Cahirciveen, County Kerry, was running along a beach known as the White Strand. Jack Griffin was leaving the beach when he thought he spotted something lodged in the nearby rocks. Closer inspection revealed that it was the body of a baby.

Griffin contacted the local gardaí. A postmortem discovered that the baby had been stabbed a number of times and a murder investigation was launched.

The net was cast wide. This was the type of crime that should be easily solved, particularly with some input from the general public. Somebody had to know a woman who was recently known to be pregnant, or had given birth, and now appeared not to have a baby.

The night before the dead baby was found on the White Strand, another woman was giving birth some 46 miles away in Abbeydorney, a village just outside Tralee.

Joanne Hayes was 25, single and living with her family on a small farm. She was the youngest of four. Her two brothers and sister, her mother and aunt all lived between two homes on the farm. They were regarded as a quiet, law-abiding family. Hayes was already a mother of one, having had a daughter with a married man, Jeremiah Locke, with whom she was having an affair. The relationship was petering out when she became pregnant again. She was determined to have the second child.

On the night of 17 April Hayes gave birth in her bedroom at home. Some of her siblings were present, as was her aunt, who was a retired nurse. The baby did not live long. A pathologist would opine that the baby may never have had a separate existence from its mother.

Some hours after her baby's death, Hayes put the body in a brown bag and walked across a few fields before lodging the bag in a water-filled hole.

Within two weeks of the discovery of the Cahirciveen baby, the gardaí had a breakthrough. Word had come back that a Joanne Hayes had been pregnant. She had earlier attended her GP and St Catherine's Hospital in Tralee.

The Hayes family were visited and brought to Tralee Garda Station for questioning. By then, a number of detectives from Dublin were on the job. The investigation section of the Technical Bureau, the murder squad, had been dispatched to the scene of the crime. A number of the detectives originated from Kerry, which may have prompted a heightened interest in the unit.

The unit was led by Detective Superintendent John Courtney, who was a native of north Kerry. Courtney had been at the centre of a number of allegations about ill-treatment of suspects, but none of the allegations had ever been proven. He was highly regarded in the force.

On 1 May the Hayes family were brought in for questioning. They were not under arrest, but, as with most people in their situation, the family probably had no idea that they were free to leave at any time. The Dublin detectives took care of the interrogations. They were accustomed to dealing with hardened criminals and terrorists; a family of farmers was unlikely to present them with any difficulties.

Later, all of the family members claimed that they were intimidated by gardaí. Joanne's brothers, Mike and Ned, claimed that they were assaulted, although a tribunal would later reject their allegations.

Hayes told gardaí that her baby had died and was buried on the farm. They did not believe her. An officer who was dispatched to conduct a cursory search of the farm found nothing.

Within hours she had signed a confession in which she admitted to stabbing her baby to death. It revealed that she had then driven to Slea Head in Dingle and thrown the body into the sea. This would support the belief that her baby was the Cahirciveen baby, the only dead infant that the detectives were then aware of. The spot where the body entered the water in her confession would make sense, in that the baby was found on the opposite peninsula, near Cahirciveen.

Joanne's siblings all gave statements supporting this story to one extent or another. The case was cracked. Once more, the culprits had come clean under the forensic questioning of the murder squad.

Infanticide was a crime that was treated with sensitivity. At the time the procedure in a case of infanticide was that the suspect would be charged with murder, which the court would subsequently revert to the former charge.

Hayes was remanded in custody to Limerick Prison on the murder charge. This young mother who had recently been through the emotional trauma of giving birth to a baby destined to die spent the night in prison under the cloud of suspicion of having stabbed her baby to death.

The others were charged with concealing birth and bailed. Joanne's siblings visited her and asked for precise instructions as to where she had buried the baby. The body was found later that day. The Hayes family contacted their solicitor and informed him. He went to the gardaí with the information.

Now the gardaí had two babies. The cause of death for one was stabbing, for the other it was indeterminable.

Following the investigation, a 130-page report was written by one of the detectives, P.J. Browne. What with the bizarre nature of the case, Browne opted to depart from the stiff prose normally employed on such reports. 'Within the covers of this Garda Report and File is told a sad tale. It occurred because a young girl in her mid-twenties was scorned by a married man she loved, had children for and wanted for herself. Hell hath no fury like a woman scorned.'

Browne even used a term that was current at the time, referring to the case as 'grotesque, unbelievable, bizarre and unprecedented'. This term had been used two years earlier by then Taoiseach Charles Haughey to describe how a wanted murderer was found in the home of the Attorney General (who had no idea about his guest's crimes). Conor Cruise O'Brien had subsequently used the acronym 'GUBU' to describe Haughey's tenure. Here now was another GUBU, according to the garda report.

The report concluded that Hayes had given birth to twins. 'By a strange twist of fate, the body of the first born was not discovered until after the charge,' the report read.

Gardaí believed that one baby had died from causes unknown and was buried in a field and that the other was stabbed to death and driven by family members to the Dingle peninsula, where it was thrown into the water, only to be washed up on the opposite peninsula the following day.

Now that two babies had been discovered, further investigation was required. An analysis of the blood groups was carried out. Hayes and Locke were both blood group O. The Cahirciveen baby was blood group A. Hayes had confessed to killing a baby to whom she could not have given birth.

The charges were dropped and an inquiry was ordered. The Kerry Babies Tribunal was chaired by Judge Kevin Lynch and sat for 77 days, hearing 109 witnesses. (The senior counsel for the tribunal was Michael Moriarty, who would later chair one of the most protracted tribunals in the history of the state. The Moriarty Tribunal investigated political corruption.)

Throughout the hearings, gardaí maintained that the babies were twins, both born to Hayes. At one stage a theory was propagated that the Cahirciveen baby's blood group could have changed due to being in the water for a prolonged period. There was also a suggestion that Hayes had become pregnant simultaneously by two different men.

The members of the Hayes family gave evidence to the effect that they were ill-treated and put under extreme duress to sign the confessions that became the basis for the initial charges. All of them maintained the original narrative that they had provided to gardaí. Joanne had given birth, the baby died soon afterwards and Joanne had buried the dead baby in a field.

Lynch's findings were published in October 1985. He wrote that he did not accept the Hayes's evidence, but he never addressed the central issue of the inquiry: how a whole family could admit to complicity in the murder of a baby that could not have been born to Joanne.

Magill magazine, which had covered in detail a whole raft of cases in which allegations of ill-treatment by gardaí had arisen, responded with an editorial:

Justice Lynch's report has made a number of things
worse. It represents the largest commitment of time
and money which parliament and the judiciary can
make to examining, supposedly, the methodology of
the gardaí.

It has manifestly failed to do so satisfactorily.
Our fears of garda misbehaviour must now be

compounded by the fear that one of the few checks against it, a full-scale judicial tribunal, has proved impotent.

By failing to answer the central question which it was established to answer, Judge Lynch's tribunal has resulted in three areas of legitimate concern; for Joanne Hayes and her family, who have been branded on evidence which we believe we have shown to be unreliable [reporter Gene Kerrigan had provided a detailed analysis showing how the judge's findings were in conflict with the evidence that was heard]; for the gardaí as a whole, over whom the shadow of this case will continue to hang; and for the citizens at large whose right to a proper accounting of the activities of those whom they employ had not been vindicated.

In addition it has raised serious questions about the suitability of this type of tribunal for investigating the behaviour of the gardaí.

There was little political fallout from the affair. Speaking during a Dáil debate on the tribunal report, Justice Minister Michael Noonan said, 'The Lynch report discloses very clearly that there were serious deficiencies in the investigation.'

Four gardaí who were involved in the case – Gerry O'Carroll, P.J. Browne, Joe Shelly and John Harrington – were assigned to desk duty. Nothing in the report warranted any form of sanction against these men.

The case brought the issue of alleged garda misbehaviour onto a new plane. This time, it had not been brushed under the carpet, but had been subjected to a public inquiry. Yet there were no satisfactory answers provided in the inquiry's report.

Glaring questions went unanswered. If they had been

properly addressed, it may have led to a scandal of sorts for the force. In the Ireland of the 1980s, institutions, from An Garda Síochána to the Roman Catholic Church, still operated on the basis that a scandal for the institution was worse than any fidelity to legal or moral standards.

The outcome of the affair implied that the political establishment simply did not have the will to investigate properly whether radical reform was required in the force.

Instead, four of the detectives who were at the centre of the affair were effectively demoted. In this respect, they were the scapegoats of a system that refused to face up to reality.

But life was changing. Society was opening up. Authority not theretofore questioned was beginning to be examined. In the media, and particularly in *Magill*, the issue of how gardaí conducted themselves simply would not go away. When the next serious allegation raised its head, nearly a decade later, all bets were off. Irish society had undergone too much change to allow this issue to be once more wished away.

* * *

Richie Barron, a cattle dealer from Raphoe, County Donegal, died early on the morning of 14 October 1996. He was walking home after an evening's drinking in the town. At 12.55 a.m. his body was spotted on the side of the road by a passing motorist. He had been seen heading out of the town at 12.25 a.m.

The motorist, a local man named Lee Parker, had seen Barron in a pub earlier that evening. He assumed that Richie had fallen down drunk on the side of the road. The stricken man was lying on his back, with his legs crossed. It was only when Parker got out of his car that he saw the blood leaking from Barron's head.

Gardaí were called and arrived within half an hour. The

scene was not preserved. Initially it was thought that Barron may have died as a result of a hit and run. Within 48 hours that assessment had been revised and a murder investigation launched.

There had been bad blood between Barron and a local family of publicans, the McBreartys. A tribunal chairman would later describe what was to unfold as 'the ability of hatred to transform myth into fact'.

On 4 December Frank McBrearty, Jr. and his cousin Mark McConnell were arrested and detained at Letterkenny Garda Station on suspicion of murder. Reporter Gerard Cunningham later interviewed McConnell, who described what he remembered of the day:

'I went to the front door and met Garda John O'Dowd. He put his hand on my shoulder, and told me he was arresting me for the murder of Richie Barron. I went weak at the knees. I was standing just in my night clothes, the child standing behind me as this was all happening.'

While in custody, McConnell says, he was verbally and physically abused. He was called 'a big fat murdering bastard' and 'pushed and hauled'. At one stage a detective told him to look at post mortem photographs of the late Richie Barron. McConnell refused.

'Eventually he (the detective) got frustrated with me. He reached for my hair, and pulled my head towards the photographs. I still tried to keep away from them, but he kept pushing my head down into the photographs and telling me to "fucking look at what you've done".'

Then a senior officer came in. He 'slapped down

a four or five page document in front of me with a smirk on his face', McConnell recalls.

'He said "that's a confession there to the murder of Richie Barron from Frank McBrearty Jr. and he's implicating you".'

The detective then read the 'confession' out to McConnell.

'I remember vividly the opening line. It was, "I Frank McBrearty Jr. am showing remorse for what I have done." I remember thinking, there's no way Frank would even use them kind of words. That wasn't his vocabulary.'

'At the end of it, after four to five pages, was a signature. I knew for a fact it wasn't young Frank's signature at the bottom of the bit of paper, he had a funny way of signing his name.'

'Young Frank was released shortly after me. They'd done the exact same thing with him, they came in with a statement supposedly from myself. Young Frank came out and said to me, "Mark, don't believe anything them bastards said to you in there," and he stormed off.'

McBrearty had a similar story of abuse. A tribunal would later fully accept McConnell's version of events and accept that McBrearty had been ill-treated in custody.

In the weeks that followed, a campaign of harassment was conducted against the McBreartys. A number of gardaí were subsequently implicated of being complicit in these acts. Dozens of baseless summonses were issued against the family's nightclub business. Intimidating phone calls were made to their homes. Garda John O'Dowd was implicated in the phone calls.

Later Frank McBrearty Sr. and nine other members of the

extended McBrearty family were arrested and questioned. A tribunal would ultimately rule that the arrests were unlawful.

Frank Senior retained a private detective, Billy Flynn, to find out what exactly was going on. In time Flynn would be credited with cracking the case by tracing the origins of the intimidating phone calls, which in turn led to O'Dowd.

A letter Flynn wrote to a solicitor soon after he was retained echoed an earlier era of garda misbehaviour.

> It was believed that Mr Barron was the victim of a hit and run and as I understand from Mr McBrearty the circumstances of Mr Barrons death took a twist which has resulted in what he has described as a horror story or a nightmare experience where Frank Sr and Frank Jr are the Gardaí's prime suspects for the alleged murder of Mr Barrons, and where the McBrearty family are the subject of Garda harassment consistent with what was known in the past as 'the heavy gang'.

The road to justice was a long one for the McBreartys. Five years later, in 2002, a tribunal chaired by former High Court Judge Frederick Morris was set up to investigate the family's claims. The inquiry soon extended to a whole range of activities by a small group of officers in Donegal. This included the planting of explosives for the purpose of claiming credit for finding them.

In total, the Morris Tribunal delivered eight reports over the course of its six years in existence. The reports formed the basis for the reformation of An Garda Síochána.

The sixth report dealt with the arrests of McBrearty and McConnell and their wider families. Morris noted that the 'unhealthy focus or tunnel vision in the course of the Barron investigation led to manufactured evidence, wrongful arrests and completely improper behaviour by gardaí towards prisoners in their custody. It cheapened the presumption of innocence and undermined the truthful resolution of a very tragic case.'

On the personal impact on those affected, Morris said, 'it dominated the lives and struck at the reputations of two families: the extended Quinn family [who were related by marriage to the McBreartys and also targeted by members of the force] and the McBrearty family. It did serious damage to the reputation of An Garda Síochána, and its integrity and professionalism.'

Morris also noted that there was no reason to believe that the behaviour of some of the officers was confined to Donegal. In an earlier report he professed himself 'staggered' at the amount of 'mischief making' and 'insubordination' that was uncovered.

Eight gardaí up to the rank of superintendent either left or were fired from the force.

In 2008 Garda Commissioner Fachtna Murphy apologised to the people associated with the case who had been mistreated in custody. He said that members of the force who do not observe professional standards do a 'grave disservice to the history and tradition of An Garda Síochána'.

The major reform of the force to emerge from the Morris Tribunal was the setting up of a Garda Inspectorate and, crucially, the Garda Ombudsman Commission, which meant that gardaí would no longer be investigating gardaí on foot of complaints.

Throughout the history of the force this had been a major problem. For instance, in the late 1990s the McBreartys had made over 60 complaints about gardaí to the Garda Complaints Board. None of them were upheld.

Any complaints deemed worthy of investigation would be

handled by a serving garda. He or she in turn would contact colleagues in the area – Donegal in this case – and would be told a history of the complainants consistent with them being troublemakers and simply causing trouble for upstanding members of the force. The powers of investigation fell well short of going behind such responses and would evidently lead to conclusions which were coloured by such responses.

The Inspectorate's function is to ensure that the best international standards are applicable to the force.

Finally, it appears that the culture that allowed the Heavy Gang to flourish has been addressed. It is inevitable that there will be some allegations of police brutality. However, a culture whereby substantial evidence of ii-treatment is ignored can no longer be sustained.

*   *   *

The controversies surrounding allegations of police brutality since the 1970s are not unique to Ireland. Other democracies have had similar problems. It is not unusual for a minority of police officers to overstep the mark of the law. The nature of the job means that constant vigilance is required.

What made the Heavy Gang particularly scandalous was the reaction of the other arms of the state. At a time when it was believed that the state was under siege, the forces of government and the judiciary turned a blind eye to what was going on. This in turn provided solace to the officers who were engaging in illegal means to extract confessions. Gardaí who disagreed with such activities were ignored and, more likely, warned in no uncertain terms that they too would be better served to turn a blind eye.

The Heavy Gang and all that flowed from it marked a low point in the history of An Garda Síochána. Had elements within the force, and the wider state apparatus, addressed the matter in the 1970s, many of the injustices suffered at the hands of errant gardaí in the decades that followed could have been avoided.

8

BLOOD SISTERS

Bridget McCole knew she was not long for this world. Her condition had been deteriorating in a dramatic fashion. The liver disease that was eating away at her life had gained the upper hand. She was weak and tired and facing into a premature death at the age of 54.

The weight of her burden was exacerbated by the thought of what she would be leaving behind. She was a mother of 12 and her husband was not a well man. Provision for her family was uppermost in her mind. It was 1 October 1996 and from her bed in St Vincent's Hospital in Dublin, Bridget McCole had a major decision to make.

Her deteriorating condition was being monitored elsewhere, for McCole was also regarded in some quarters as an enemy of the state. In the summer of 1995 she had launched a legal action against the state and the Blood Transfusion Service Board (BTSB) for negligence.

McCole had been infected with contaminated blood from which she contracted hepatitis C, a debilitating and sometimes fatal condition and the underlying cause of her pending demise.

The infection occurred during one of her pregnancies in 1977, when she received an injection of a blood agent, anti-D. This agent was used to treat haemolytic disease, where antibodies in the mother's blood attack the red blood cells running through the veins of her baby. The anti-D used to treat McCole was contaminated by blood received from a donor the previous year.

The nature of the infection emerged in public in 1995. McCole, and up to 1,000 other women, were told that they could receive compensation for the poisoning of their blood by applying to a tribunal set up by the government. No liability would be admitted. Anybody who accepted compensation would forfeit the right to sue the state or its agencies. No answers as to how the women had been infected with hepatitis C would be provided. Monetary compensation, decided in an arbitrary fashion, was all that was on offer.

Most of the women involved were not happy with the set-up, but it had been made known to them in no uncertain terms that the alternative was to square up against the might of the state in court.

Publicly, the Minister for Health, Michael Noonan, announced that it was up to the women themselves. They could either apply for compensation to the ad hoc tribunal or they could go to court.

Privately, those women who indicated that they would go the court route received letters from legal representatives of the state, saying it was difficult to understand why they did not just go to the tribunal. They were told that any legal action against the state would leave them facing 'uncertainties, delays, stresses, confrontation and costs'. Any cases the victims might take would be defended by the state 'if necessary to the Supreme Court'.

The message was clear. Take the money. Do not ask any more questions as we will make life difficult, if not unbearable, for you. The subliminal threat carried further potency as many of the women it was being issued to were already ill, some extremely so.

McCole was not happy with the offer. For over a decade she had suffered in silence. Like the other women who became ill, she did not know what was wrong with her. She was determined to get answers.

* * *

McCole lived in the remote Gaeltacht area of north-west Donegal, in Loughaugher, near the village of Crolly. There was a great community spirit in the area, but it was also a difficult place in which to rear a large family. During winter snowstorms, the area was often cut off. The McColes, like other rural families, did not have a phone in their home.

McCole did not drink or smoke. Her husband, Brian, had farmed sheep, but he had been ill for some years. The older McCole children worked locally. They were a close family in a tight-knit community.

For over a decade before the identification of her illness, McCole had not been feeling well. Some days were better than others. She visited her GP's surgery, 14 miles away, on a number of occasions, describing her condition, hoping for something that might put her on the road to recovery. But hepatitis C was not identified at the time.

After her death, her GP, James Brogan, spoke about her visits to his surgery. 'A woman with 12 children and an ill husband is going to be a tired person,' he said. 'We did the usual bloods and things and they turned up normal.'

After McCole turned 50, her condition began to worsen.

She experienced blood clots. The pain increased. According to her eldest daughter, Brid, who later gave evidence to a tribunal, other members of her family would lie awake at night listening to her screams.

'She was so upset by the fact that for so many years she had been going to hospital and she had been seen by so many doctors and had so many blood tests … she was beginning to doubt herself if it was all in her mind,' her daughter said.

Then, in 1994, she read in the newspapers that the government intended to investigate how an unknown number of women may have become infected with bad blood from transfusions. The article referred to the women being infected with hepatitis C, a condition that had only been identified in the previous few years.

Symptoms of the condition were immediately apparent but grew progressively over a prolonged period. The disease had been a subject of speculation for nearly 20 years, loosely identified as 'non-A, non-B hepatitis', but was now confirmed as a condition in its own right. The prognosis was not good, with no known cure and the high possibility of progressive liver disease.

Something told McCole that this was what had been ailing her. She organised for a test with her GP and the condition was recognised. Like other women who would finally be made aware of what had been wrong with them for years, she felt confused and frightened. The future had just been writ large and it was not an inviting picture.

Treatment followed, first of all in Letterkenny General Hospital. After a while it became necessary to attend Beaumont Hospital in Dublin. The journey took nine hours and would involve her leaving her home at 6.00 a.m. to travel by taxi to Letterkenny and from there on to Dublin by a hospital bus, which had to stop along the way for other passengers.

Some of her stays in Dublin stretched into weeks and even months. The McColes had no relations in the capital. For a woman from a remote yet close community, the loneliness can only be guessed at. As a result of her frequent stays, the family had a telephone installed in their home, which provided some comfort to her.

Once hepatitis C was identified and her condition was attributed to infection by the BTSB, McCole was provided with counselling at a local psychiatric centre. Most local people would not have been aware of her condition, as it was a private matter. But in rural Ireland, little goes unnoticed and, even in the 1990s, a certain stigma attached to any apparent psychiatric frailties. It was one more of the little things that collectively were placing a great strain on an already gravely ill woman.

McCole joined Positive Action, the group representing infected women, and it provided her with huge support. In November 1995 she was part of a delegation from Positive Action received in Áras an Uachtaráin by President Mary Robinson. She treasured the day, and retained near her thereafter a photograph recording the meeting.

Meanwhile, the business of living was getting tougher.

In February 1995 an expert group set up to examine the infection of thousands of women by the BTSB presented its report to Minister Noonan. In April he established an ad hoc compensation tribunal for the women. Positive Action was told in no uncertain terms that its members could avail of the tribunal or face a protracted and adversarial fight in the courts.

McCole refused to take the compensation route. It would have meant there was no explanation as to how she had been poisoned, who was responsible and why it took so long for the infection to be identified. She wanted answers, to which she felt she and her family were entitled.

The action was launched against the state and the BTSB. Immediately the screws were turned. The threat to impose stress and worry on any litigant was given life.

From the off, the government knew that it was liable for the infection, yet it persisted in fighting the action. A few months before McCole launched her case, the government received legal opinion that any case brought by any of the infected women had 'been greatly strengthened by the expert group's findings'. The opinion, from senior counsel Ian Finlay, went on to state that unless a compensation scheme provided attractions a court could not offer, claimants were likely to sue.

This was exactly what McCole was now doing. The government, which was supposed to represent her as a citizen, had advice that it was liable for her infection, yet it was fighting her every inch of the way, despite her deteriorating condition.

A variety of legal tactics were then put to use. McCole applied to take her action under an assumed name in order to preserve her anonymity. The state objected to an application for anonymity.

In the wings, other infected women were observing McCole's progress. The objection to anonymity was reported to have sent a shiver through their collective body. Many of the women were private about their condition. Through regular contacts with Positive Action, those in government circles knew that anonymity was highly valued by the women. Yet now, one of these women was being denied even that dignity.

On 28 September 1995, in a letter from the Attorney General to the Chief State Solicitor's office, a comment was made that opposing McCole's wish for an alias had a 'tactical value' in promoting the government's compensation scheme. In other words, refusing to grant her wish for privacy may dissuade others from going to court and persuade them to accept an award from the compensation tribunal.

Other tactics were applied. The product that had poisoned McCole, anti-D, had been manufactured by the BTSB. For the sake of the legal action, however, the board denied that it had even manufactured anti-D.

Then the BTSB put a lodgment in the court. This legal device means that if any award subsequently made by the court does not exceed the value of the lodgment, then the plaintiff is liable for at least some of the legal costs. Ordinarily the costs follow an award. In order words, if a lodgment of €100,000 is made with the court by a defendant, and a judge subsequently awards only €90,000 to a plaintiff, then the plaintiff is liable for any costs incurred after the time of the lodgment. In reality, the legal costs could gobble up most, if not all, of any award made.

Making a lodgment is a device commonly used to put pressure on a plaintiff to settle. In normal circumstances, in legal contests of equals, it is part of the cut and thrust of battle. In this case, it represented the might of the state attempting to try every which way to ensure that the truth of how it wronged an innocent woman would not emerge.

The deterioration in McCole's condition continued to accelerate. She applied to have an early hearing in June 1996. The request was prompted by a suggestion from her consultant that she may not be up to participating in a court action later in the year.

The state treated McCole as a legal enemy against whom any tactic within the rules could be used. The request was resisted by the state and the BTSB. They stated to the court that they required more time to prepare a defence.

In May the BTSB offered Bridget McCole £175,000 in

settlement of her claim. The figure was probably more than she might have received at the compensation tribunal, but it would mean she would have to relinquish her quest to find out the truth. The liver disease was kicking in by that time and she was enduring regular, torturous journeys to Dublin for treatment. She refused the offer. The truth remained her objective.

After the state requested further time to prepare the case, the hearing was set for 8 October.

During the summer, McCole's condition forced her to spend more and more time in hospital in Dublin. On 16 August she received special permission to leave hospital for the wedding of one of her children. The following Monday, she returned to Beaumont. She would never go home again.

The case was raised in the Dáil and in the media. Reacting, Noonan said that the forthcoming case would act as an inquiry of sorts into what had happened. It was an extraordinary position to take. The government was unwilling to set up a public inquiry into the poisoning of women, and now, when all efforts to aggressively resist a legal action by one of the women had failed, the case was being portrayed as some class of inquiry.

McCole's condition was rapidly deteriorating. She told her daughter that if only Noonan could see how sick she was it would make all the difference to the government's position. But the minister was not approaching the problem from a human perspective, but rather from one of defending what he was being told were the state's interests.

Noonan was reacting to the strongest professional advice from both lawyers and his department. From civil servants who saw their role as protecting the Department of Health from any financial fallout. From lawyers who applied tactics that are standard arrows in the quiver of legal strategy.

Ultimately, the decision on how to approach the case was the responsibility of Noonan, but as with many of his predecessors in cabinet – and many successors – he effectively outsourced the decision making and hid behind the advice proffered. Noonan would subsequently be heavily criticised for the heartless position the state took against a dying woman. Neither for the first nor the last time, the interests of a public institution – in this case the Department of Health and the BTSB – were perceived by civil servants and advisers as of greater importance than the interests of the citizen whom the institutions were intended to serve.

On 9 September the BTSB received a joint opinion from three senior counsel that it was their 'unanimous and unequivocal advice that it is imperative for the Blood Transfusion Service Board to concede on the issue of negligence'. The case had been in train for over a year, yet only at this late stage did the board seek an independent legal opinion.

It was the first time the BTSB had been given legal advice to that effect. The government had received similar advice the previous year, but in legal terms the parties were separate defendants in the case. Why the BTSB had not obtained detailed legal advice prior to this time has never been satisfactorily answered. Why the government did not share its advice with the BTSB is a matter for conjecture.

Talks with McCole reopened. Despite admitting liability, the state was unwilling to concede aggravated damages. The value of the settlement remained the same, £175,000, take it or leave it.

By the end of the month, it became obvious that McCole had only weeks to live. She knew that even if she lived until the beginning of the hearing, she was unlikely to see the end of it.

She would hardly be in a position to give evidence. She had been beaten by the clock ticking down on her illness, and the state had played the situation to its full advantage.

On 1 October, from her sick bed, she agreed to the settlement. It meant that her family would have at least something for the years of pain and upheaval they had suffered. The following day, 2 October 1996, Bridget McCole died.

Her final months had been weighed down with the worry and stress caused by the ongoing battle of the state to keep her at bay. Her courage and the circumstances in which she died ensured that her death would make a difference. The true story of how a state had negligently poisoned over 1,000 women would be brought to light.

* * *

A bitter irony attaching to the scandal of blood poisoning is that its origins can be traced back to an attempt by the state to provide better services for its citizens. In 1970 the Blood Transfusion Board began producing the blood product anti-D immunoglobulin. The product is administered to rhesus negative blood type mothers who are due to give birth to rhesus positive babies.

Anti-D, which is manufactured from plasma, is regarded as an excellent treatment for the potential complication of haemolytic disease, in which antibodies in the mother's blood attack the red blood cells in the veins of the baby. Up to 5,000 Irish women are treated for this condition each year.

The decision to manufacture anti-D in Ireland meant there would be more control over the blood used as a raw material. The board would not have to import blood, the origins of which may not be traceable. It was a development that a tribunal would later find was a 'particularly noteworthy and splendid' achievement.

Through the early 1970s anti-D was manufactured and used without incident. Later it would emerge that best practice was not always adhered to in the storage of the product. In 1975 the entire stock of anti-D in the board's headquarters at Pelican House in Dublin was placed in a fridge in a special hepatitis laboratory. This exposed the product to the possibility of cross-infection. A biochemist working in the board demanded that the entire stock be destroyed. He was assured that this would be done.

Later he discovered that only the outer wrappers of the bottles containing the anti-D were actually discarded. The product itself was retained. There is no evidence that this incident had any bearing on what was to transpire, but it is an indication of the manner in which business was done in the board at the time.

In the second half of 1976 a pregnant woman, Patient X, had to undergo a number of blood transfusions. She was a patient in the Coombe Maternity Hospital but was transferred to Crumlin Hospital three days a week for plasma exchange treatment, which involved a complete change of blood. Over 25 weeks, Patient X received a successful course of plasma exchange. Unknown to her, some of her plasma was taken to be used in the production of anti-D.

On 4 November 1976 Patient X suffered a reaction to a transfusion. Two weeks later she became jaundiced and was diagnosed as having hepatitis. Samples of her blood were sent to the BTSB for testing. It yielded a negative result for hepatitis A and B. (Hepatitis C would not be identified as a defined condition for another 15 years.) Yet it was obvious that the woman was suffering from something.

Over the following month another ten samples of her blood were examined by the BTSB in relation to her ongoing treatment. In each case, the sample was accompanied by a form referring to her clinical condition and carrying the words 'infective hepatitis'. By this stage it was well known in the board that Patient X was displaying jaundice.

Despite the prevailing circumstances, further supplies of the woman's plasma were taken from her in January 1977 and included in pools used for the production of anti-D. Patient X was not a donor. Her blood was used without her knowledge or permission in 16 batches of the product, which translated as over 5,000 doses. Every one of those doses was potentially contaminated.

Six months later the result of this sequence began to manifest itself. On 18 July 1977 Dr Dermot Carroll, a GP working as a locum in the Dublin suburb of Raheny, was visited by a patient, M McG, who had complaints that he recognised as the symptoms of jaundice.

A month later she returned with a more serious case of jaundice. The doctor diagnosed her as suffering from hepatitis 'non-A, non-B' and he also identified the source of her infection. She had received an anti-D injection in the Rotunda Maternity Hospital the previous May.

The doctor was required by law to inform the local health board, which he did. In addition, he contacted the BTSB and spoke to one of the medical staff there. The notification could not have come as a surprise. From 12 July the board had received alarming reports of at least seven and possibly ten women who had recently been given anti-D and were displaying the symptoms of hepatitis.

There was now a clear connection between specific batches of anti-D and the infected women. The BTSB looked into the connections. On 25 July the person in charge of the board's laboratory where the anti-D was manufactured, Cecily Cunningham, was told not to use Patient X's plasma in any more donor pools.

Cunningham would later testify that she received no instructions as to what to do with the already manufactured batches or with those issued but not yet used. As a result, 16 batches containing Patient X's blood continued to be used.

On 5 November Bridget McCole received an injection of anti-D from one of those batches. The poisoning of her blood was inadvertent, but had been preceded by numerous examples of negligence in the BTSB. In all, up to 1,600 women received anti-D injections that contained the infected blood of Patient X.

The following years were lonely and frightening ones for hundreds of the infected women. The jaundice receded, but other health problems manifested themselves.

In 1989 hepatitis C was identified as a specific condition in the United States. Two years later alarm bells should have been going off at the BTSB. Following an examination of a sample of Patient X's blood in Middlesex Hospital in England, it was discovered that she was hepatitis C positive. The news was relayed to the BTSB. The reaction seems to have been offering up hope that if the problem was ignored, it might go away.

In 1993, in a series of routine tests of 100,000 blood donors, it emerged that there were 30 hepatitis C carriers. The records of 15 of these carriers were then examined and it was found that 13 of them had received the anti-D agent. A connection had been established that simply could not be ignored.

In February 1994 the BTSB announced that the agent had been contaminated and given unknowingly to women about to give birth. It was this notice that alerted McCole and hundreds of other women to their condition. After years of not knowing or understanding why their health was deteriorating, somebody had finally come clean on what had happened.

Women who had received anti-D in 1977 were invited to attend at the board for testing. Later, the testing was extended to all women who had received the agent, amounting to 70,000 cases. Of these, over 1,200 tested positive for hepatitis C antibodies, of which around half tested positive for the active virus.

One woman who had tested positive was Jane O'Brien, a journalist. She asked the BTSB to put her in touch with other women in the same situation. The board refused. She persisted in her endeavour and managed to get word out that she was attempting to bring together those who were affected.

A meeting was eventually convened in the offices of the Council for the Status of Women in Dublin. Thirty affected women attended and the support group Positive Action was formed. Positive Action would go on to play a vital role in bringing the facts into the public domain and highlighting where the state was continuing to deny its citizens' basic rights.

An investigation into the whole contamination was announced by the Minister for Health, Brendan Howlin. It was to consist of an expert group, chaired by Dr Miriam Hederman O'Brien. Meanwhile, Positive Action continued to push its case and to garner support through the media and the sheer force of will of the organisers and the moral ballast of their cause.

The BTSB arranged for counselling for the women, but once again the state's approach to those it had poisoned lacked both sensitivity and responsibility. The counselling personnel were employed by the blood board, the same organisation that had contaminated the women. Some women reported being asked extremely invasive questions during the process, such as how many sexual partners they had had while infected. Eventually, Positive Action was able to secure funding for independent counselling.

When the expert group reported in March 1995, there had been a change of government and Noonan was the new Minister for Health. The expert group reported that there had been further infections all the way up to 1994. Despite the discovery in the Middlesex Hospital in 1991, the BTSB had ploughed on with its existing policy.

It also found that the BTSB was aware in 1976 that Patient X was infected with environmental jaundice, yet her blood continued to be used. (It would later be established that the board was aware that Patient X had infectious hepatitis and not environmental jaundice.)

Following the publication of the report, Positive Action entered into negotiations with the Department of Health for appropriate compensation. The negotiations were protracted as a result of the department's concern that it would have to pay out huge sums. Negotiations broke down in September 1995 and resumed in November.

Ultimately, the department offered to set up an ad hoc compensation tribunal, where the women would be arbitrarily awarded a sum of money. Crucially, the process would involve no admission of liability. Positive Action was not happy with the outcome, but had little choice but to go along with it.

In many instances members adopted a twin-track approach of applying to the tribunal and initiating legal action as well.

McCole was early out of the blocks, issuing High Court proceedings and determined to find out in public the truth about how she had been infected and why her life and her family were subjected to protracted upheaval and the terror of not knowing what had happened.

It would be some years later, following the release of the legal strategy in the McCole case, before it became apparent that the government was prepared to do everything it possibly could to dissuade women from going down the legal route. While in theory the government was acting as an honest broker, offering the victims the opportunity of receiving compensation without recourse to the courts, in practice, the strategy it employed against the women was intended to herd them towards the tribunal.

It was in such an environment that McCole was growing weaker, the prospect of the end of her life blighted with the stress being inflicted by an agency of state that had poisoned her blood some 18 years previously.

* * *

When Bridget McCole died on 2 October 1996, it was six days before her case was due to go to a hearing in the High Court. If she had not agreed to settle the case, the maximum her family could have been awarded in the High Court after her death was £7,500. As it was, they received £175,000.

Almost immediately, the political fallout from the case began to manifest itself. Within a week the government had agreed to set up a judicial inquiry. That it had taken the death of one of the women to bring about this change of course – five months earlier Noonan had ruled out a judicial inquiry – added to the sense of scandal around the whole affair.

Announcing the setting up of the tribunal in the Dáil, Noonan admitted that what happened was 'nothing less than a public health disaster'. He went on to defend the decision to set up the original compensation tribunal before lurching into a gaffe that would haunt the rest of his political career.

Noonan's ham-fisted attempt to target the lawyers who

advised McCole backfired spectacularly. He posed the question as to whether:

[O]n reflection, would not the solicitors for the plaintiff have served their client better if they had advised her to go to the compensation tribunal early this year?

Is it not accepted in the legal profession that the tribunal is working well and that Mrs McCole could have received a significantly higher award by going before it? She would not have had to face the enormous stress of court proceedings. Could her solicitors not, in selecting a case from the hundreds of hepatitis C cases on their books, have selected a plaintiff in a better condition to sustain the stress of a High Court case? Was it in the interest of her client to attempt to run her case not only in the High Court but also in the media and the Dáil simultaneously?

Up in the public gallery, a delegation of women from Positive Action had been watching proceedings. Immediately after the foregoing contribution, they got up and walked out. It was a dramatic gesture.

Within an hour, Noonan realised he had made a major blunder and sought to rectify it, returning to the chamber in sackcloth and ashes mode. He told the House that he now realised his comments had caused:

[U]nderstandable offence to her family, to other victims and to those in the organisation associated with the campaign and I would like to avail of this opportunity to apologise unreservedly for any offence ... I certainly did not mean to question in any way the right of Mrs McCole and her legal

> team to take the course of action which they did ...
> I was making criticisms of the adversarial legal
> system and in the course of an adversarial legal
> system sometimes contending parties can cause
> difficulty. I made the remarks in that context. There
> was no intention of hurting or offending Mrs
> McCole's family in any way whatsoever.

The damage had been done. One clumsy gaffe ensured that Noonan, perhaps unfairly, would thereafter be regarded as one of the main culprits in the wrong done by the state in how it dealt with citizens whose lives had been irreparably damaged by a state agency.

That same week the McCole family wrote a letter to Noonan that would substantially form the terms of reference for the public inquiry.

> We write to you as the husband and family of Mrs
> Brid McCole, who died on October 2nd from liver
> failure as a result of her infection with the hepatitis
> C virus following the administration of Anti-D
> Immunoglobulin in November, 1977.
>
> We refer to recent events and the admission of
> liability by the Blood Transfusion Service Board in
> their letter of September 20th, 1996, copy annexed.
> We would like you to answer the following
> questions, which are questions about which our
> mother was concerned and remain unanswered:
> 1. Why did the Blood Transfusion Service Board use
> plasma from a patient undergoing therapeutic
> plasma exchange when it was unsafe to do so?
> 2. Why did the Blood Transfusion Service Board
> ignore the ample warnings of jaundice, hepatitis
> and adverse reactions to Anti-D in 1977 and again

take no steps when they were informed of the infection of Anti-D with hepatitis C on December 16th, 1991?

3. Why did the Blood Transfusion Service Board not inform the infected women in 1991, and why did they not report the infection to the Department of Health, as they were obliged by law to do?

4. Why was the Blood Transfusion Service Board permitted to manufacture Anti-D unlawfully and without a licence under the Therapeutic Substances Act 1932 from 1970–1984?

5. In their letter of September 20th, 1996 the Blood Transfusion Service Board did two things. They admitted liability and apologised, but only in the context of a threat that, were she to proceed with a case for aggravated/exemplary damages, and not to succeed, they would pursue her for costs. What was the justification for this threat?

We are asking these questions in the knowledge that our mother, were she alive, would have pursued her court action to get answers to these questions. We are confident you have the answers and can get them.

* * *

The tribunal was chaired by Judge Thomas Finlay and began its work on 5 November 1996. Among the early witnesses called was 27-year-old Brid McCole, eldest daughter of Bridget.

She told the inquiry that her mother had 'gone through hell' because of her infection. She referred to Noonan's statement earlier in the year that the then pending court action would be an inquiry in itself. 'That put an extra burden on her,' she said. 'I feel very strongly that only because my mother died, this tribunal would not have come through. It is only a shame that someone had to die for this to happen.'

The tribunal reported in March 1997, less than six months after it had been established. Among the findings made by Judge Finlay was that the plasma used in the manufacture of anti-D was in breach of the BTSB's standards; medical staff at the BTSB failed to respond to reports that recipients of the contaminated anti-D had suffered jaundice and/or hepatitis; and the BTSB had acted unethically in obtaining and using the plasma from Patient X.

Three employees of the blood board were named as sharing responsibility for the failures that led to the crisis. These were the blood bank's national director, Jack O'Riordan, former assistant director, Terry Walsh, and biochemist Cecily Cunningham. Finlay's report also recommended a complete overhaul of the BTSB.

The policy and conduct of the Department of Health and the National Drugs Advisory Board were criticised.

There were also criticisms of government policy once the infection became known to the authorities, but they were not politically explosive.

Following the publication, Positive Action lobbied the government once again for a statutory compensation tribunal with powers to award punitive damages. This time around, the government complied.

Later in 1997 the newly elected Fianna Fáil-led government made public the file containing the legal strategy pursued by its predecessor in the McCole case. It made for damning reading, showing how, at every turn, McCole had faced the might of a state determined that her case would not succeed.

The file also revealed that the BTSB had had information since April 1995 that it was negligent (the official legal advice the board claimed to have got to that effect was in September 1996, some weeks before McCole's death), yet continued to fight the case tooth and nail.

As is often the case in Irish life, nobody was ultimately held responsible for what had occurred. The Finlay report was forwarded to the Director of Public Prosecutions, who decided in October 1997 that no prosecutions would be forthcoming in the case.

The following month, both Positive Action and the McCole family made official complaints to An Garda Síochána about the conduct of the BTSB in contaminating the women and how senior staff conducted themselves as information became available.

In a detailed complaint, Positive Action outlined how it believed gardaí should take a wide-ranging approach to any investigation to cover all aspects of the saga, including the failure to act on the information that became available in 1991 from the UK.

The force was then obliged to investigate and forward its findings to the DPP in a completely separate procedure. As a result, Walsh and Cunningham were arrested and charged with seven counts of grievous bodily harm. (By that stage O'Riordan had died.) Walsh died in 2006. In 2008 all the charges against Cunningham were dropped owing to the death of a crucial witness.

Two years after the Finlay Tribunal completed its work, another group of victims who had been injected with poisonous blood finally got the public inquiry they had sought. Over 250 haemophiliacs had been infected with HIV and hepatitis C as a result of infection through the BTSB.

The Lindsay Tribunal, chaired by judge Alison Lindsay, reported in September 2002, but the results were not greeted positively by the victims. Lindsay did not refer her report to the DPP and found that most of the problems that led to the infections were historic and had since been corrected. Again, systems were responsible, but nobody was to carry the can for poisoning hundreds of vulnerable recipients of blood.

* * *

The infection scandals involving the BTSB were among the worst in the history of the state. At stake were people's lives and they were treated in the most cavalier manner. Something that required the highest standards of care – the transfusion of blood – was reduced to an exercise in seeing, hearing and speaking no evil in the hope that any issues might go away or be buried.

The scandal was informed by the worst elements of administration in the state, with incompetence being followed by desperate attempts to save the institutions from any fallout rather than rushing to inform and assist the stricken citizens. The first instinct was to protect the institution by fighting the citizen all the way through the courts. It was a shameful episode from start to finish.

9

DOING THE STATE SOME DISSERVICE

It was a Saturday night in Dublin in the mid-1980s. The audience in the main hall of the RDS had been worked into a frenzy of excitement. People were standing, dancing, on the chairs. But they were not responding to U2, Bruce Springsteen or one of the other international rock acts that periodically lifted the gloom in the recession-hit Ireland of the era. No, their adoration was directed exclusively towards a politician.

This, however, was no ordinary politician, but one Charles J. Haughey, leader of Fianna Fáil and the dominant and most controversial figure in Irish politics in the second half of the 20th century. A man whose career began with warnings from veteran Fianna Fáilers that he would drag the party into the mire and concluded with a senior judge declaring that he had devalued democracy.

Haughey was out of government that night. The disgrace of his spell in office was still fresh in the memory, as was his Houdini-style survival in a series of incredibly bitter leadership challenges. The slightly ageing figure standing at the podium had served two terms as Taoiseach, neither of which could have been considered remotely successful.

Yet the reception Haughey was receiving was akin to a returning Messiah. The strains of 'Rise and Follow Charlie' filled the hall and the swaying masses made clear their unbridled passion for their leader. Jack Lynch before him and Bertie Ahern after him may have enjoyed wider popularity with the general public, but neither man ever attracted such devotion from the Fianna Fáil masses.

Haughey revelled in the moment, a chieftain being acknowledged by 'his people', for that was how he saw himself. He played up his 'Republican' persona. But he certainly was not republican in the French egalitarian sense. Not for him the traditional de Valera values of austerity and simplicity. He was an expert judge of champagne, vintage port, and a good claret and had a taste for French cuisine, handmade designer shirts and high art, buying a period house filled with antique furniture and fine paintings and hunting with hounds wearing, of all things, a top hat.

It was one of many contradictions in Haughey's extraordinarily complex persona. The darling of the working classes who lived like the lord of the manor; the brilliant minister who was seized by indecision on becoming Taoiseach; the politician who caved into vested interests but had the courage to embrace visionary concepts such as the International Financial Services Centre (IFSC); the wrecker of the economy in the early 1980s turned saviour seven years later; the 'teapot diplomat' charming Margaret Thatcher whereas earlier he had been at the centre of the arms trial; the Fianna Fáil tribal hero who stole from his party; the super-confident, at times arrogant, wunderkind who still felt the need to surround himself with the trappings of an aristocrat.

Haughey despised the bourgeois values of businesspeople, regarding them as boring, dull and uncultured, but was happy to rely on handouts from them to fund his opulent lifestyle. He was the politician who told Irish people 'we are living way beyond our means' at a time when his personal debt to income ratio was off the scale. He regarded himself as a man of destiny yet, within hours of finally becoming Taoiseach, he was seeking a substantial cash injection to bolster his ailing finances from 29-year-old businessman Patrick Gallagher, who famously asked him, 'Tell me the truth. How much do you fucking owe?'

Despite, or maybe because of, these contradictions, Haughey's influence over four decades of the Irish state's existence was enormous. And he continues to cast a long shadow over a political culture that has become irrevocably debased in the eyes of many citizens.

In his resignation speech in 1992, he famously quoted from *Othello*, 'I have done the state some service and they know it, no more of that.' But Haughey was less Othello and more Iago. The harsh, undeniable reality was that while he did have his achievements, overall he did the state an enormous disservice, the effects of which will be felt for some time to come.

As far back as 1960 one of the grizzled old 1916 veterans in Fianna Fáil, Gerry Boland, forecast that Haughey would one day 'drag down the party in the mire'. It was an open secret in the party that other founding fathers and veterans of de Valera cabinets, such as Frank Aiken and Seán MacEntee, were seriously worried about Haughey's growing influence. Yet such views did nothing to delay a meteoric rise within the party.

* * *

Haughey had qualified as an accountant and set up the firm of Haughey Boland in 1951 with his old school friend, Harry Boland. The firm quickly became extremely successful and looked after the affairs of a large number of companies, many of them in the property field. But Haughey's real ambitions were clearly political.

He was elected to the Dáil in 1957 and was promoted in 1960 by the Taoiseach, his father-in-law Seán Lemass, to parliamentary secretary, as the rank of junior minister was then known.

In the same year, he acquired a house in Grangemore in Raheny, Dublin, on 45 acres of land. During the 1960s he somehow managed to amass further wealth, acquiring a farm in Meath, racehorses and a chicken hatchery. His first racehorse, Miss Cossie, received enormous press attention.

In 1961 Haughey was elevated to the cabinet as Minister for Justice. He was a young man in a hurry. The powerful Secretary of the Department of Justice, Peter Berry, later wrote that 'while he was in Justice, Haughey was a dynamic minister. He was a joy to work with and the longer he stayed, the better he got.'

But the top civil servant also recalled a less attractive side to Haughey's personality. When Berry objected to a blatantly political promotion in the immigration service, Haughey flung the departmental file at him and the papers were strewn across the floor of the minister's office. It was a small insight into what was to come.

While Haughey's next job, as Minister for Agriculture, was less successful, his flamboyant lifestyle ensured that his profile continued to soar. As Conor Cruise O'Brien, later to become an arch political opponent, would write in 1969 of him:

Haughey's general style of living was remote from the traditional Republican and de Valera austerities. He had made a great deal of money and he obviously enjoyed spending it, in a dashing 18th century style, of which horses were conspicuous symbols. He was a small man and, when dismounted, he strutted rather. His admirers thought he resembled the Emperor Napoleon, some of whose better known mannerisms he cultivated. He patronised, and that is the right word, the arts. He was an aristocrat in the proper sense of the word: not a nobleman or even a gentleman, but one who believed in the right of the best people to rule, and that he himself was the best of the best people. He was at any rate better, or at least more intelligent and interesting, than most of his colleagues. He was considered a competent minister, and spoke in parliament with bored but conclusive authority. There were enough rumours about him to form a legend of sorts.

Haughey added to the legend by socialising with cabinet colleagues such as Donogh O'Malley and Brian Lenihan, becoming, in the memorable words of Tim Pat Coogan, 'the epitome of the men in the mohair suits'.

Stories about their drinking exploits in the Fianna Fáil haunt of Groome's Hotel were legion. They also frequented the upmarket Russell Hotel, where Haughey socialised with financiers and builders, with whom he was probably closer than he was with anybody in Fianna Fáil.

By the mid-1960s Haughey was a candidate for the leadership of Fianna Fáil, along with George Colley, a school friend who had become an intense rival. However, amid fears that the party would split between the Haughey and the Colley factions, Haughey made a tactical decision to withdraw from the 1966 leadership contest and backed Jack Lynch.

In return, Lynch made him Finance Minister. Ireland was in

the middle of an economic boom, allowing Haughey scope for some imaginative reforms. He introduced free travel, subsidised electricity for old age pensioners and endeared himself to the arty crowd by abolishing income tax for artistic work.

He also introduced a special provision in the 1969 Finance Act that opponents would claim directly benefited him financially.

In the 1969 general election, Haughey's wealth, long a subject of fascination, became a central issue. The *Evening Herald* revealed that the minister had sold his home at Grangemore to well-known property developer Matt Gallagher for over £200,000 and bought the Abbeville estate and its 250 acres for £140,000. Abbeville, in north County Dublin, was the former summer home of the lord lieutenants in Ireland and was partly designed by James Gandon.

When questions were raised about the origin of his wealth, Haughey's line of defence – one he was to stick to right up to the establishment of the tribunals in Dublin Castle – was to object 'to my private affairs being used in this way. It is a private matter between myself and the purchaser.'

But Fine Gael's Gerald Sweetman claimed that Haughey had benefited from legislation he had introduced himself, amending part of the 1965 Finance Act so that he did not have to pay tax on the profits on his property dealings. Haughey referred the matter to the Revenue Commissioners and was left in the clear when they reported that 'no liability to income tax or surtax would have arisen' even if the Act had not been amended.

At the time, that verdict seemed emphatic enough. But looked at with the benefit of hindsight, and knowing the 'privileged treatment accorded to him by the Revenue over more than three decades, it may simply have been another case of the institutions of the state acting under duress to protect him,' Stephen Collins wrote in his brilliant 2001 book on Fianna Fáil, *The Power Game*.

Fianna Fáil was also facing criticism over what were believed to be growing links between politics and business, best epitomised by Taca, the fundraising organisation of 500 businesspeople who attended monthly dinners and, in return for contributions to the party, were given special access to ministers (see Chapter 5). Although traditionalists in the party also attended Taca dinners, Haughey, who organised the first dinner, was the politician most associated with it.

There was also persistent speculation in political circles concerning Haughey and property developer John Byrne, who had built O'Connell Bridge House, which was then leased by the government.

Byrne and Haughey were close friends. And Des Traynor – who it would emerge decades later was Haughey's bagman – was a director of both Byrne's principal property vehicles, Carlisle Trust and Dublin City Estates.

There had always been rumours – emphatically denied – that Haughey was a silent partner in Byrne's business empire. The rumours gained such currency that in 1979 Byrne had serious difficulty finding a state tenant for an office block he had on St Stephen's Green.

'Wherever he turned he found himself facing a brick wall. And this wall, it transpired, was the Minister for Finance George Colley. He personally vetoed any and all proposals to lease Sean Lemass House because he was convinced that his arch-rival Charlie Haughey had a stake in Byrne's property empire,' Frank McDonald wrote in his 1985 book *The Destruction of Dublin*.

In 1983 Byrne's solicitors took the unprecedented step of issuing a statement denying that Haughey was involved in Byrne's controversial plans to build over 2,000 homes in the green belt area between Baldoyle and Portmarnock in north County Dublin.

What can be said for certain is that Haughey liked to socialise with high fliers, including auctioneer John Finnegan, developer Ken O'Reilly-Hyland, who was appointed by Fianna Fáil to many state boards and who would also chair Fianna Fáil's fundraising committee, celebrity architect Sam Stephenson, car dealers Denis Mahony and Brian Dennis, and the builder he sold his home at Grangemore to, Matt Gallagher.

Traynor, along with O'Reilly-Hyland and others, was also a director of a consortium set up to redevelop the old Fitzwilliam Lawn Tennis Club at Wilton Place in the heart of Dublin's business district. Like Byrne's Carlisle Trust, the vast bulk of the ordinary shares in the consortium, Marlborough Holdings, were held by a Guinness & Mahon trust company, and as a result the shareholders' identity was not known.

Traynor, as it would emerge decades later, was developing something of a speciality in setting up trust companies. He put that expertise to good use for his close friend Haughey. The two men had met when Traynor began working at Haughey's accountancy firm in the early 1950s and Haughey became his mentor.

Traynor quickly proved something of a financial whizz and was made a partner. He went on to become a leading figure in Irish business in his own right, becoming chairman of CRH in the early 1980s and before that de facto chief executive of blue-chip merchant bank Guinness & Mahon. Despite holding such prominent positions, he was a low-profile character who eschewed media interviews.

From the early 1960s Traynor was arranging for all of Haughey's bills to be paid via a single bank account, the Haughey Boland No. 3 account, held in the Allied Irish Bank (AIB), Dame Street, Dublin. The funds in this bill-paying service came from accounts held in Guinness & Mahon and controlled by Traynor, which formed an integral part of the operation of the so-called Ansbacher accounts.

These accounts become infamous in Ireland in the late 1990s when it emerged that Ansbacher, a clandestine bank in the Cayman Islands, was used by 200, often high-profile, Irish figures to deposit tens of millions of pounds. The scheme facilitated widespread tax evasion for the great majority of the many Irish resident account holders.

Clients' deposits with Ansbacher were treated for tax purposes as if they were lodged offshore, but Traynor was actually holding the cash in Ireland and running the business from his central Dublin headquarters – for a time this was in the head office of one of Ireland's leading companies, CRH.

There were other sites bought for development around Dublin and linked to Haughey in speculation but nothing was ever substantiated, despite many people wondering how a politician could afford such a lavish lifestyle. McDonald highlighted Haughey's developer links in *The Destruction of Dublin*, but once again most people chose not to probe further.

While Ireland was in the middle of a boom in the 1960s, within Fianna Fáil there was a growing sense of unease about the party's changing values. In 1967 George Colley spoke of 'low standards in high places', a comment widely regarded as a reference to Haughey.

But that unease turned to outright horror when Fianna Fáil

was plunged into the greatest crisis in its history. Haughey was at the epicentre.

* * *

Haughey had never been seen as a particularly hardline Republican in the mould of Kevin Boland or Neil Blaney, who both sat alongside him at the cabinet table. It had not gone unnoticed within a party obsessed by history that his Fianna Fáil lineage was non-existent – his father had been a Free State Army officer. However, his parents had come from Swatragh in County Derry, and the plight of Northern nationalists was a regular dinnertime conversation in the Haughey household when the future Taoiseach was growing up.

On VE Day in 1945 Haughey, a student in University College Dublin, burned a Union Jack outside Trinity College. But that incident had been long forgotten, particularly given Haughey's tough approach to the IRA during his time as Minister for Justice in the early 1960s.

When the situation began to deteriorate in the North during 1969, Haughey was put in charge of a £100,000 fund to relieve distress for the nationalist population there. There was nothing remarkable about this, but shortly afterwards garda intelligence sources began reporting contacts between subversives and certain cabinet ministers.

They were extraordinary times in the North and respected and moderate nationalist politicians were calling for arms for citizens' defence committees to protect Catholics who had been under attack from loyalist pogroms during the height of disturbances that August.

Lynch, despite pressure from Blaney and Boland, was ensuring his government took a careful approach so as not to inflame the situation. But the evidence available suggests that

Haughey and Blaney followed their own Northern strategy, unbeknownst to Lynch.

When the IRA announced on 18 August that it was resuming its military campaign, Lynch responded firmly that the government would not tolerate any group usurping its powers. Yet around that time senior gardaí informed the Department of Justice that a cabinet minister had held a meeting with Cathal Goulding, the Chief of Staff of the IRA, 'at which a deal had been made that the IRA would call off their campaign of violence in the 26 counties in return for a free hand in operating a cross border campaign in the North'.

The IRA believed the cabinet minister had been speaking to the chief of staff with the authority of the government, or so Berry was told. The name of the minister was not given to Berry, but when the Minister for Justice, Michael Moran, read out Berry's report at cabinet, Haughey interjected, 'That could have been me. I was asked to see someone casually and it transpired to be this person. There was nothing to it. It was entirely casual.'

Amazingly, Haughey's version was accepted and even Berry, who had something of a reputation as a conspiracy theorist, was reassured. Because of Haughey's previously tough line with the IRA as Minister for Justice, Berry did not believe that Haughey could be involved in plotting with Republicans.

Yet many who have studied this period believe that Haughey, along with Blaney, was doing exactly that. Certainly he seemed to be running an alternative government from his home, summoning army intelligence officers and IRA leaders to meet him, and even inviting the British Ambassador, Andrew Gilchrist, to Abbeville to discuss the future of the North.

At that meeting in early October, Haughey told Gilchrist

there was nothing he would not sacrifice, including the position of the Catholic Church and neutrality, if the British would give a secret commitment to move towards Irish unity. He offered NATO bases on Irish soil as part of the deal.

Meanwhile, moves were afoot by IRA activists to import arms using money from the Irish government's relief fund. In the early months of 1970, Irish Army intelligence officer Captain James Kelly – acting, he would argue, with the full authority of his superiors in the army and government – organised the purchase of arms on the continent, which were due to be shipped from Antwerp into Dublin in March.

Haughey, in his role as Minister for Finance, instructed customs to clear the cargo without inspecting it, but it was never loaded because the paperwork was not in order. The following month, Berry learned of a plan to bring 6.8 tons of arms and ammunition into Dublin Airport within days. He got a call from Haughey:

'You know about the cargo that is coming into Dublin Airport on Sunday?' asked Haughey.

'Yes, Minister,' replied Berry.

'Can it be let through on a guarantee that it will go direct to the North?'

'No.'

'I think that is a bad decision. What will happen to it when it arrives?'

'It will be grabbed.'

'I had better have it called off,' said Haughey, ending the conversation.

Berry went to Lynch with all that he knew. After some prevarication by a no-doubt stunned Lynch, the Taoiseach's hand was forced when the leader of the opposition, Liam

Cosgrave, was briefed on the affair by senior gardaí who were hugely concerned about what was going on.

Matters came to a head in May 1970 with the sensational sacking by Lynch of Haughey and Blaney from the cabinet. The two men were brought before the courts – Haughey was arrested by detectives at his Abbeville mansion – and charged with conspiracy to import arms. The meteoric rise had come to a shuddering halt.

Captain Kelly, Belfast Republican John Kelly and Belgian-born businessman Albert Luykx were also charged. Many have questioned the decision to charge them. The argument has been made that Captain Kelly was acting under orders – although there is also a counterargument that he far exceeded his brief. John Kelly had reason to believe he had the tacit support of the Irish government and Luykx was sucked into the affair though his association with Blaney.

The charges against Blaney were dismissed in the District Court because of a lack of evidence, but Haughey and the others were returned for trial in the Central Criminal Court, charged with conspiring to illegally important 500 guns and 180,000 rounds of ammunition.

Haughey denied all knowledge of the attempt to import arms, in the process leaving his co-defendants in the lurch. They had admitted their role in the affair but stated that it was legal because it was sanctioned by the Minister for Defence, Jim Gibbons. Gibbons became the main state witness and his evidence was directly at odds with Haughey's.

Gibbons said he had made it clear to Haughey the previous April that the Departments of Defence, Justice and Transport were aware of the plot to import arms through Dublin Airport. He said that when Haughey had told him that the 'dogs in the street are barking it' and promised to stop the process 'for a month', he had replied, 'For God's stake stop it altogether.' Haughey denied this conversation had happened.

In his summing up, the trial judge, Justice Henchy, said the only conclusion was that either Gibbons or Haughey was guilty of perjury. There was a direct conflict of evidence between Haughey and Gibbons and one of them must be lying.

However, on 23 October the jury found Haughey and his co-defendants not guilty. 'That night Haughey threw a party to celebrate and among the revellers was at least one member of the jury. The whole affair had a Sicilian whiff about it,' Collins wrote in *The Power Game*.

Acquitted of the charges, Haughey made vague challenging noises in the direction of his party leader, but it quickly became apparent that Lynch was in total control of Fianna Fáil.

In any other democratic state, Haughey's political career would surely have been finished, despite his acquittal. Leaving aside the suggestion of perjury, there was, as Collins argues:

... overwhelming evidence that Haughey and Blaney were involved in encouraging the Republican split and that arms were promised in return for a commitment by Republicans to confine their campaign to the North. On this score, there is the detailed diary of a dedicated public servant, Peter Berry, the intelligence reports of the Gardaí, the testimony of leading members of the Official IRA, some of whom met Haughey, and the fact of the plot to import arms.

Even if it is not accepted that Haughey was encouraging a Republican split, he was conducting meetings with known subversives and effectively usurping his Taoiseach. Even allowing for how high emotions were running at the time, that alone should have ensured Haughey was finished politically.

But, not for the last time, Haughey showed his incredible survival instincts.

While Blaney and the ever principled, if inflexible and misguided, Boland left Fianna Fáil, Haughey stayed and, more incredibly, was allowed to stay. It is easy to understand why he chose to stay – he knew he would never be Taoiseach if he left the party – but less clear is why he was allowed to do so. Presumably the leadership did not move to banish him from the party because they feared it would tear Fianna Fáil asunder.

To many, Haughey was a hero and he had strong support among the grass roots. Even while he was firing Haughey, Lynch was expressing the view that Haughey may still have a future in the party. However, many in Fianna Fáil would come to lament the missed opportunity.

* * *

Haughey had to swallow some particularly unpalatable medicine to stay in the fold. Not only did he have to suffer the indignity of backing Lynch, but he had to vote confidence in Gibbons, whose testimony at the arms trial had flatly contradicted his own.

As well as eating humble pie, Haughey had to stomach hundreds of chicken-and-chip meals as he set about his own rehabilitation by travelling the length and breadth of the country talking to any group in Fianna Fáil willing to invite him. P.J. Mara, who was to become one of his closest political confidants and a legendary government press secretary to Haughey's governments, accompanied him on many of these trips.

It was hard work, but the slog paid off, building on the huge reservoir of support for him in the grass roots of the organisation. Although he had always denied the gun-running charges, the arms trial only added to the whiff of sulphur around him and appealed to the many fireside Republicans in the party who remained steadfastly anti-partition.

But those in the party who had actually walked the Republican walk, as opposed to just talking the talk, were far less impressed. The day after the general election of 1973 was called, party veteran Frank Aiken stunned Lynch by informing him that if Haughey was nominated by his local constituency organisation and then ratified by the Fianna Fáil national executive, he would refuse to stand as a Fianna Fáil candidate and notify the media he was retiring in protest at Haughey's nomination.

Understandably, Lynch was horrified at this development. Coming just as the election campaign was beginning, the potential for electoral damage was obvious.

Haughey was selected and then ratified by the national executive and Aiken, true to his word, withdrew his nomination, signalling to Lynch that he intended to give his reasons to the press.

Huge pressure was brought on Aiken to back down. Senior figures – Lynch, Colley, Seán MacEntee, Paddy Smith and even Eamon de Valera – weighed in to try and talk Aiken out of it. With time running out, Lynch went to Aiken's right-hand man in Louth, Joe Farrell, asking him to try and get through to Aiken.

During their conversation, the former Tánaiste told Farrell he was motivated by a desire to help Fianna Fáil. 'The reason I didn't do it sooner is that I thought I would not have to do it, that somebody else would. But when nobody else did it, I believe that I owe it to the men who went before me in this party. I'm convinced of that,' he said.

Farrell replied that all the work Aiken had done during his

career – helping found Fianna Fáil, setting up Bord na Móna, his achievements as Minister for External Affairs – would be forgotten if he went ahead. He asked Aiken for his permission to go to Lynch and 'tell him to say that you are standing down on doctor's orders'.

After a long pause, the honourable political veteran said, 'All right. Go ahead.' Aiken never attended another Fianna Fáil ard fheis or played any role in party affairs after that. In fact, his son Frank Junior stood for the Progressive Democrats in Louth in 1987, narrowly failing to win a seat.

There is no doubt that Lynch had been put in an incredibly difficult position. Any move to stop the national executive from ratifying Haughey would have split the party during a general election campaign – something no leader could have countenanced. It is hard to disagree with Paddy Smith's argument, in a letter to Aiken at the time, that the opportunity to stop Haughey had been missed a couple of years earlier.

But should Lynch have allowed Aiken to speak his mind at the time? It would have been an embarrassment for Fianna Fáil, but the party ended up losing the election anyway. A public denouncing of Haughey from such an eminent Fianna Fáil figure might have proved fatal for his leadership ambitions.

Throughout Haughey's career too many decent and honourable figures bit their tongue or, in the case of Aiken, were talked out of speaking out.

By the beginning of 1975 Lynch bowed to the huge pressure to bring Haughey back to the front bench. Some in Fianna Fáil believed Lynch did so because he feared by leaving him outside the tent, he would become a rallying point for the party's anti-Lynch faction. The theory was that it was better to have him back on the inside, close to, and associated with, Lynch.

If that was Lynch's thinking, it backfired badly. Did he

really need to do it? There was pressure from the Fianna Fáil grass roots, but given Lynch's authority in the parliamentary party, nobody would have challenged the leader if he had refused to reinstate Haughey. And once Haughey was back in the fold, he was able to position himself as a leadership contender again.

Traditionalists in the party looked on askance. Rita Childers, wife of the recently deceased president, Erskine, refused to attend the annual Fianna Fáil Mass shortly after Haughey's reappointment. Her husband had been publicly critical of Haughey after the arms trial and at the ard fheis of 1972, where Haughey very publicly returned to the fold, Erskine had pointedly kept his head buried in his newspaper on the podium and ignored the cheers as Haughey slipped into the seat beside him.

Now his widow went even further, declaring that 'the late president would not benefit from the prayers of such a party. Happily for him he is now closer to God and will be able to ask his intercession that his much loved country will never again be governed by these people.' There was outrage in Fianna Fáil at these comments. Childers was regarded as a natural Fine Gaeler and was perceived as having a personal grudge against the party for stymieing moves to succeed her late husband as president.

Two years later Fianna Fáil was back in government with a 20-seat majority and, seven years after being fired from cabinet, Haughey was also back, this time as Minister for Health.

He worked assiduously to build support among a parliamentary party, many of whom found Lynch and his coterie aloof and out of touch. Lynch started to lose his grip on Fianna Fáil. The party establishment was firmly behind

Colley to succeed Lynch, who, it was widely known, intended to step down.

If Colley had the insiders in his camp, Haughey was relying on newer, younger and hungrier TDs outside the centre of power, the likes of Ray MacSharry, Albert Reynolds, Pádraig Flynn, Seán Doherty, Charlie McCreevy and the man who would become his protégé, Bertie Ahern.

There was a feeling among some sections of the party that Fianna Fáil under Lynch had drifted from its Republican roots and that Haughey was the man to return them there. Ever ambitious, Haughey stoked the discontent against Lynch. In December 1979 Lynch announced his resignation as Taoiseach and Fianna Fáil leader in an ill-thought-out attempt to catch Haughey cold.

Unlike 13 years earlier, there would be no compromise candidate. It was a straight fight. Colley against Haughey. They may have been of the same generation but they represented different eras. It was the Old Guard against the Young Turks.

It was not just a contest for the leadership, it was a struggle for the soul of the party – something that became much more apparent with the passing of time. Colley was upright, sober, correct – a suitable heir for the likes of de Valera, Aiken, MacEntee et al. Haughey was the very antithesis: brash, dangerous and (regrettably) probably more in tune with a changing Ireland.

The entire cabinet bar Haughey and Michael O'Kennedy supported Colley, but it was not enough. To the horror of the Colley camp, Haughey won the day by 44 votes to 38. The party was hugely divided and the atmosphere was very tense, with – not for the last time – rumours of intimidation of TDs in the run-up to the vote.

It was that knowledge of the bitterness and division in Fianna Fáil that would colour the speech made by opposition leader Garret FitzGerald on the day of Haughey's nomination for Taoiseach. While FitzGerald's reference to Haughey's 'flawed pedigree' might have been unfortunate, the rest of the Fine Gael leader's criticism proved highly perceptive.

> I must speak not only for the Opposition but for many in Fianna Fáil who may not be free to reveal what they know and what led them to oppose this man with a commitment far beyond the normal ... We cannot ignore the fact that he differs from all his predecessors in that those motives have been and are widely impugned, most notably but by no means exclusively, by people within his own party, people close to him who have observed his actions for many years and who have made their human interim judgment on him ... Many of those who may vote for him will be doing so in the belief and hope that they will not have to serve long under a man they do not respect, whom they have fought long and hard, but for the moment in vain, to exclude from the highest office in the land.

While the speech was strongly criticised, many in Fianna Fáil privately agreed with it, so much so that a number of them had seriously considered not voting for Haughey as Taoiseach. But, as happened with Aiken six years earlier, this nuclear option was ultimately not utilised.

If what we now know about Haughey's personal finances had been known then, Colley and not Haughey would certainly have become Taoiseach and politics would have been radically different – and certainly for the better.

At a press conference on the day he became Taoiseach,

Haughey was asked if he would be disclosing the sources of his wealth. He responded, 'That question assumes that I am a wealthy man but I would not necessarily assume that if I were you. Ask my bank manager.'

The comment was interpreted as a pat answer but Haughey was in fact engaging in a double bluff. His aura of wealth was a charade.

* * *

Haughey owed AIB £1.14 million and the bank was pressing for the enormous debt to be repaid. To put Haughey's debt into context, the bank was making post-tax profits of around £28 million a year at that time.

Haughey had basically bullied AIB into allowing this situation to develop and continue, warning them in 1976 that he could prove to be 'a very troublesome adversary'. Two years later his debt was almost £600,000, large enough to be considered by the AIB board, but the bank exhibited what a quarter of a century later the Moriarty Tribunal would describe as 'a marked deference in its attitude to Mr Haughey'.

A few days after becoming Taoiseach, Haughey told property developer Patrick Gallagher – son of Matt Gallagher – that he needed £750,000 to clear his debts.

The issue was finally sorted in January 1980 when Traynor negotiated a deal whereby of the £1.14 million owed, AIB would settle for a payment of £750,000 within weeks and a further £110,000 to be paid within a reasonable period of time. In return, AIB agreed to hand back the title deeds of Abbeville.

The £750,000 was paid to the bank by means of three bank drafts all drawn on Guinness & Mahon, where Traynor was a senior figure. Needless to say, the remaining £110,000 was never paid.

Patrick Gallagher, whose business empire would collapse three years later and who was sent to prison in Northern Ireland for fraud, had stumped up £300,000 of the £750,000 needed by Haughey – purportedly for an option on 35 acres of land at Abbeville which was never exercised. Other benefactors, never identified, came up with the rest.

It was around this time that Haughey addressed the nation on television saying, 'As a community we are living way beyond our means.' In retrospect, the hypocrisy was breathtaking.

Thanks to the investigations of the Moriarty Tribunal, we now know that between 1979 and 1996 – during which period Haughey was Taoiseach for over seven years – he lived a lifestyle and incurred expenses far beyond the scale of his public service remuneration, which was his sole apparent income. 'This was primarily enabled by the bill-paying service set in place for Mr Haughey by Mr Desmond Traynor.' The tribunal's report on Haughey added:

After Mr Haughey first became Taoiseach at the end of 1979, the borrowings receded and the funds were derived primarily from clandestine donations and recourse to the [Fianna Fáil] Leader's Allowance Account, including not merely accounts of public monies, but money intended for the medical expenses of the late Brian Lenihan.

Moriarty dismissed the former Taoiseach's claim that he knew virtually nothing of his financial arrangements and described some of his evidence as 'unbelievable'.

The report also said that the acceptance by Haughey of 'secretive, opaque' large-scale personal donations – frequently involving off-shore vehicles – when governments led by him were championing austerity 'can only be said to have devalued the quality of a modern democracy'.

The tribunal identified that Haughey had received over €11.5 million (the equivalent of up to €45 million in today's money) in funds during this 17-year period and that excluded his income/pension from political life.

While Haughey's supporters insisted he had done nothing in return for this largesse, Moriarty did not agree. The tribunal concluded that in return for payments from Ben Dunne, Haughey 'acted with a view to intervening improperly in a pending tax case of great magnitude'.

At the time Revenue was seeking £38.8 million in capital gains tax from the Dunne family trust. As the newly elected Taoiseach in 1987, Haughey asked the then Revenue chairman, Seamus Pairceir, to meet Dunne. Revenue's approach to Dunnes Stores then changed and this crystallised in an offer to settle for £16 million. In the event, Dunne won an appeal with the appeals commissioner.

Moriarty found that the terms of the settlement offered to Dunnes Stores constituted a 'valuable and substantial' benefit to Dunne 'directly consequent on Mr Haughey's actions, irrespective of how matters ultimately unfolded'. The tribunal concluded:

> [A]t a time when the finances of the State were under extreme pressure, Mr Haughey, as the head of the government, had a particular duty to maintain the paramountcy of Revenue in collecting taxes, and this ought to have been reflected in a studious avoidance of unnecessary contact as opposed to his persistence in advertising to Revenue his interest in Dunne's affairs so as to signal his support for a radical reduction in the amount of tax being demanded by the Revenue.

Moriarty said that in the evidence given to the tribunal, while there was an acknowledgment of much diligence and capability in the manner in which Haughey discharged his duties, there were also 'elements of fear and domination engendered by him in individuals in both private and public sectors'.

The tribunal threw further light on where Haughey's money had come from. It uncovered two loan accounts in Guinness & Mahon in the early 1980s in the name of businessman P.V. Doyle. These were applied exclusively for Haughey's benefit and constituted payments to Haughey amounting to over £300,000.

It found that Haughey directed the granting of an Irish passport to a Lebanese girl in 1989 because of her connection to Mahmoud Fustok (see Chapter 12), who gave £50,000 to Haughey in 1985.

It revealed that Haughey used the leader's allowance account, which was supposed to be for Fianna Fáil's parliamentary expenses, to meet his personal expenditures in places such as Le Coq Hardi restaurant in Dublin and the Parisian shirt-making firm Charvet.

Perhaps most damaging of all was the tribunal's finding that Haughey 'personally misappropriated' donations to a fund set up to finance medical treatment in the United States for his old ally Brian Lenihan. Haughey 'deliberately sought to raise funds in addition to what he knew, or must have known, was required to meet the cost of Mr Lenihan's treatment'. As much as £265,000 may have been collected for Lenihan's benefit, but only £70,000 went towards the cost of his medical treatment in the US, with Haughey misappropriating for his personal use a sizeable proportion of the excess funds collected.

He also retained £85,000 of £160,000 in donations made by

two well-known businessmen to Fianna Fáil in the run-up to the 1989 general election – using the opportunities provided by the raising of funds for the election campaign to 'advance his personal finances'.

It emerged that after his retirement from public life, businessman Dermot Desmond made two sterling payments to Haughey: one for £100,000 in 1994 and another for £25,000 in 1996. The tribunal said these:

> ... followed in the path of an established pattern of support by Mr Desmond of the business ventures of Mr Haughey's family and they further followed the conferring of an indirect benefit of £75,456 on Mr Haughey by Mr Desmond, through the financing of the refit of the Haughey family yacht, *Celtic Mist*, all of which occurred during Mr Haughey's tenure as Taoiseach.

The tribunal concluded that while only a limited number of decision made by Haughey to facilitate donors had been identified, this did not mean that all his other acts or decision in public life were 'devoid of infirmity' – legal speak for a moral flaw or failing.

Even if the tribunal had found there was no 'infirmity' in his acts in public life, Haughey was still left hopelessly compromised by being a kept man for his political career.

The contrast between the frugality and simplicity of his predecessors and his delusions of grandeur are best illustrated in a story told to leading political journalist, Stephen Collins. In Paris at a European Union summit in 1982, Haughey summoned Foreign Minister Brian Lenihan, press officer Frank Dunlop, special adviser Pádraig Ó hAnnracháin and some civil servants to accompany him on a mystery outing, which turned out to be a visit to the Charvet shop.

The manager of the shop made quite a fuss of 'Monsieur Prime Minister' and ordered staff to start loading boxes into the car. Haughey explained to his entourage that the boxes contained shirts. One asked how he could be sure they were the right size, to which Haughey replied, 'They have a bust of me here.' When the manager looked quizzically towards the rest of the group, Haughey responded, 'My security people.'

Ó hAnnracháin got back into the second car outside and good humouredly quipped to his colleagues, 'Would you credit it? The little shite from Donnycarney.'

The same 'little shite from Donnycarney' never wore a watch – if he needed to know the time he asked a minion who was expected to respond immediately.

1982 is also remembered as the year of 'GUBU'. The year when the most-wanted man in the country, Malcolm Macarthur, was apprehended in the home of the Attorney General (who was unaware that Macarthur was a fugitive). Haughey described the strange series of events as 'grotesque, unbelievable, bizarre and unprecedented', to which Conor Cruise O'Brien applied the acronym 'GUBU'.

But it would not be until Haughey's government collapsed that a fuller picture would emerge of what was going on behind the scenes, such as the tapping of two leading political journalists' phones. Seán Doherty, who was a controversial Justice Minister during that short-lived government, took the fall for the phone taps, but there was enormous pressure on Haughey and it appeared that his enemies in the party would finally be able to overthrow him.

An internal Fianna Fáil committee of inquiry into the phone tapping affair cleared Haughey. David Andrews, who later described the inquiry as a farce, refused to go along with this, issuing his own minority report in which he said Doherty's phone taps had been motivated by 'internal party considerations rather than by considerations of national security' and suggested that Haughey should take ultimate responsibility for the whole affair.

A fierce lobbying campaign by his supporters saw Haughey once again defy the odds and scrape through. Despite everything that had emerged, the vast majority of the Fianna Fáil rank and file party members wanted him to stay.

The three challenges to Haughey's leadership in the early 1980s took their toll on everyone. The party organisation reacted almost hysterically to every challenge and there were stories of threats, intimidation and inducements. The pressure was enormous, with a number of Fianna Fáil TDs suffering physical collapse under the strain.

After the attempted heave in November 1982 Jim Gibbons was punched by a member of a crowd of angry Haughey supporters. Charlie McCreevy was chased across the car park, kicked and jostled and called a 'bastard' and a 'Blueshirt'.

One story from the time speaks volumes about the atmosphere within the party. Martin O'Donoghue was dropped from the cabinet in 1979 when Haughey took over as Taoiseach. A couple of days later he received a special delivery at his home. When he and his wife opened the parcel, they found two dead ducks inside along with a short message from Haughey: 'Shot on my estate this morning.' Understandably enough, O'Donoghue regarded this as both a bad joke and a menacing gesture.

By the mid-1980s Haughey was finally in control of Fianna Fáil. Colley had died and Des O'Malley was expelled from the organisation for refusing to vote with the party against the government's Family Planning Bill. O'Malley's speech on the night he abstained was one of the most powerful ever heard in the Dáil:

> The politics of this would be very easy. The politics would be to be one of the lads, the safest way in Ireland. But I do not believe that the interests of this state or our constitution and of this Republic would be served by putting politics before conscience in regard to this. There is a choice of a kind that can only be answered by saying that I stand by the Republic and accordingly, I will not oppose this Bill.

But the rest of Fianna Fáil opted for the more narrow, blinkered Republicanism of Haughey.

Two years later Haughey was back as Taoiseach for a five-year spell that started impressively, but in its final stages re-raised all the old question marks about his character.

A series of business scandals broke, which led to claims of a 'Golden Circle' involving people with whom Haughey had an association. At a parliamentary party meeting, Seán Power told Haughey, 'The people of Ireland are disgusted with the scandals and the relationship you, Taoiseach, have with some of the people at the centre of those scandals.' Haughey was not used to being spoken to like that.

Haughey won a no-confidence motion put down by Power. At the parliamentary meeting to vote on the confidence motion, Albert Reynolds – by now Haughey's clear rival for the leadership – claimed that a prominent business associate of Haughey's had tried to dig up dirt on Reynolds' business dealings in the Midlands. He also alleged that people in a white Hiace van had conducted surveillance of his house in Longford and that a man was seen acting suspiciously near his Dublin apartment. Two backbenchers also claimed their phones were being tapped.

Yet again Haughey survived the vote, but his past was about to finally catch up with him. It later emerged that a week after this no-confidence vote, supermarket magnate Ben Dunne famously handed Haughey three bank drafts worth £210,000, saying, 'Look, that is something for yourself.' The gesture prompted the then Taoiseach to respond with the now immortal words, 'Thanks, big fella' (see Chapter 11).

Haughey was now widely seen as a liability. Labour Party leader Dick Spring lacerated him in the Dáil, likening him to a virus causing a 'cancer on the body politic'. The political end came in early 1992, when Doherty went on RTÉ television's *Nighthawks* programme and told the nation that Haughey had known about and indeed authorised the phone tappings of the early 1980s. Haughey, aware there were other skeletons in the cupboard, jumped before he was pushed.

*   *   *

If Haughey had hopes of a quiet, dignified retirement where he could enjoy the usual mellowing of public opinion towards departed public figures, they would be shattered a few short years later. The dark secret of his personal finances finally came into the public domain because of a massive row in the Dunne family (see Chapter 11). Payments to Haughey were mentioned in affidavits that were part of the litigation.

The *Sunday Tribune* was the first to break the story about the references to a senior Fianna Fáil figure in the affidavit, creating the momentum for the establishment of the McCracken Tribunal to investigate payments by Dunne to Haughey and to a former Fine Gael minister Michael Lowry.

It emerged that Dunne had paid Haughey more than £1 million, the majority of it routed through Cayman Islands banker John Furze, an associate of Traynor. This evidence revealed for the first time the existence of the Ansbacher accounts.

Haughey's reputation and his legacy, which he dearly valued, were in tatters. The revelations about his extravagant private life, the £16,000 a year spent on Charvet shirts, the expensive dinners at top restaurants funded by party money, and the many millions he had received from various benefactors and businesspeople would change the public perception of him forever. Protestors lobbing coins at him during his appearance at the subsequent Moriarty Tribunal replaced the adoration of the masses at ardfheiseanna.

Charges of obstructing the work of that tribunal were suspended indefinitely on the grounds that he could not get a fair trial. But in the court of public opinion, Haughey was tried and found guilty – unfortunately in the eyes of many, so too was the entire political system.

Some of Haughey's advocates have suggested that history may well judge him more kindly. That is nonsense.

It will recall his many achievements, not least his belated role in laying the foundations for the Celtic Tiger when his minority government of 1987 finally took decisive action on the public finances. Undoubtedly, he was a politician of enormous intelligence, imagination and vision, but that only emphasises the lost opportunity.

Garret FitzGerald said Haughey had the potential to become one of the best Taoisigh the country ever had. However, his preoccupation with wealth and power clouded his judgement, and ultimately this is what history will focus on.

Haughey was a crooked politician who used his position as Taoiseach to confer favours on donors who made secret payments to him. Horrifying and all as the Moriarty Tribunal report was, we only know a fraction of the complete story. For example, who other than Patrick Gallagher came up with the money to settle with AIB back in 1980?

Haughey was in possession of information that would have been very valuable for some of his benefactors relating to, for example, currency devaluations or budgetary measures. We do not know if he ever misused this information, but his actions in taking millions means it is impossible to entirely dismiss the possibility.

He was fatally compromised. Given what we now know about his debts with AIB, Ansbacher and his relationship with Gallagher and other developers, how as Taoiseach could he have been expected to act against AIB over the DIRT scandal or clamp down on tax evasion? How can we expect ordinary citizens not to think the worst of why Gallagher was never brought to justice here, as happened in Northern Ireland, or of why governments Haughey was part of oversaw the destruction of Dublin during the 1960s and 70s?

Other politicians who served at that time and took money from businesspeople – Ray Burke, Pádraig Flynn, Bertie Ahern and numerous other TDs and councillors – are accountable for their own actions. Haughey's role in creating that culture, however, cannot be underestimated.

But Ireland is also compromised for allowing Haughey to become Taoiseach, despite his fatal flaws as a politician and despite what it knew about the arms trial and what it suspected about the funding of his lifestyle. The mansion, the private island, the yacht, the fine suits could not be supported on a politician's salary.

There were some media reports over the years that deserved greater investigation. Nobody, or very few, wanted to know.

In five general elections under Haughey's leadership,

Fianna Fáil won between 44 and 48 per cent of the popular vote, a figure his successors have never come close to.

And what is deeply ironic is that the people Haughey most appealed to were conservative and devoutly Catholic. Haughey's lifestyle was the antithesis of their values, but they adored him and were almost magnetically drawn to him and his brand of tribal, nationalistic politics.

It is pretty much inarguable that Haughey could only have been successful in a country where many people have a deep ambivalence to politics and the law. It is doubtful whether in modern times a politician with so many question marks surrounding him could become US President or British Prime Minister. But the reality in Ireland was that those who were in a position to know what was going on looked the other way. And large numbers either did not want to know or did not care either way.

Tragically, for Haughey personally and for Ireland generally, the fears inside and outside Fianna Fáil that he would corrupt the standards of public life if he obtained power proved to be entirely justified. If anything, even his biggest critics underestimated what he was capable of.

It is this ambivalence to the normal everyday rules that is central to the mess that Ireland finds itself in after the economic meltdown of the late 2000s. It is a cliché that a country gets the politicians it deserves, but in this case, it has more than a ring of truth. On four separate occasions, Haughey was elected Taoiseach and that says more about Ireland than Irish people might wish to acknowledge.

10

BANKING ON THE STATE

Garret FitzGerald had taken to his bed. It was Friday 8 March 1985 and the Taoiseach had a serious dose of the flu. The night was closing in when there was a knock on the door of his home on Palmerston Road in the Dublin suburb of Rathmines. At the door were his two senior lieutenants, Finance Minister Alan Dukes and the Trade Minister John Bruton. They wore faces as long as that on the suffering Taoiseach. Their tidings had the potential to completely undermine the state's shaky financial edifice.

Earlier that day executives in Allied Irish Bank (AIB) had dropped a bombshell on the Department of Finance. The bank was no longer willing to prop up its insurance subsidiary, ICI, which was haemorrhaging millions of pounds. It was going to allow the insurance company to go to the wall.

While such a decision on the face of it might be deemed a matter for a private company, there were far higher stakes at play. AIB had a major exposure to international institutional investors. If the bank was to default on its obligations to ICI, the investors would in all likelihood run for cover, leaving AIB open to possible collapse. That in turn might threaten the financial stability of the state. AIB put it up to the government. Save us to save the country. Hand over the money.

His conversation with Dukes and Bruton left FitzGerald feeling even worse than before. He had little choice. The state would have to take control of ICI. Taxpayers would have to clean up the mess created by buccaneering bankers, whose pursuit of profit had lurched into craven recklessness. It was time for a bail-out. It was time to ignore the most basic rules of capitalism and intervene to save the poster boys for that very philosophy, the banking sector.

* * *

The Insurance Corporation of Ireland (ICI) had a long and largely distinguished history by 1981 when AIB took a stake in it. Established in the 1930s, it grew out of a company that provided marine insurance for merchant shipping. Gradual and prudent expansion saw it grow to a position in 1980 in which it was the second largest non-life insurer in the state. It had offices in Britain, North America and Australia. The British operation was about to move into a higher gear.

ICI was a perfect fit for a bank eager for expansion. The concept of a one-stop shop for financial products was not yet common, but AIB saw the insurance company as ideal for drawing in customers.

In 1981 AIB bought a 25 per cent stake in ICI for £10.5 million. Little thought appears to have been invested in how best to run an insurance company. The commercial possibilities were obvious, but what was not apparent to the bank executives was that running an insurance company was entirely different from running a bank.

The next move was forced on AIB. In July 1983 a US insurance firm with an 8 per cent share in ICI decided to cash in its chips. The selling of the stake presented problems for AIB. If an aggressive or predatory company bought into ICI, then the bank's position might be threatened. The only sensible move was for the bank to buy up the extra stake itself. In doing so, however, it crossed the 29 per cent threshold above which – the stock market deems – a company must be bought outright.

The bank had to move quickly. Due diligence of ICI was carried out prior to the takeover. The due diligence would come to be hugely significant. In September 1983 ICI became a wholly owned subsidiary of AIB.

Meanwhile, at the coalface of the insurance industry, far away from the corporate manoeuvring, business appeared to be booming. ICI's London office in particular was showing tremendous results, amounting to half of ICI's gross revenue. The manager of the office, John Grace, was expanding the business at a rate of knots. He was a gregarious character who enjoyed the high life, particularly when he was being entertained by brokers.

Grace aggressively went on the trail of high-risk business, such as insuring fairground attractions and circuses. These were the kind of operations that usually found it difficult to get insurance, and as a result the premium income was high, relative to other sectors. Of course the risk of having to pay out was also high, but that was for another day, one that may not even arrive.

Back in AIB head office in Dublin, all the executives could see winging its way over from London was the bottom line. But the never never was looming on the horizon.

A downturn in the insurance market affected ICI in a particularly bad way. The company had meagre cash reserves and the high-risk business that Grace had brought in began to require serious payouts. In 1983 the company suffered a loss of

£63 million, of which £50 million was attributable to the London office.

AIB as a whole had pre-tax profits of £85 million in 1983. ICI, therefore, had effectively gobbled up two-thirds of the bank's profits. Less than a year after assuming full ownership of the company, AIB began to recognise its folly.

In July 1984 the Department of Trade, Commerce and Tourism examined the books of ICI. What the officials saw was far from reassuring and a meeting was set up with AIB management. The civil servants were told that things were fine and the company was well capable of trading out of its difficulties.

By the autumn, however, it was apparent that the problems were not going away. Rumours of the ill health of ICI swept through the business community. The influential *Business & Finance* magazine published an investigation into the company in November under the headline, 'The Can of Worms at ICI'.

The same month, executives at AIB and ICI met with Minister Bruton. They were led by Gerry Scanlan, the recently appointed chief executive of the bank. They told Bruton that 'corrective measures were being taken to rectify matters', as the minister later reported. His department had hired actuaries after the July meeting, and they reported that the bank would be able to ship the losses at ICI. Still, the money kept pouring out. The insurance company was literally bleeding its parent dry.

The following March the bank took the decision to abandon ICI. By then, AIB had spent £86 million in acquiring and shoring up the insurance company. In separate meetings with the Central Bank and the Department of Finance on 8 March 1985, bank executives told of what they intended.

The implications were immediately obvious to the civil

servants. Either the state stepped in or the bank might go to the wall, dragging the precariously balanced finances of the country with it. The choice facing the government was stark. Let the market take its course, allow ICI to fail and offer up prayers to St Jude that AIB would not follow. Or, commit as yet unquantifiable millions of taxpayers' money to discharging ICI's debts and to save AIB from catastrophe.

∗ ∗ ∗

Within a week of being appraised of the situation, FitzGerald's government acted to save ICI. The company would be bought by the state for a nominal sum.

The politicians were furious at being placed in a corner by the bank. During the Dáil debate to introduce the requisite legislation on 27 March, Bruton gave vent to his feelings. Some of what he had to say was prescient in light of the later scandals to engulf AIB in particular and banking in general:

It is almost incomprehensible and more than a little disquieting that it apparently took so long for senior management in both ICI and AIB to begin to realise that there might be fundamental problems with the London branch operations of the insurance company, which after all accounted for about 70 per cent of total business in gross terms. This is even more difficult to understand when one considers that problems had arisen within the head office operations of ICI in Ireland, and corrective measures were taken during 1984.

The facts are far from clear even at this stage, and it is difficult to say how much of the London branch's problems arose while AIB were a minority shareholder and how much actually arose during

1984, at which stage ICI were under the full control and ownership of AIB. It is obvious that a serious lack of management control, particularly in relation to the flow of information between London and Dublin, contributed in no small measure to the present problem. If the problem had been spotted and the position established at an earlier date, then the magnitude of the present difficulties would not be as great.

Bruton went on to comment on how the affair reflected on general corporate governance in the banking industry, something which would be at issue repeatedly over the following decades:

The problems which have come to light in this case clearly raise the most serious questions about the role of management, directors, shareholders and of auditors of companies.

The chain of responsibility is clear. The primary responsibility for ensuring the satisfactory conduct of company affairs lies with the shareholders and is exercised through the directors and management of the company. The secondary responsibility for the correct presentation of the financial activities and standing of any company rests on the auditors.

The response of the leader of the opposition, Charles Haughey, would be repeated after the property bubble collapsed in the late 2000s. Haughey, of course, had a greater knowledge of banks and how they dealt with clients thanks to his own considerable dealings with them, both legitimate and illegitimate:

It would be an absurdity, an unacceptable injustice and totally ridiculous if the general public, the great majority of whom have never benefited one iota from banking profits and many of whom have had very unhappy experiences at the hands of bankers, were asked to step in and take up an additional burden because of someone else's mistakes – mistakes made in this very specially privileged sector of our economy.

And so the state came to the rescue. In what was a game of chicken between the government and the executives of AIB, the government blinked first.

Hindsight would one day look unfavourably on the government for not taking a stake in the bank and tying the fortunes of AIB to the state. After all, if the state was bailing out this private entity, surely, under the basic rules of capitalism, it was entitled to a reward for its risk.

Other incidents during the crisis showed where exactly the bankers stood. On the night of 15 March, when the deal for the state takeover was arranged with the government, AIB hosted a celebratory drinks party in its headquarters. While it is understandable that there was relief, the optics showed a different situation. Bankers were celebrating the rescue of their fortunes by the taxpayers of a state that was itself on the brink of insolvency.

The day before the deal was announced, Scanlan bought 50,000 shares in the bank. In the two days that followed the announcement, the AIB share price rose by 25 per cent, delivering a tidy profit to the chief executive. Scanlan denied that he had done anything improper. He said he had told the AIB chairman, Niall Crowley, about the planned purchase and the bank's board had signalled its approval.

The stock exchange also accepted that Scanlan's dealings

were above board. Whether such questionable activity on the market would be accepted in today's world is a moot point.

Around the same time, AIB released its annual results for 1984. The strapped bank that had gone cap in hand to the government made a tidy £84 million for the year, coincidentally nearly the same amount it had ploughed into ICI. Despite its disastrous investment, the bank was now free to start out again with a clean slate. The taxpayers were stepping in to stump up for the losses.

The main cost to the exchequer was the advancement of interest-free loans to cover some of the losses. Then, in 1992, Des O'Malley changed the terms on which the bail-out had been offered to the bank. He wanted the bank to contribute more. He refused to issue AIB with an insurance licence until it agreed to put another £170 million towards the costs of winding up ICI.

O'Malley's intervention certainly saved huge sums for the taxpayers. In 1997 Professor Patrick Honohan – who would be appointed Governor of the Central Bank in 2009 – estimated that the cost of the bail-out was around £400 million. Of this, the state only had to bear £34 million. The remainder was paid by AIB through a bank levy and from the accountants who had done due diligence of ICI prior to AIB purchasing it.

In the end, the state did not get as bad a deal as was originally feared, although it could legitimately be asked why taxpayers were forced to contribute anything towards a highly profitable public company.

Irrespective of the fact that AIB bore a relatively significant portion of the cost, the overriding feature of the episode was that when the bank got into trouble, the state came to its rescue. If a private company, and particularly a bank, knows that it has this safety net, then the concept of risk is eliminated.

Any venture to make money thereafter is simply a case of heads the bank wins, tails the taxpayers lose.

Under such circumstances it might be reasonable to assume that some gratitude to the state would be in order. The following year, 1986, the banks in general, and AIB in particular, had an opportunity to show their gratitude.

* * *

For many years, officials in the Revenue Commissioners and the Department of Finance had concerns about the system whereby bank depositors were obliged to declare the interest earned on their money for tax purposes. Tax was due on the interest, as it was considered to be earnings. Many depositors ignored their obligation to report the earnings and pay tax on it.

In 1986 Dukes introduced new legislation that put the onus onto the banks to collect a new deposit interest retention tax (DIRT). From then on, banks would deduct the tax due at source and hand it over to the Revenue.

One category of depositor was exempt from the tax. Anybody living overseas and opening an account in the jurisdiction of the Republic was classified as a non-resident account holder. Traditionally, due to decades of emigration, there had been a large number of non-resident account holders.

Non-resident accounts were usually owned by Irish emigrants who returned home frequently or perhaps had a business interest in Ireland. The ranks of emigrant account holders were about to swell beyond all comprehension.

Pretty quickly, depositors copped on to how to avoid paying DIRT. Those lodging money – anybody from a person running a small business to a wealthy professional – simply deposited the cash in an account bearing an overseas address. In a country where everybody knew the local bank manager, it was even possible to ascribe a fictitious name to the account. Thus, DIRT was avoided.

There was another, greater attraction to setting up a bogus non-resident account. The money deposited therein would be beyond the reach of the Revenue Commissioners. Therefore, non-taxed income, or hot money, could just disappear into the bogus account, available to the whims of the depositor, but beyond the scrutiny of the tax inspector.

In effect, throughout the 1980s and into the 1990s there was a two-tier tax system for most earners in the country. There was the PAYE sector and those businesspeople who were wholly tax compliant, and then there were those who were shovelling large amounts of their earnings into bogus non-resident accounts. Of course, there were also the gold-plated scammers who were facilitated with offshore accounts in the Ansbacher bank run by Haughey's bagman, Des Traynor (see Chapter 9).

Undertaking this homespun scam would not have been possible without co-operation, and in many instances guidance, from banking personnel. And so the banks – with AIB to the fore – became involved in one of the greatest tax evasion schemes known to the state.

Instead of undertaking their legal duty to collect tax from their customers, the banks colluded in a massive tax evasion scam that not only deprived the state of DIRT, but hid hundreds of millions of pounds in taxable income from the Revenue Commissioners.

This scam was at its height at a time when Ireland was barely solvent, and major cutbacks to services such as health care caused serious hardship, pain and even the deaths of many citizens. There was no money in the state coffers to provide adequate services and at the same time tens of thousands of 'citizens' were evading their obligation to pay their way.

Who bore culpability within the banks for this scam? In the first instance, the teller, and more often the manager, of the local branch was the facilitator. Most customers received assistance in completing the non-resident forms and in some instances a bank employee even supplied the false address.

Branch managers were themselves under major pressure to boost business. If one made an ethical or moral stand and refused to go along with the scam, he or she would not be long for the world of banking.

When the scam was uncovered, the senior executives all claimed to be largely ignorant or even powerless to stop what was going on, but all the evidence suggests there was a culture of seeing, hearing and speaking no evil on the matter.

Everybody knew what was afoot, but little discussion was had about it. The senior executives just accepted the bottom line. Business was booming. No questions were asked. Whether or not the bankers were aware of it, they were operating in a culture of effective impunity.

An internal Revenue Commissioners memo issued in July 1986 directed tax inspectors not to ask banks for declaration forms on non-resident accounts pending 'further instructions'. This memo, known as SIM 263, meant there was little prospect of a forensic audit of the non-resident forms. The author of the memo has never been discovered.

One man in banking who began asking questions was the internal auditor of AIB, Tony Spollen. He first became aware of the issue following an inquiry in the UK into its equivalent of DIRT in 1989. That inquiry by the British Inland Revenue discovered a number of non-resident accounts were bogus. As

# #

a result, AIB was forced to pay £3.7 million sterling on the bogus accounts held in its British branches.

The British inquiry sparked some interest among bank executives in Dublin. One senior executive, Henry O'Brien, penned an internal memo to Spollen:

> I feel decidedly uncomfortable about the position in the Republic of Ireland. When DIRT was first introduced there was a move to clean up the situation, but then word went round the branch system that Revenue would not exercise their rights to review the position at branches and progress more or less ceased.
>
> We carried out a 100 per cent sample at a number of branches and the outcome was disconcerting. In general there is not a major problem in Dublin or the east coast area but from West Cork to Donegal the position is bad in a large number of branches.

O'Brien acknowledged that any serious efforts to clean up the system would likely lead to a 'loss of deposits'. But Spollen was a highly principled man who saw his duty to his office as superseding any loyalty to the institution. He forwarded the letter to the bank's finance director. Later, the chief executive, Gerry Scanlan, would say he had not been informed of this potential crisis situation.

Spollen continued to investigate the matter. He did the sums and found that for one six-month period the bank had a potential DIRT liability of £10 million. If correct, it meant that AIB was facing an overall bill of nightmare proportions.

An internal examination of the bank's non-resident accounts found that of 87,000 such accounts, around 53,000 were bogus. These bogus accounts contained roughly £600 million. While the bank had no obligation to investigate the origins of the money held, it would not have taken a genius to work out that most of that money was being hidden from the Revenue Commissioners. Spollen's overall estimate was that the bank was sitting on a potential DIRT liability of £100 million.

In 1991 the bank fell under the impression that the state was about to do it another favour. At a meeting in the bank's headquarters on 13 February, a senior Revenue inspector, Tony McCarthy, met with bank executives. The bankers would later claim that McCarthy told them, or at least indicated, that there would be a general amnesty over the bogus non-resident accounts. According to the bankers, McCarthy's offer was that if the banks cleaned up the system, there would be no tax sought on interest accruing before April 1990.

McCarthy vehemently disputed that he had offered any amnesty. 'A settlement wasn't even on the agenda, or on my mind,' he later told an inquiry into the matter. 'An amnesty wasn't even within my remit.' Crucially, there was not one scrap of paper originating in Revenue to suggest that an amnesty had been offered.

Within the bank, Spollen continued to make waves. He corresponded with the internal auditor for the Irish operations, Don Walsh. 'Please quantify immediately the amount of false Form F [the non-resident application form] money on the books of the group. The estimate (£350m – £450m) is frightening.'

Scanlan would later tell an Oireachtas inquiry that he had little knowledge of Spollen's serious concerns. For a man who was earning a fortune running the biggest bank in the state, Scanlan seems not to have been clued in to the potential financial disaster facing his organisation.

Eventually, Spollen had to go. There would be some dispute

in later years over the exact reason for his departure, with Spollen claiming he was eased out because of the awkward issues he raised. The bank always denied this contention, but there is no doubt that his capacity to raise uncomfortable (but entirely valid) questions for the bank did not sit easily with the prevailing culture.

The bogus non-resident account scandal may have rested there, remaining dormant for the rest of eternity. However, on 4 April 1998 the *Sunday Independent* published a front-page story based on Spollen's 1991 report estimating the bank's potential liability at £100 million. Reporter Liam Collins had managed to get his hands on material that was dynamite.

A report into the matter was compiled by the Comptroller and Auditor General. It largely vindicated the position that Spollen had adopted. It also opened the eyes of PAYE workers to what had been going on in a secret economy during the lean years.

The report revealed that every financial institution in the country had been operating the bogus accounts. ACC, for instance, the state-run bank used primarily by farmers, was involved. In fact, three ACC employees, based respectively in Tallaght, Tullamore and Tuam, had opened bogus non-resident accounts themselves. The bank eventually coughed up £17 million, which was based on an initial liability of £1.5 million.

Following the publication of the report, the Dáil's Committee of Public Accounts (PAC) began hearings into the matter in August 1999. Over the following six weeks various bankers and politicians were grilled about their knowledge of what had gone on during the 1980s and 1990s.

Five Ministers for Finance were questioned. All claimed to have no knowledge of what was afoot, either in their overseeing of financial policy or in their role as the nominal shareholder of ACC. The PAC report would eventually conclude, 'None of the [finance] ministers appear to have discharged their responsibility for the ACC in an appropriate manner.'

The PAC hearings were televised live on TG4, and provided not a little satisfaction to the general public, who were pleased to see bankers being exposed to the glare of forensic questioning on their activities.

Scanlan remained defiant, largely relying on the defence that he saw, spoke or heard no evil. 'I wouldn't be wasting my time dealing with areas where I had competent management to deal with them and to whom responsibility had been delegated,' he told the inquiry.

He did not accept Spollen's estimate of the potential liability in the 1991 report. 'I have long since concluded that £100 million is total fiction,' he told the committee. 'The only way it [compiling the estimate] could have been done was to go into the branches and examine every single deposit.'

At one stage, Scanlan claimed that the amnesty that the bank alleged it was offered took place at a football match. When McCarthy angrily rejected the allegation, Scanlan withdrew it. (Scanlan was later exposed as one of six bankers who had benefited from a tax evasion offshore vehicle known as Faldor. In 2006, he settled with the revenue for 206,000 euros as a result of his involvement with the company.)

Scanlan's opposite number in Bank of Ireland at the height of the operation of the bogus accounts was Mark Hely-Hutchinson. He came under questioning from committee member Pat Rabbitte TD about how bank employees had assisted customers, in this case farmers, in filling out Form F.

'Have you ever seen a livestock headage payment?' Rabbitte asked. The banker said he had not. 'Well, you can take it from me, they are immensely complex. How is it that the same farmer who manages to fill in an application form for a headage payment has a difficulty with a non-resident form?'

Hely Hutchinson replied, 'Well, if he is a farmer, which means by definition he is a resident, part of his difficulty might be that he doesn't quite know what answers he ought to make sure that he evades the tax.' The answer brazenly acknowledged that bank officials were assisting with tax evasion.

Following the publication of the report in 2000, the Revenue Commissioners went after the banks for money owed. In total, €225 million was recovered from 25 financial institutions, including €133 million in penalties. By 2006, the total amounts collected from the holders of non-resident accounts was €840 million.

Even allowing for a high proportion of interest and penalties, this was a major tax evasion scam and it was facilitated by the banks. Once again, however, there was nobody to blame.

Once again, the state had been taken for a fool. Not one bank executive was deemed responsible for the scam. There was a bill to pay but it was small beer compared with the profits the banks were making in what was by then a booming economy. In 2000, for example, AIB's pre-tax profits amounted to €1.25 billion.

The PAC report into the DIRT scandal set out what was at the root of the problem: 'a particularly close and inappropriate relationship between banking and the state and its agencies ... [which] were perhaps too mindful of the concerns of the banks and too attentive to their pleas and lobbying'.

The message was clear. The banks were too big to fail.

They knew that they could act with impunity when it came to pursuing the highest profits attainable.

* * *

This was the background against which the property-related bubble was blown for most of the first decade of the new century in Ireland. Banks lent at will because the concept of risk was a notional one.

Central Bank figures show that property-related loans between 2002 and 2007 increased by 43 per cent. In the same period, bank profits went through the roof. Once again, AIB was the leading light. By 2007 its profits had increased to €2.5 billion, around half of which was attributable to the Irish market.

Warnings were issued, but largely ignored, along the way. In 2004 the Central Bank warned that the rapid increase of credit 'would give rise to serious problems before too long'. The following year it stepped up its concern: 'The construction sector now accounts for nearly 13 per cent of total employment, an exceptionally high fraction by international standards.'

Nobody heeded the warnings, least of all the banks. Meanwhile, in the United States a similar bubble was about to burst. When it did, Ireland was ill-equipped to deal with the fallout.

The world began to change in September 2008. In the first week of the month, the US mortgage providers Fannie Mae and Freddie Mac were nationalised. If left to their own devices these institutions would have collapsed, with horrendous consequences for millions of homeowners.

A week later, on 15 September, the merchant bank Lehman Brothers did collapse. The US government decided not to intervene. The market was allowed, in this case, to be the final arbitrator. If Lehman had been nationalised, the right-wing strain in business and government would have derided creeping nationalism. In retrospect, nationalisation would probably have been the correct course of action.

The panic that was engulfing Wall Street spread across the world like a pandemic flu. In Ireland, the illusion of a boom built on sound fundamentals was coming apart. Irish banks began reaping the whirlwind. Billions of euro took flight from Irish banks in the two weeks after Lehman's collapse. Investors began shying away from them, fearful that their solvency levels were plunging.

On 29 September shares in Ireland's main financial institutions tumbled dangerously. AIB lost 15 per cent, Bank of Ireland was down 17 per cent and Anglo Irish Bank fell a whopping 46 per cent. Rumours began circulating that Anglo Irish would not open for business the following day. It was time to go to the government once more with the mantra first used during the ICI debacle: save us to save yourselves.

Phone calls were made from the main banks to Government Buildings. The top bank honchos required an urgent meeting.

Some time after 9.00 p.m. four of Ireland's leading bankers made their way into Government Buildings. AIB's chairman, Dermot Gleeson, and chief executive, Eugene Sheehy, were joined by their counterparts in Bank of Ireland, Richard Burrows and Brian Goggin.

They were brought into the Taoiseach's office for a meeting with Brian Cowen and his Minister for Finance, Brian Lenihan. The two politicians said little as they listened to the bad tidings. Both banks claimed that they had enough cash to trade for a few weeks only. The rate at which money was flowing out of the system meant that they would soon be insolvent. The consequences for the Irish economy were not worth thinking about if the top two banks went bust.

AIB's Sheehy later recalled the character of the meeting. 'Our interest in stability and the government's would have been very much aligned. That meant staying open for business.' Sound familiar? AIB was once again putting it up to the government: if you let us fall, we will take the whole economy crashing down with us.

When the bankers finished pleading, they were asked to wait outside. The two politicians had more or less already decided what the course of action would be. After earlier discussions with the Attorney General and the Governor of the Central Bank, it was agreed that the government would underwrite all banking deposits, loans and obligations. The whole system was to be insured.

It was an unprecedented move. In the short term it meant that the run on the banks would be halted. The long-term consequences included the underwriting of bad loans. If some debtors were unable to repay their loans, the bank's exposure would be taken up by the taxpayers.

The earlier sentiments, however deeply ironic, expressed by Haughey when he was leader of the opposition in 1985 were once again salient and are worth repeating:

> It would be an absurdity, an unacceptable injustice and totally ridiculous if the general public, the great majority of whom have never benefited one iota from banking profits and many of whom have had very unhappy experiences at the hands of bankers, were asked to step in and take up an additional burden because of someone else's mistakes – mistakes made in this very specially privileged sector of our economy.

Absurdity or not, it was done. Those who had not benefited from the enormous banking profits were going to be hit for the enormous losses that followed a few years of reckless lending.

The bankers were invited back in and told what the government was proposing. They were given time to consider it, but none was really needed. The banks were in a jam and the government had just handed them a free ticket to ride.

The required legislation was passed the following day. The main opposition party, Fine Gael, went along with the proposal. The Labour Party opposed it. Fine Gael's spokesperson on finance, Richard Bruton, summed up what many were feeling about the banks:

Everyone in this House will agree that huge mistakes have been made in Ireland in recent years that have undermined the successful model that we had. It was a model of an economy based on strong export growth, tight management of public finances and a financial sector that had a proper balance in its approach to funding. The problem was the dangerous flirtation with the property sector that occurred in recent years. Those who were in a position to exercise restraint on this, in my view, failed to act.

He went on:

There was warning that our financial structure was going down a road that was dangerous but, in my belief, little was done to address that. Indeed, we have been exposed by dangerous levels of credit expansion, particularly in the property sector and by a false belief, often promulgated by Government, that this was based on sound fundamentals when the sound fundamentals of a small open economy clearly lie elsewhere. Indeed, the Government itself became excessively reliant on the product of this property boom and I am sure we will have another day to discuss that when we debate the budget.

The Irish solution to an Irish problem made headlines across the world.

Reaction was mixed. In time, other countries would follow the same route, but in a more discerning fashion, not guaranteeing absolutely everything as the Irish had. The bank guarantee thus became the cornerstone of all government policy that followed in relation to the banking crisis.

A few days after the deal was done, the chairman of Anglo Irish Bank, Seán Fitzpatrick, was interviewed on RTÉ radio. He told Marian Finucane that he was a grateful banker. 'I am saying thank you unashamedly, because we owe our lives to the government and what they did. We are incredibly grateful for the guarantee.'

The interview included a number of barefaced lies about the exposure of Anglo. In less than three months, Fitzpatrick would be unmasked as a central cog in the crazed lending spree that took hold of Irish banks from 2004. Much of the anger that was to manifest itself in the public consciousness would be directed at him. By December, Fitzpatrick had resigned.

He was followed by the chief executives and chairpersons of most of the leading institutions. The four horsemen of the apocalypse who had arrived at Government Buildings on 29 September all eventually stepped aside from their positions.

There followed a programme of recapitalisation of the banks and the setting up of the National Asset Management Agency (NAMA). NAMA was effectively designed as a vehicle to socialise the banks' debts. Once again, taxpayers were picking up the pieces.

In May 2009 Lenihan introduced the legislation to set up NAMA. 'It is important to be reminded that the reason for the Government's interventions to date, including the establishment of the National Asset Management Agency, is to stabilise the banking sector,' he said, before explaining:

> The banking system is unique. Its proper functioning is critical to the smooth running of the economy and therefore must be protected by Government – the recent global financial crisis has given rise to numerous interventions across the developed world. Here in Ireland, through the bank guarantee, bank recapitalisation and the protection of public ownership, we have provided very substantial support to the banking sector. Our overriding objective is clear – maintain a functioning banking system that will ensure a flow of credit to the real economy.

When the investigations into all that went wrong during the property bubble are complete, it is widely accepted that one finding will be that the banks were not subjected to a tough enough regime of regulation.

History suggests that the culture of impunity that the banks enjoyed over the previous 20 years was also a factor. As long as the banks were too big and too important to fail, the state was always going to step in and save them whenever the need arose. In relation to banking and its relationship with the state, it might reasonably be asked: Have we learned anything?

Some would say that the establishment of NAMA means that we have not. The agency was set up in order to manage the banks' huge property loans, which were not being repaid and which were weighing down their balance sheets. The loans were bought at a discount with a view to either managing or selling the properties on which they were secured.

The government has received kudos from the International Monetary Fund (IMF) and the Organisation for Economic Co-operation and Development (OECD) for adopting this approach to the banking problem. But a whole army of critics suggest that it is just one big bail-out for the banking system, for which the citizens are footing the bill.

NAMA is projected to have a lifespan of seven to ten years, after which all the assets are expected to be disposed of in an orderly manner. Only time will tell whether NAMA ends up being a prudent route taken by a government with its back to the wall, or the biggest bail-out for the banks in the history of the state.

11

BEN THERE, DUNNE THAT

It was approaching midnight on Wednesday 19 February 1992 when Ben Dunne rang the escort agency. Dunne was alone in his suite in the Grand Cypress Hotel, Orlando, Florida. He was bored. All he had for company was a big bag of cocaine, which he had procured a few nights earlier.

The agency was advertised in the local telephone directory. Its tagline was 'Escorts in a flash – We can be with you in an hour'. Dunne dialled the number and left a message.

Somebody called him back with a price list. He could have a female escort for two hours for $300, and anything extra could be negotiated with the girl. This was no problem for Dunne, who had around $9,000 playing money in the safe in his suite. Soon after, a man called for the money. Dunne handed it over. Then he waited.

For the previous few years, Dunne and about ten friends flew to Florida at the beginning of February for some rest and relaxation, golf in the sun and a few beers in the shade. This golfing trip so far had been uneventful.

They had arrived the previous Saturday. On Tuesday, on a whim, Dunne decided they would all upgrade to the Grand

Cypress because it had an adjoining golf club. He booked the accommodation in the hotel with his Bank of Ireland credit card. His ten companions were each staying in rooms costing $255 a night. He took a suite at $1,320.

On Wednesday evening he stayed in his suite on his own rather than dining with his friends. It is unclear when exactly he started into the coke or how much he had ingested, but, as midnight approached, he was in serious party mode.

In another part of town, Denise Wojcik took a call from the agency. A client was waiting at the Grand Cypress. Wojcik worked for the agency most nights of the week, but she always claimed that there was no prostitution involved. Six months earlier she had lost her job as a librarian. Her fee for escorting came to around one-third of the $150 an hour that the client was charged.

At 1.30 a.m. Dunne answered the door of his suite. He was holding a glass of Dom Perignon champagne. He welcomed Wojcik in and gave her a tip of $400. After some initial chit chat, Dunne produced the bag of coke. They did a few lines and then he led her to the bedroom area, which included an en suite bathroom.

They both got into the large bath. The lines of coke kept coming. Dunne was chopping them up with a plastic membership card from the K Club, the exclusive Irish golf resort in County Kildare.

One of the most basic effects of cocaine is a loss of inhibitions to the extent that some who use it cannot stop talking. The conversation in the bath was non-stop, most of it coming from Dunne.

Later, Wojcik suggested that her friend, with whom she shared a trailer, join the party. It was around 5.00 a.m. when she gave Dunne the number of the trailer. He rang it and asked

Delta Rittenhouse to come join them. Rittenhouse had a baby, so she had to find a babysitter, no easy job at five in the morning, but she said she would try.

Dunne and Wojcik had been shovelling cocaine up their noses for the best part of four hours. Dunne's stash was something north of 40 grammes, enough to get arrested for trafficking. But the millionaire was not interested in making money from the drug. He just had an insatiable appetite for it, particularly when he went abroad on golfing trips.

Some time later, Dunne went to open the safe in the suite. He tried the combination lock. It would not work. He began pacing up and down the room. He was out of his mind on coke, in a hotel room with a woman from an escort agency and a big bag of cocaine and somebody apparently had fixed it that he could not open the safe where his money was. Under the circumstances, paranoia was quite easily induced.

What unfolded over the following hours would transform the life of 42-year-old Dunne. It would also ultimately lead to the break-up of Ireland's best-known retailing empire, bring down a government minister and unmask as a kept man Ireland's most controversial politician. The sequence of events would also provide the impetus for judicial investigations of a type never seen before in the Irish state.

* * *

By 1992 Dunne had led an extraordinary life. He was born in Cork in 1949, the fifth of Ben and Nora Dunne's six children. The Dunnes had moved to Cork in the early 1940s. After a brief spell working for Roches Stores in the city centre, Ben Senior and a friend opened their own shop across the road from the chain store in 1944.

The venture was an immediate success and led to further

shops in the newly created Cork suburbs. Within a few years, Ben parted from his business partner. He opened his fifth Dunnes Stores in Limerick in 1954, and another in Wexford the following year. The first Dublin store opened in 1960.

The Dunnes philosophy was to pile the goods high and sell them cheap on a tight margin. The customer was king and the crowds quickly came whenever he opened a new shop. It was a different form of retailing, copied from the United States. The niceties of traditional shops were set aside in order to sell as cheaply as possible.

The company's early marketing slogan would persist for decades: 'Dunnes Stores Better Value Beats Them All'.

Ben imparted a steely work ethic to his offspring. He himself worked all hours, six days a week, and rested on the Sabbath. Any time not spent working was spent with the family and there was no spare time for anything else.

The family moved to a large house outside the suburb of Blackrock, but did not become part of the Cork social scene. Young Ben attended Presentation Brothers College. He displayed little interest in academia and less in the dominant sport at the school, rugby. His free time was spent helping out in the stores.

By then, further horizons were beckoning the Dunnes. In 1965 Ben Senior and his eldest son, Frank, came across an overgrown site in Cornelscourt in south County Dublin. The city suburbs were fast spreading out towards the area and the retailer saw a future that would replicate the drive-in stores that were a feature of US cities. He bought the site and began developing what would become a flagship store.

Throughout the 1960s Ben Senior and Nora spent an increasing amount of time in Dublin, while Ben Junior and his youngest sister, Therese, remained in the family home in Cork.

Despite the vast wealth that his father was accumulating, nobody could ever say that Ben Dunne was born with a silver spoon in his mouth. He left school at 16 and went to work full-time with his father. By the age of 17, he also was spending most of his time in Dublin.

The family lived in Jury's Hotel and worked the week in the various stores, returning home to Cork some weekends. Eventually, Ben Junior relocated to Dublin to head up the company's footwear and menswear divisions.

In 1972 he married Mary Goodwin. His parents did not approve of the union. Goodwin was from a middle-class background in Kilkenny and, despite the wealth that he had acquired, Ben Senior remained somewhat suspicious of what he saw as the snobbery of the middle class.

Ben and Nora were also acutely aware that their wealth, and the high-profile nature of it, might attract suitors to their children for the wrong reasons. When their eldest son, Frank, had married a Danish woman a few years earlier, they did not attend. So it went when Ben got married.

Throughout the 1970s Ben Junior's influence in the company grew to the point where he and Frank were relieving their father of much of his responsibility. By 1976 the company was the seventh largest in the state, with 42 stores in the Republic and another eight in Northern Ireland and a total turnover in excess of £75 million per annum.

Then, on one fine autumn morning in 1981, Ben Junior was kidnapped. He was driving north in his black Mercedes on Friday 16 October to open a new branch in Portadown, County Armagh. Just south of the border another vehicle pulled across the road in front of his Merc. Four armed and masked men got out of the vehicle and dragged Dunne from his car. They put him in the back seat of their vehicle and drove off in a southerly direction.

Dunne was thrown on the floor and a hood was placed over his head. He provided the men with phone numbers for his father and his wife. It became apparent to him from early on that what they were after was money. At a time when the violence in the North often lurched into bare sectarian murder, that thought must have been some comfort to him.

Within hours, the ransom demand was issued. The kidnappers wanted £500,000 in used banknotes. Word was carried to the family through intermediaries. Two days after Dunne was taken, a family friend, Fr Dermot McCarthy, met with masked men in County Louth. He gave them a note for Dunne.

Gardaí were kept up to date with developments. The force was left in no doubt from Government Buildings that standard policy must be followed in the case. Irrespective of the wealth or status of the hostage, no ransom could be paid. Although it was never confirmed that the Provisional IRA carried out the kidnapping, it was believed that the money would go towards buying arms to kill and would also incite others to invest in kidnapping as a handy fundraising exercise.

Ben Senior was not worried about government policy. His son had been kidnapped. He would do what was necessary to get him back. Pleas from the government not to trade with the kidnappers were ignored.

Acquiring the sum of cash in used notes was no problem for the Dunnes. The nature of their business meant there was no need to withdraw it from a bank.

There are believed to have been at least four attempts by the Dunnes to pay the ransom. In one instance, a family friend, Noel Fox, was intercepted by gardaí outside Dundalk, close to the border, with a large amount of cash. One theory is that Fox was a decoy set up to allow another intermediary to deliver the money.

On the following Wednesday evening, Dunne, who had been hooded for most of his nearly six days in captivity, was taken from a house and put into the back of a car. Shortly before midnight he was released at the gates of a church in Cullyhanna in south Armagh, which was a Republican stronghold.

As a memento of his time in captivity he was handed three bullets from the guns that were used to guard him. The car drove off. Dunne ran into a graveyard that adjoined the church and jumped into a grave that had been dug for a burial due the following morning. The terror he felt can only be guessed at.

Some time later, a journalist from Belfast, Eamonn Mallie, walked into the graveyard. He had been tipped off that Dunne could be found there. The two men met and Mallie offered to drive Dunne home.

Both the British and Irish governments denied that any ransom had been paid for Dunne's release. However, Dunne himself later claimed that money was paid.

Nearly 20 years after the event, Fox was asked about it briefly at a tribunal. When it was put to him that he had been instrumental in securing Dunne's release, he replied, 'That is correct.' What role Fox could have played beyond organising or delivering a ransom is a matter for conjecture.

It was later reported that £350,000 had been paid, although other sources close to the matter suggest that up to £500,000 sterling was handed over. Whatever the sum was, it is widely accepted that a large amount of money was paid to secure Dunne's release.

True to his breeding and character, Ben Junior took only

one day off work when he got back to Dublin. He did not go to counselling, which might have been advisable considering what he had been through. In later years, he would ascribe his behaviour, and particularly his coke habit, partly to his ordeal and how he dealt with it in the immediate aftermath.

Eighteen months later, in April 1983, Ben Senior died after suffering a heart attack. Ben and Frank were appointed joint managing directors of the business, which by then had an annual turnover of £300 million.

The company expanded through the rest of the 1980s. Ben had inherited his father's obsessive work ethic.

Ben and Mary had four children but, in the second half of the decade, he began to stray. He was introduced to cocaine, a drug that then was the preserve of a small, wealthy clique. He was en route to the night in February 1992 when the whole edifice would come crashing down.

* * *

Dunne tried the combination of the safe again. Same result. He had the number written on a crumpled piece of paper. Slowly, he read out the numbers and tried once more. Nothing budged. Wojcik told him to calm down, to take it easy.

Dressed in nothing but his boxer shorts, Dunne, a man of considerable bulk at the time, began pacing up and down the room.

'Leave me alone,' he told her. 'Leave me alone.'

She suggested that he ring security. He rang security, explained his problem and then got up on the bed and began jumping up and down. Wojcik, who was also in her underwear, was growing uneasy. She went to get dressed.

Wojcik then noticed that Dunne had picked up a piece of wood and was swinging it around. He was 'like some crazed

King Kong, jumping up and down and swinging this object over his head,' she later described.

A security guard called to the door. He was dressed in a black boiler suit, which seemed to set off further panic in Dunne's head. 'Get the police,' he said.

Dunne moved towards a balcony that looked down on the hotel lobby 17 floors below. The security guard thought he might jump.

The hotel managers were contacted. There was a drug-crazed Irishman on the 17th floor, threatening to jump. Initially, they thought the crazy Irishman must be attached to another Irish party staying on the 17th floor that night.

U2 were in town to launch their US tour, which was to begin in Orlando the following night. Perhaps this was some expression of rock 'n' roll Babylon. Perhaps it was a member of the U2 crew living up to the caricature of rock music tours.

Two of the U2 security detail were asked to accompany hotel security up to the 17th floor to talk this guy down. When they got there, they saw it had nothing to do with them and left. Downstairs, Bono noticed the commotion. He later said he had never seen anything like it.

Meanwhile, Dunne's friends were already out on the golf course, unaware that the man himself was behaving like a suicidal baboon.

At 9.00 a.m. the cops arrived. One of them talked Ben down and got him away from the edge of the balcony for enough time for three other officers to hold him down and cuff him. He was still screaming and roaring and it was decided that the only way to get him out of the hotel was to hogtie him to a pole.

Guests looked on as the police officers walked through the hotel lobby with a man tied hands and feet to a pole, as if he was a beast being brought off to roast over a fire. Dignity was entirely absent from the spectacle.

Dunne was taken to hospital initially, but later that morning he was transferred to Orange County Jail and handed a prison uniform. Inside the hotel suite, the police officers found a bag with 32 grammes of cocaine and thousands of Irish pounds and US dollars. It was inevitable that he would be charged with trafficking.

The following day he was released on $25,000 bail. Most of his friends had flown home by the time he got out. Who could continue golfing in the wake of Ben's travails?

Word began filtering back to Ireland. The *Sunday Tribune* news desk got a call from a stringer reporter it used in the US. She had heard from a diplomatic source that Dunne had been arrested and charged over a drugs bust involving a call girl.

Tribune reporter Diarmuid Doyle began digging for information on Saturday morning. The police in Florida filled in all the details. Then he made the necessary but unenviable call to the Dunne home in Castleknock in Dublin. He told Mary Dunne what the paper was going to publish and asked whether her husband would like to respond.

An hour later a chipper Ben Dunne put through a call to the *Tribune*. He betrayed no signs of a man whose world was disintegrating. He neither confirmed nor denied the story. 'Be careful what you publish,' was all he would say.

Doyle wrote the story and the paper hit the streets on Saturday night, right about the time that Ben was boarding a plane for the long flight home. 'Ben Dunne, the chairman of Dunnes Stores, was charged with drug-trafficking in Orlando, Florida on Thursday last,' the front-page story on the paper opened.

The charge is believed to have arisen from a search

of a room at the Grand Cypress Hotel, where Orange County deputy sheriffs had gone having been alerted that a man was believed to be threatening to commit suicide by throwing himself from a railing on the 17th floor.

Mr Dunne, who is due home from Florida early this week, told the *Sunday Tribune* yesterday that he was not a drug trafficker and denied that he had attempted to commit suicide.

'These events arose from an extraordinary set of circumstances which will become public in the appropriate place.'

The story dominated the media over the weekend and into the next week. On advice from his solicitor, Noel Smyth, Dunne decided to give a press conference at his home and to do an interview for RTÉ television. It was a masterstroke.

Dunne appeared on TV looking somewhat unkempt, and entirely contrite. 'I can blame nobody but myself,' he said.

No, I'm not a cocaine user. In a weak moment I took the goddamn stuff and in no way am I looking for pity. I took it. I shouldn't have taken it. Just the same way, I am not an alcoholic. I took cocaine and I won't be taking it again. It was hard to be arrested as a dealer, but it is something I will overcome. I was weak and that is why I took it.

If the situation arose where it came up again, I wouldn't do it again. I am admitting that nobody put a gun to my head to make me take cocaine. I had a free choice about whether to break the law or not. I am not addicted to any drugs, legal or otherwise. There is an awful lot of prescribed drugs that I wouldn't take. I don't drink shorts, I drink beer. I

am not interested in drinking shorts because I'm
afraid to. I have caused a lot of hardship to my wife
and kids.

The interview immediately won over the public to his side. He
was a sinner who was attempting to repent. Who but the most
righteous could quibble with a man who had fallen from the
path briefly and was doing his utmost to get back?

The interview also had a major impact on the business of
Irish public relations. Appealing to the better nature of the
Irish people when in trouble is a tactic that has often been used
since. In Dunne's case, it was not even a PR professional who
advised the approach, but his solicitor.

The public were onside. Over in Florida, the trafficking
charge still loomed, but Dunne had the best lawyers money
could buy and, when all was taken into consideration, no judge
would really think he was a drug dealer. Besides, the manner in
which the drugs were discovered in his suite constituted an
illegal search.

His lawyers suggested a plea bargain that might involve
Dunne pledging to get treatment but would mean he would
never see the inside of a US prison. Not all parties to the affair
would be so easily appeased.

Some of Ben's siblings, and particularly his sister Margaret
Heffernan, were horrified at the spotlight that had been thrust
on the family.

The Dunnes' parents had been private and very religious.
The episode in Orlando and the fallout from it were the
antithesis of everything they stood for. Within weeks of Ben's
return to Ireland, there were rumblings that all was not well in
the family.

Dunne's case in Orlando came up on 1 May 1992. The state
dropped the trafficking charges and he pleaded guilty to

possession of a small amount of drugs. A number of character references, including two from professional golfers Des Smyth and Christy O'Connor Jr., were presented in court.

There was also evidence of Dunne's charity work and suggestions that his kidnapping 11 years previously may have been responsible for post-traumatic stress disorder. His lawyers said he was willing to undergo treatment in a London clinic. The judge ruled that he was to do so and the court was to be updated on his progress.

In June Dunne entered the Charter Group clinic. A few days later, a radio scanner in the Phoenix Park picked up a telephone call between Margaret Heffernan and Noel Smyth. The contents were leaked to the media. Heffernan was heard berating Smyth that the clinic was a holiday home and that Ben could have done with six months in prison. She also suggested that Smyth was a bad influence on her brother.

In July the Dunne siblings voted at a board meeting to change the rules that governed the company. The following February, one year on from the Orlando episode, Frank and Margaret moved against Ben. With the support of one of their other two sisters, Ben was removed from his role as chairman.

He immediately pledged to leave the company. He said the family trust which governed Dunnes Stores should be broken up. He alleged that some of his siblings had not abided by the rules of the trust and that it was a sham.

His siblings in turn commissioned a report into how Ben had run the business when he was in charge. The accountancy firm Price Waterhouse was retained. The resulting report would be devastating, not so much to Ben, but to two major political figures.

* * *

Michael Lowry was already going places before Ben Dunne

latched onto him. He was born in 1954 in Holycross, County Tipperary. Like Dunne, he did not complete his second-level education, leaving early to join a local company, Butler Refrigeration, where he worked as an engineer.

Lowry threw himself into politics at a young age. He joined Fine Gael and rose quickly through the ranks, displaying an ability to get on with people and to get things done.

He gravitated towards GAA politics, ultimately serving as chairman of the Tipperary County Board. He was also instrumental in fundraising to pay off the debt on Semple Stadium in Thurles, where the GAA was founded.

In 1981 he stood for the Fine Gael nomination in the Tipperary North constituency, but was defeated. His chance came again in 1987, when he was selected and romped home.

By then he was a major cog in the Butler firm. He cut a deal whereby he would continue to work part-time while concentrating more of his energies on politics.

One of Butler's main contracts was with Dunnes Stores. Fitting and maintaining the refrigeration units of most of Dunnes' 90 outlets constituted a large chunk of Butler's business.

In the course of their business dealings, Dunne spotted talent in Lowry. He approached him with an offer. Leave Butler, set up your own company and work exclusively for Dunnes.

Dunne told him, as recounted at a tribunal years later, 'If you are good for Dunnes Stores and if you achieve the savings that I think are possible, I will certainly make it worth your while and your company will be successful and you will be a wealthy man.'

In January 1989 Lowry left Butler, taking with him some of the company's key personnel and the Dunnes contract.

It soon became known that Lowry's company, Streamline,

had Dunnes Stores as a major client, but it was much later before it became public knowledge that Dunnes was Streamline's only client.

The young ambitious TD was working for one of the biggest retailers in the state. If that was the extent of the relationship, Lowry might have sailed through any revelations. The real problem arose in the manner in which Lowry was remunerated.

The contract he signed with Dunnes Stores – the only one Dunnes was offering – was designed such that his company would earn a small annual profit of up to £50,000. Bonuses above that would be paid separately through Ben Dunne himself.

Most of the cheques subsequently paid to Lowry were drawn from a company bank account that Ben's siblings – and fellow directors – were unaware of. Payments ranging in size from £6,000 to £12,000 were made to Lowry between 1989 and 1991.

There were other larger payments also. Dunne arranged for the opening of two offshore accounts in the Isle of Man to receive payments. Lowry himself opened an offshore account in Jersey with £100,000 in September 1991, which included a £34,000 sterling payment from Dunnes Stores. Ben made a number of other payments to the Isle of Man accounts.

Lowry has always maintained that all of these payments were for work done by Streamline. However, he often lodged the money to personal accounts, effectively therefore taking it from the company for his own benefit. Dunne's pledge to make him a wealthy man was taking shape, but by the standards of any sort of corporate governance, it was a highly unorthodox arrangement to say the least.

There was also the question of how much of the money

Lowry was declaring for tax, particularly as he was building up large balances in his offshore accounts.

Lowry's political career also benefited from his commercial relationship with Dunne. He introduced Dunne to some of the Fine Gael grandees and organised for party leader John Bruton to have dinner at Dunne's Castleknock home in 1991. Therein, Ben produced a cheque for £50,000 to put a dent in the party's £1 million plus debt.

During the 1992 election campaign, Lowry invited Fine Gael frontbencher Michael Noonan to speak at a rally in north Tipperary. Afterwards, he handed him a cheque for £3,000, which he said was a political donation from Dunne.

Another frontbencher, Ivan Yates, took a call from Lowry during that campaign. Lowry said he had a cheque for him from Dunne for £5,000. Yates had never met Dunne. The previous highest political donation Yates had received was £500.

There was nothing improper about any of the donations Dunne made to Fine Gael or the campaigns of some of its leading candidates. Politicians are always grateful for donations within the rules at election time. But Lowry's role as conduit was significant. Apart from anything else, he was demonstrating his importance to the party.

In 1992 Lowry also decided to move his family to a larger home, one better befitting his new-found status as a wealthy entrepreneur and an up-and-coming politician. He bought a Georgian house for £140,000 just up the road from where he had been living in a bungalow. The house needed some serious repairs.

Lowry rang Dunne and told him about his domestic difficulties. He did not have the cash on hand to undertake the extensive work. Dunne put him in touch with an architect and builders who had worked for Dunnes Stores and on Ben's house. Dunnes Stores was about to fund the refurbishment of Lowry's stately pad.

The total bill for the refurbishment came to £395,000. In the books of Dunnes Stores the payment was treated as work done on the company's Ilac Centre store in Dublin's city centre. It was actually a beneficial payment to Lowry, on which he was not paying any tax.

Meanwhile, Fine Gael had had a poor election and was in opposition. The party was now in major debt. In September 1993 Lowry organised for a political donation of £100,000 to be made by Dunne to the party. Lowry said Dunne's only condition was that the donation be strictly confidential. It was thus treated, and another chunk was taken off the party's debt.

When the Dunnes went to war, Lowry was in serious hock to the chairman of the company and Fine Gael had been a major beneficiary of the retailer. A legendary figure on the other side of the political divide, however, had as much reason, if not more, to be grateful for the generosity of 'big Ben'.

* * *

Charles Haughey was not a favoured figure among some of the Dunne siblings. In the 1960s he had insulted their father at a trade fair in New York by telling him his merchandise was too cheap and tacky for a display of national wares. Some within the family never forgot the slur. Ben Junior, however, was an admirer of Haughey.

The story of Charlie Haughey is dealt with elsewhere in this book (see Chapter 10). Suffice it to say here that by 1987 he had debts of over £1 million.

Des Traynor dealt with Haughey's finances. In November of that year he compiled a list of businesspeople who he felt might be willing to make contributions of at least £100,000 to the Haughey lifestyle fund.

The first name on the list was Ben Dunne. Traynor approached Noel Fox, the Dunne family confidant and trustee on the family board. Fox told Dunne about the plan to gather together at least half a dozen people to tackle Haughey's debt.

Dunne replied, 'I think Haughey is making a huge mistake trying to get six or seven people together … Christ picked twelve apostles and one of them crucified him.' He said he would pay the whole debt, which he was under the impression was around £700,000. He said he would need time to come up with it, but Traynor did not have much time.

A few days later, Dunne instructed that a sterling cheque for the equivalent of £205,000 be drawn from a store in Bangor, County Down.

The following July, another cheque was sent, this one for £471,000 sterling. In April 1989 a cheque for £150,000 was issued. Another for £200,000 sterling followed in February 1990. In total, over the course of 26 months, Dunne contributed over £1 million to Haughey.

All of the above payments were made through the Dunnes Stores company and involved Haughey's bagman, Traynor. Haughey never handled any of the money. There was, however, one transfer that was directly between the two men, Dunne and Haughey.

During this period Dunne often called on Haughey at home in Abbeville in Kinsealy. On one occasion in November 1991, Dunne was playing golf in Portmarnock and before leaving the club, he rang Haughey, whose home was on Dunne's route back to Dublin. He had in his pocket three bank drafts made out to fictitious individuals.

Haughey was at a low point. The previous week, he had

repelled the latest internal challenge to his leadership. It was the first since Des O'Malley had left to form the Progressive Democrats in 1985. This time, though, it looked as if the game might be up.

Haughey looked wretched when Dunne called. 'He looked like a broken man,' Dunne later said. Dunne felt sorry for him and wondered whether he might be able to cheer the old dog up. As he was leaving, he dug the three drafts from his pocket and handed them to Haughey.

'Look, that's something for yourself,' he said.

'Thanks, big fella,' Haughey replied, having just been handed another £210,000 for his trouble.

When the Dunne family lined up for a battle royal in the courts a few years later, Ben would claim in a statement that the three drafts were originally destined for three of his siblings.

He alleged that they were irregular payments to be made to offshore accounts in names provided by his siblings. The veracity of such a claim was never ultimately tested. However, irrespective of who the drafts were destined for, Haughey received them, and in time, he would wish that he never had.

On one of his visits to Abbeville, Dunne had injured his foot and was using a wheelchair. The two men were idling near a lake on the extensive grounds. Years later, when the extent of their relationship became public, Haughey would say to one friend, 'If I'd known what was coming, I'd have pushed him into the fucking lake.'

* * *

Once Margaret Heffernan and Frank Dunne moved against Ben at board level, the scene was set for a family to go to war. Initially, Frank and Margaret offered Ben £40 million just to

300

relinquish his stake in the family trust. Ben refused. The High Court beckoned.

From July 1993 the writs began flying between the parties. Ben was stripped of his executive function, but he was still a board member and he continued to attend at the office.

In one instance, Heffernan was conducting a meeting with representatives of another company from Waterford when Ben marched into the room.

'I'm a 20 per cent owner of this company and I'm here to see what's going on,' he announced, a cigarette dangling from his fingers.

'The meeting is over,' Heffernan replied. The others in attendance got up to leave. Ben walked over to his sister.

'You better get used to it,' he said, and with that he stumped out his cigarette in her glass of mineral water. Nobody else said a word.

The temperature was turned up as both sides armed themselves with the best lawyers money could buy. At times, Ben let his emotions get the better of him as he saw what was unfolding.

In one reported case, he walked into the offices of the company's accountants, Oliver Freaney, and shouted, 'You fucking bollocks. I'm a street fighter and you won't get me out of the company as easy as you think.'

Throughout this period, Ben boasted more than once to Heffernan that he had given Haughey more than £1 million, but added the rider, 'you'll never find it'.

On foot of his claims, Heffernan visited Haughey in Abbeville in August 1993. She asked him whether her brother had advanced him large sums of money. Haughey replied that he could not be responsible for what her brother said. She also arranged a meeting with Traynor and asked him the same question. He said he knew nothing whatsoever about it.

At a time when Haughey was regarded as enjoying his retirement, and as his contribution to public life was undergoing a favourable re-evaluation, he must have been despairing that his carefully constructed public persona was going to come crashing down as a result of a family feud among the Dunnes.

The Price Waterhouse report was compiled and pointed towards numerous unorthodox payments made by Dunne to Haughey and Lowry.

In November 1994 solicitors for Dunnes Stores wrote to Haughey asking for the money to be returned. Haughey invited Heffernan to his home, where he emphasised to her that a full-blown court battle would do enormous damage to both the Dunne family and their company's brand. He might have added that it would also destroy his reputation.

On the night before the High Court was due to hear the case, the lawyer for Dunnes Stores, Niall Fennelly, rang one of Ben's legal team, Dermot Gleeson. Let's break bread was the message.

The case was settled with Ben receiving £125 million from the family trust. His tax bill of around £30 million was believed to be the highest ever paid in the state. His legal fees came to around £5 million, with his siblings facing a similar bill.

A highly damaging court battle had been avoided. Many family secrets would have been disseminated in such an encounter, something that would have made old Ben Dunne shiver in his grave.

Probably the most relieved person was Haughey. Once again, he had escaped. There would be no exposure of his status as a kept man while he ran the country. Another person feeling some relief must have been Lowry. The Price Waterhouse report would also have stopped his political ascent in its tracks, just as he was about to reach ministerial office.

*　*　*

Watergate haunted a generation of reporters throughout the world. The investigation by two *Washington Post* reporters into the activities of the Oval Office was a high water mark in journalism. Few scoops thereafter have been able to live up to it.

In Irish journalism, Sam Smyth's scoop in November 1996 came at least close. Smyth was working for the *Irish Independent* as an investigative reporter of some repute. In late 1996 he had been writing for some time about the apparently bizarre conduct of the Minister for Transport, Energy and Communications, Michael Lowry.

Lowry had been appointed to the office in December 1994, when Fine Gael, Labour and Democratic Left formed a coalition after the Fianna Fáil/Labour administration collapsed. Lowry's ascent occurred just a month after the Dunnes case was settled out of court. A lucky escape.

Lowry was colourful and controversial from the off in government. He declared that he was going to clean up the semi-state sector. He began cutting a swathe through the sector, although it was difficult at times to distinguish what he classified as 'cleaning up' from blatant politician manoeuvring, often targeting figures who were associated with Fianna Fáil.

In 1995 anonymous letters began appearing in political and media circles alleging serious corruption in the semi-state sector. There were also allegations that Lowry was under surveillance from a private detective, the implication being that powerful vested interests were attempting to divert the fearless minister from his righteous track.

Smyth followed the story closely. He began to notice that Lowry was making plenty of claims that did not add up. There was no evidence that powerful interests had put him under surveillance.

Throughout 1996 Smyth followed Lowry's progress in, as the minister saw it, tackling the wrongs in the semi-state sector. Smyth wrote a number of stories on the matter for his newspaper. Out there among the paper's large readership, somebody was taking notice of the reporter's by-line on stories written about Lowry.

As he later revealed in a book about the affair, *Thanks a Million, Big Fella*, it was late one Thursday evening in October 1996 when Smyth picked up his house telephone. The caller had rung twice previously but had not left a message. Smyth knew him, but not well. He told Smyth he had a story for him about Lowry.

The next afternoon the pair met. The man was sweating, agitated and nervous that they might be seen together. He told Smyth that Dunnes Stores had paid for the refurbishment of Lowry's County Tipperary home. Over £200,000 was involved and the job was done through the company's architect and builders.

Smyth was taken by the story, but he explained that he would require substantial documentary proof before the newspaper's lawyers would ever let it reach print. A number of further meetings followed. At each, the contact gave a little more, beginning with the photocopies of cheques for the work done.

Smyth did his own homework. He knew a report had been compiled for the High Court action between the Dunne siblings a few years previously. Could the contact get a copy of the report? Initially the man said no way, but in the end he showed Smyth a photocopy of the pages involving Lowry.

It was a scoop in every meaning of the word. Smyth's story got the nod from his editor and the newspaper's solicitor. The one proviso the legal people put on it was that Lowry be given every opportunity to refute or comment on the story.

As the minister was in Brussels on European Union business, Smyth put together ten questions relevant to the story and faxed the document to the minister's press office.

Later that day, while Lowry was chairing a European Council meeting on Internet pornography, the questions were passed to him by an aide. He looked at the sheet of paper and said nothing. Then word came through that his wife wanted to talk to him. A plane had been flying low over their house in Tipperary. She was distressed about it and did not know what to do.

The plane had been hired by the newspaper to take aerial photographs of the house that Dunne helped to build.

Lowry flew home that evening and informed the Taoiseach, John Bruton, and the Tánaiste and Labour Party leader, Dick Spring, that a story was going to break about him the following morning.

When the sheet did hit the street, all hell broke loose. The minister's department was inundated for media interviews. The Taoiseach was asked for his opinion of the story. Bruton replied that the private dealings of a TD were a different matter to how that TD conducted himself once appointed to ministerial office.

Opposition TD Michael McDowell of the Progressive Democrats captured the public mood when he reacted to Bruton's comments. 'Are we really to believe that John Bruton thought it acceptable for his party chairman and a prominent front bench public representative to have his home massively refurbished at the expense of a large commercial company under any circumstances?'

Lowry was returning to his constituency for a family matter that day, and he agreed to give RTÉ an interview in the Green Isle Hotel in the western suburbs of Dublin. Charlie Bird was dispatched. But by then the media frenzy had heightened, and both Lowry and the RTÉ crew were followed to the location by other reporters.

In the interview, Lowry suggested that he was a victim of that old hoary chestnut – the witch-hunt. This specific witch-hunt was being conducted by one journalist in particular. He said he would not be hounded out of office. And on he went, talking and talking around the main issue, dancing past the glaring question – how is your position tenable, now that you have been exposed as a kept man?

Back in Leinster House, all eyes were glued to the item on the six o'clock news. The reaction was uniform. Lowry's body language spoke a lot louder than his words. He was finished.

As he de-miked after the interview, Lowry engaged in his own little effort at spin. He told some of the reporters that the real story was that over £1 million had been given by Dunne to another politician. He did not offer any names, but it did not take too long for the penny to drop.

After years of Haughey dodging inquiries into his lavish lifestyle, decades during which he fobbed off any suspicion about his income, the chickens were coming home to roost in the grand environs of Abbeville.

Lowry lasted in power for another 24 hours. After intense meetings the following day, culminating in an exchange with the Taoiseach, Lowry emerged from Government Buildings to declare that he had resigned in the best interests of the government.

He returned to the bosom of his people in north Tipperary. As is the norm in situations like this, he received a champion's welcome. A report in the following Monday's *Irish Independent* stated, 'It seemed more a triumphant send-off than a homecoming for a humbled hero.'

And so it would remain. In the following three general elections, and counting, the people of north Tipp returned Lowry to the Dáil, despite a drip drip of information that showed him up as a tax dodger and one who referenced the truth with great economy.

But behind the scenes on his first weekend as a deposed minister, Lowry continued to spin to a few choice reporters. The real story is elsewhere. Somebody had got £1 million from the 'big fella'.

* * *

It would be two months before Haughey was unmasked as the beneficiary. In the interim, the papers would begin referring to 'Mr You Know Who', until Cliff Taylor in the *Irish Times* finally got his hands on the relevant section of the Price Waterhouse report.

It was all downhill for Haughey from then on. A tribunal of inquiry into the Dunnes Stores payments to politicians was set up under Judge Brian McCracken. Haughey was hooked by Dunne's solicitor Smyth, who told the inquiry about the money handed over in Abbeville.

When Fianna Fáil returned to power the following June, the new leader Bertie Ahern publicly disowned Haughey without naming him.

The McCracken Tribunal begat the Moriarty Tribunal, charged with delving deeper into the financial affairs of both

Haughey and Lowry. The reputations of both men were effectively shredded over the following decade as the tribunal slowly picked its way through a myriad of bank accounts. The inquiry was ongoing when Haughey died in 2006.

Others were drawn into the web. The businessman Denis O'Brien had won the state mobile phone licence when Lowry was the line minister in 1995. That competition came under scrutiny at the tribunal as a result of what were regarded as a suspicious series of business activities and transactions involving Michael Lowry.

O'Brien had become a billionaire in the interim, the foundations of his business empire rooted in the mobile phone licence. He launched a campaign against the tribunal, forcing it to admit to making mistakes along the way.

As of the summer of 2010, the process is ongoing, with Lowry, among others, still awaiting the tribunal's final report. The cost of the tribunal is expected to run into hundreds of millions of euro.

The only player to emerge from the whole process with his reputation relatively intact is Ben Dunne. It was his coke and hookers habit that kicked off the chain of events that led to the fracturing of reputations of two government ministers, one of them a former Taoiseach and a legendary figure in Irish politics. Yet Dunne remains well regarded by the Irish public at large.

He moved into the fitness business after leaving Dunnes Stores. He also later became the unlikely proprietor of an art gallery, making regular contributions to media programmes and publications. To a large extent his indiscretions have been forgotten, largely because he presents an amenable and unpretentious face to the public. But how different it all might have been if he had been able to open the safe in his suite that night in Orlando.

If Dunne had not lost control, he might have sailed on for years, powdering his nose to beat the band until finally going into rehab on the advice of those around him. He might still be chairman of Dunnes Stores, Michael Lowry might now be leader of Fine Gael and Charlie Haughey's 30 years of double living may never have been exposed. Instead, however, the activities of those individuals were exposed, the Revenue Commissioner's coffers replenished and a salutary lesson was issued to any other politician who might had had difficulty interpreting right from wrong.

12

PASSPORT TO A NEW LIFE

Singing star Natalie Cole stepped out of a stretch limousine at Peak House, a $20 million, 24,000-square-foot mountain 'chalet' in an ultra-exclusive residential enclave in Aspen, Colorado, playground of the rich and famous.

It was just a few days before Christmas 1997 and Cole was the star entertainer at the self-styled 'party of parties', a housewarming for Aspen's newest resident. As she walked into the house, the daughter of legendary crooner Nat King Cole passed a sofa sewn from the skin of 33 alligators and a collection of carvings from elephant tusks reputed to be worth $1.8 million. Her audience included Goldie Hawn, Ivana Trump and many other stars, politicians and businesspeople.

Even by the heady standards of this jet set crowd, this million-dollar shindig was something else. Bowls of caviar greeted the guests, who also dined on Pacific lobster, Texan beef, expensive champagne and a particularly fine wine from the Montrachet vineyard – producers of what many believe is the finest dry white wine in the world.

A credit card was left in the nearby ski store for guests to pick up their own choice of Christmas presents. As the guests left, they also received gifts from Asprey & Garrard, the exclusive London jewellery store.

And the man throwing this extraordinarily lavish event was an Irishman – well, an Irishman of sorts. Viktor Kozeny is not your typical Irish name, and the tall, cherubic, blond host certainly does not look Irish. Kozeny was in fact born in the Czech Republic, but he had bought his Irish passport two years earlier.

As Kozeny and his beautiful third wife, Ludka, charmed and schmoozed their guests, the main question of the night at Peak House was who is this Gatsby-type character? It was a good question, but one that nobody in Ireland seemed to ask until well after he had been granted citizenship. And, to the cost of at least some of his party guests in Aspen, by the time they found out the answer, they were already co-investors with the man dubbed the 'Pirate of Prague' and the 'bouncing Czech'.

* * *

Viktor Kozeny was born in a Stalin-era block of flats in Prague in the summer of 1963. His family then moved to West Germany. As a student he met an eminent US physics academic who, like so many others over the following years, took a liking to the super-confident young Czech and urged him to study in the United States.

Kozeny did not need to be asked twice and shortly afterwards turned up at the professor's front door. Although the professor quickly realised that Kozeny knew nothing about physics, he persuaded a colleague to take the 18-year-old into his home. Within a few months, the young Czech had run off with the man's wife, a 37-year-old mother of three.

Next, Kozeny managed to talk his way into Harvard, finally

graduating with a degree in economics after six eventful years. He started working for London investment bank Flemmings, but was fired after six months. His home country, newly freed from the yoke of communist oppression, beckoned.

* * *

On his return to Prague, Kozeny immediately spotted an opportunity with the Czech government's privatisation scheme. Czech citizens were encouraged to buy a booklet of vouchers for a relatively small sum (around $30), which could be used to buy shares in newly privatised state companies. But people unused to the ways of capitalism were reluctant to dip their toes into the market.

Kozeny realised this and set up a group of so-called mutual funds – professionally managed schemes that pool money from many investors and invest it on their behalf, which he called the Harvard Capital and Consulting Funds, after his alma mater.

A slick, Western-style advertising campaign, including television ads, urged Czechs to sign over their vouchers to Kozeny with an extraordinary guarantee that they would get ten times their money if they wanted to cash out after a year. It had all the hallmarks of a pyramid or Ponzi scheme.

Working out of an attic with two telephones, Kozeny and his secretary, later to become his third wife, worked day and night to recruit investors. And incredibly, almost one million people, seduced by the promise of high returns, signed up to the Harvard funds. This was enough for Kozeny to control more than 15 per cent of the Prague stock market, including banks, steel mills and breweries.

Kozeny's legendary networking skills ensured that he quickly made friends in high places, giving him the inside track on identifying where best to invest. When the Harvard funds began trading on the stock market, their value increased 20-fold, giving them a market value of $1 billion and peaking far in excess of that. Early investors made a serious return.

By the early nineties, Kozeny was close to being the most powerful man in the Czech Republic. In response, the government quickly introduced a law stopping mutual funds from owning more than 20 per cent of any one company. The measure was directly aimed at the Harvard funds.

The media also started to ask questions. It took the arrest of a former Czech secret police agent in 1992 before things began to go wrong for Kozeny. The former agent claimed that he was paid $20,000 to sell Kozeny secret government documents.

With the privatisation process in full swing, anybody who knew what state-owned businesses were going to be sold off, and at what price, stood to make millions. Kozeny was not charged in the case but was asked to appear before a hearing, at which he alleged that he was trying to trap the agent in a government sting operation.

A little over a year later, with his dealings increasingly under the microscope, Kozeny left the Czech Republic and moved to the Bahamas.

* * *

Kozeny bought a property in Lyford Cay, the private gated community that is one of the world's wealthiest and most exclusive neighbourhoods. There he met Michael Dingman. In the 1980s Dingman was a hugely controversial business figure in the US, where he operated as an industrial turnaround specialist and became enormously wealthy in the process. Although a generation older than Kozeny, the two men hit it off and teamed up in business.

First, though, Kozeny set about obtaining a new homeland. In April 1995 he and his two daughters, Brigitte and Jenny, applied for and were granted Irish passports. The application followed his investment of £1 million in an Irish software company. In keeping with the terms of the controversial passports for sale scheme, Kozeny bought a flat in Carysfort Hall in Blackrock on the southside of Dublin city.

The new Irish citizen then embarked on a stunning play in the Czech Republic. He and Dingman secretly became major investors in eight key Czech stock market companies. Dingman apparently committed $140 million of his own money in tandem with cash from Harvard Capital and Consulting Funds. Kozeny's mutual funds, which included other people's money, were buying heavily into stock market companies that he happened to have an interest in.

In October 1995 Kozeny and Dingman announced that they had bought large blocks in these companies and stated that their goal was the restructuring of Czech industry. However, when their early moves at restructuring met with local resistance, they changed tack. Assets were traded forwards and backwards, in over 1,000 different transactions, between Dingman's investment company and the different Harvard funds. Assets were sold off and cash was taken out.

'When all the dust had settled, Kozeny had built a fortune variously estimated at between $200m and $700m,' *Fortune* magazine later revealed. The Czech authorities contend that much of this wealth was stolen.

Kozeny announced his intention to convert the Harvard mutual fund family into a new industrial holding company. But the head of the Prague Stock Exchange warned investors to avoid Kozeny's companies, prompting an investor stampede to the exits. By the end of 1996, Harvard funds had lost over 80 per cent of their value, causing huge damage to investor confidence in the Czech Republic in the process.

In July of that year, the Czech Finance Ministry fined Kozeny's Harvard operation the equivalent of €25,400 – the maximum fine allowed under Czech law – and he was forced to repay the equivalent of €5.5 million to the Harvard funds, which later went into liquidation.

Thousands of ordinary Czechs were left high and dry. Meanwhile, Kozeny was living the high life overseas. He famously paid £13,000 sterling for a dinner for three at Le Gavroche restaurant in London's Mayfair. One bottle of wine ordered, priced at a little under £5,000, was sent back for being 'too young' by Kozeny, who suggested the kitchen staff be allowed to have it.

Such conspicuous consumption was also on display when he paid £12.5 million sterling in 1998 for Andrew Lloyd Webber's six-storey Eaton Square mansion in Belgravia, regarded as one of the finest properties in London.

It was also in 1998 that Kozeny finally came to public prominence in Ireland. RTÉ television's *Prime Time* programme broadcast a report on Kozeny and his activities in the Czech Republic. The programme makers travelled there to prepare the report and interviewed those who had lost their life savings.

The *Prime Time* report, which prompted calls for the Irish government to rescind his passport, clearly set alarm bells ringing for Kozeny. A public relations offensive was called for.

Kozeny recruited Frank Dunlop, one of Ireland's leading PR operators. More than a decade later, Dunlop was jailed after pleading guilty to making corrupt payments to councillors in return for their support for developers on land rezonings (see Chapter 6).

It was decided that Kozeny would talk to one journalist to

put forward his case. Dunlop contacted the *Sunday Tribune* and the newspaper's then Business Editor, Shane Coleman (co-author of this book), met up with Kozeny in the penthouse suite of the Berkeley Court Hotel.

All of Kozeny's renowned charm was on display as he affected a wounded innocence. Describing Ireland as his 'home country', he said, 'This is a lawful society. I've earned the right to be a citizen [of Ireland]. I am a citizen of this country. It is similar to saying that someone who is controversial should lose their Irish citizenship as well. Once you are a citizen, you are equal to other citizens.'

Ignoring the obvious point that he lived in the Bahamas, Kozeny claimed that he opted for an Irish passport because 'it gave me the opportunity to live in a country that is lawful, civilised and close to my heart – and I like beer'.

He rejected the allegation that his Irish passport had facilitated any wrongdoing, stressing he had never been charged with any crime.

It's pure nonsense, absurd. I had to submit proof that I had no convictions from the Czech and US police. I was investigated by Interpol. I've been scrutinised in a very thorough fashion. The fact that one is controversial, in political opposition [Kozeny at the time was a supporter of the main opposition party in the Czech Republic] doesn't make you a criminal. By doing new things you are bound to be controversial. If you cause a social change, you are bound to be under attack.

Comparing himself to Robin Hood, taking money away from 'fat, lazy bureaucrats', Kozeny said he had no remaining investments in the Czech Republic, but was instead focusing on Azerbaijan.

Azerbaijan, the small but hugely oil-rich state bordered by Russia, Georgia, Armenia, Iran and the Caspian Sea, was described by *Fortune* magazine as having 'no stock market, no meaningful financial regulation, and a rich history of graft and cronyism'.

Just as in the Czech Republic, the Azerbaijan government was offering its citizens vouchers that they could exchange for shares in the formerly state-owned companies.

Kozeny's plan was to build up a fund of $150 million to buy vouchers and the goal was to buy the one company in Azerbaijan of interest to Western investors, the huge national oil company, SOCAR. Investors could be getting in on 'the next Kuwait', Kozeny said, declaring they could get returns of up to 100 times their investment.

By this point 'Robin Hood' had his own personal jet, a seaplane, a 165-foot yacht, a fleet of luxury cars, a 500-acre private island in the Bahamas, an oceanfront mansion in Lyford Cay with its $14 million swimming pool the size of a small lake, and a 'chalet' in Aspen, which was to be his base for luring ultra-rich investors. Last, but by no means least, he had also, seemingly almost effortlessly, acquired an extremely valuable Irish passport.

* * *

Kozeny's next-door neighbour in Aspen was Frederic Bourke, co-founder of the luxury handbag company Dooney & Bourke, who quickly fell for Kozeny's 'Irish' charms. He was to be in good company.

Dingman, who also had a home in Aspen, introduced Kozeny around the area. The list of blue-chip investors he drew into his Azerbaijan adventure included insurance giant AIG, legendary Wall Street hedge fund manager Leon Cooperman and former senator George Mitchell, who played such a key role in the Northern Ireland peace process.

Bourke and his friends put up $8 million. Richard Friedman, a Boston property billionaire who has loaned his Martha's Vineyard holiday home to former President Bill Clinton, was in for $1 million.

But the really big money came from Cooperman's hedge fund, Omega Advisors, which invested $110 million plus $15 million of Omega partners' own money. A further $15 million came from Columbia University, $15 million from AIG and $25 million from other big investors.

The investors clearly believed that Kozeny's supposedly excellent connections with the Azerbaijan President and other key decision makers would see the deal home. The fund ended up totalling $450 million, including, Kozeny claimed, 'hundreds of millions' from his own pocket.

But as time went on there was no sign of SOCAR's privatisation and the investors began to worry. Their concerns turned to outright panic when they saw a European Union report detailing the money the Azeri government had raised from the sale of privatisation 'options'. The reported figures represented a fraction of the money Kozeny had been given to purchase those options.

Kozeny has claimed he was double-crossed by the Azeris, who pocketed the missing millions in payoffs. 'They sucked us in. We got fucked and hosed,' he told one US magazine. This claim is strongly denied by the Azeris.

Whatever happened, the scheme, like most others of the get-rich-quick variety, collapsed, leaving a lot of very powerful people very disgruntled. SOCAR was not privatised and when Kozeny attempted to use some vouchers to buy a stake in a small company that was being privatised, the Azeris would not accept them.

The investors in Oily Rock Group Ltd., the name given by Kozeny to the venture, were soon branding Kozeny a crook, with some of them suing him in the Bahamas, London and the US in 1999 and 2000. A British judge froze his assets.

Kozeny had made some very powerful enemies and in 2003 he was indicted in New York on charges of stealing $182 million from investment funds managed by Cooperman's Omega Advisors. He was then indicted on a new set of related charges in New York, with prosecutors saying that he paid more than $11 million bribing Azeri officials in 1998 in relation to the anticipated privatisation of SOCAR. If convicted, Kozeny faced up to 25 years in prison.

The Manhattan District Attorney said his office was seeking Kozeny's extradition in 2003. By the summer of 2010, that had yet to happen, although Kozeny did spend over a year in Nassau's Fox Hill Prison, where he was remanded to await extradition to the US. A Bahamian court refused to grant him bail because it emerged he had six Irish passports and one each from Venezuela and the Czech Republic. However, in 2007, with the extradition proceedings running into problems, Kozeny was eventually released on $300,000 bail.

There was more good news for Kozeny in January 2010, when the Court of Appeal in the Bahamas upheld a lower court's decision to refuse the extradition request. The judge said that while Kozeny's actions were morally reprehensible, they were not illegal under Bahamian law and as a consequence were not extradition offences. The court also found that the US government's failure to disclose information that could be beneficial to Kozeny made the request an abuse of process.

The prosecutors plan to appeal this decision to the Privy Council, the final appellate court, which is based in London.

But while Kozeny remains at liberty, others associated with the Azerbaijan adventure have not been so fortunate. In late 2009 Bourke was sentenced to a year in prison and fined $1 million, under the Foreign Corrupt Practices Act in the US, for conspiring to bribe leaders in Azerbaijan.

Bourke denied knowledge of the bribes and his lawyers argued that Kozeny stole from Bourke and other investors. However, jurors found that Bourke conspired with Kozeny to bribe leaders in Azerbaijan to fast-track the sale of SOCAR.

* * *

Despite the fact that the US and the Czech authorities believe Kozeny has serious questions to answer, 'the bouncing Czech' still retains his Irish passport.

There are very narrow grounds on which Irish citizenship can be revoked. If it could be established that Kozeny has been acquiring multiple passports or that he was a citizen of another state when he received an Irish passport and did not inform the authorities of that, it may be possible for the state to revoke his Irish citizenship under section 19 of the Irish Nationality and Citizenship Act 1956.

There were reports after Kozeny's arrest that the Irish Department of Justice had been in touch with the authorities in Grenada in relation to his status there. Kozeny apparently obtained a Grenadian passport under its now-defunct economic citizenship programme and was made Grenada's honorary consul to the Bahamas. Nothing seems to have come of those inquiries.

If there are questions about why greater efforts have not

been made to revoke Kozeny's Irish passport, there are many others about how he was granted one in the first place.

Prime Time reported in 1998 that at the time Kozeny applied for an Irish passport there was an FBI file accusing him of being a KGB agent; that Kozeny was under investigation by the Czech police in relation to the controversy over the purchase of state secrets; and that he was also under investigation by the Czech Finance Ministry for unethical share dealings.

It seems that the only research carried out in Ireland was to ask the Czech authorities if Kozeny had a criminal record there. He did not. On that basis he was deemed fit to become an Irish citizen, once he stumped up the cash, of course.

It is all a long way from the original ideals of the Irish Republic. W.B. Yeats' lines in 'September 1913' spring to mind, but which is more appropriate: 'Was it for this the wild geese spread/The grey wing upon every tide' or 'But fumble in a greasy till/And add the halfpence to the pence/And prayer to shivering prayer, until/You have dried the marrow from the bone'?

Romantic Ireland, it could certainly be argued, was dead and gone the day the government put a price on the ultimate representation of Irish sovereignty, the Irish passport.

Although Kozeny remains the most extreme example of all that was wrong with the grubby 'passports for sale' scheme, he is far from the only one.

* * *

At least 178 people, including well over 50 spouses and children of investors, were naturalised under the scheme, which was established in the late 1980s.

Successive Ministers for Industry and Commerce

throughout the 1980s had advocated a scheme whereby citizenship was given to foreign nationals in exchange for investment. To be fair to those ministers, business confidence – and investment – was on the floor in what was a very difficult period for the Irish economy. Despite this, however, successive Ministers for Justice opposed the idea.

In 1986 Minister John Bruton, later to become Taoiseach, raised the idea of such a scheme to attract investment from abroad after returning from leading a trade delegation to Asia. There was correspondence between the departments but nothing came of it.

The idea was reactivated when Charles Haughey's Fianna Fáil returned to power in 1987. The following year guidelines for the scheme were brought to cabinet. The Department of Justice opposed the idea, endorsing what was presumably regarded as a rather old-fashioned notion that Irish citizenship was something that should be earned in the normal way and not something that it should be possible to buy.

Haughey, who ruled his governments with a firm hand, overruled the Department of Justice. The scheme was put in place. No regulation or legislation was required. A section of the Naturalisation and Citizenship Act 1986 allowed for the creation of the scheme. Under the section, the Minister for Justice could waive normal conditions and grant citizenship to a person who had 'Irish associations'. Normally a person would have to be living in Ireland for five years before qualifying for naturalisation.

The Haughey government drew up a 'statement of intent', which defined 'Irish associations'. It stated: 'The Minister [for Justice] will be satisfied, on the advice of a Minister of the Government, that the applicant has established a manufacturing or international services or other acceptable wealth and job-creating project here that is viable and involves a substantial investment by the applicant.'

Other conditions were that the applicant must have a 'residence' in Ireland and must be of good character. Both conditions were simply box-ticking exercises. The 'residence' requirement meant that a property had to be purchased, but not necessarily occupied. And the reader has presumably enough information at this point to assess how seriously the requirement for applicants to be of 'good character' was taken.

The size of the investment required when the scheme was first launched was £500,000. For that price, the spouse and children of an investor would also be issued with passports.

Although the establishment of the scheme was not made public, word about it began to spread in business, legal and accountancy circles.

The first passports under the scheme were issued to a number of Chinese and Hong Kong nationals in December 1988. The investors were behind the establishment of a clothing factory that employed hundreds of people in north Dublin for a number of years before it went into liquidation.

Following the general election of 1989, Fianna Fáil was joined in government by the Progressive Democrats. Bobby Molloy, a PD minister in that coalition, revealed to the *Irish Times* a number of years later that Haughey told him to bring any foreigners wishing to avail of the scheme to him. Molloy had not known of the scheme's existence before that conversation. He said the scheme was 'controlled' by Haughey.

* * *

During his tenure as Taoiseach, Haughey became involved in two controversies over the granting of Irish passports to Middle Eastern families.

The first involved the securing of an Irish passport for Kamal Fustok, a younger brother of Saudi Arabian diplomat Mahmoud Fustok, and other members of his extended family.

The Moriarty Tribunal investigated the payment in February 1985 of £50,000 by Mahmoud Fustok, a brother-in-law of Saudi Crown Prince Abdullah, to Haughey, allegedly for a horse. In its report, the tribunal concluded there were 15 inter-related applications in the 1980s for passports – all 15 applicants were relatives of, or connected to, Mahmoud Fustok.

The tribunal found that each of these applications was proposed or promoted by Dr John O'Connell, who during those years was a TD, a close associate of Haughey and, for a portion of that period, the Ceann Comhairle of the Dáil. It concluded:

> The evidence heard undoubtedly demonstrates a clear pattern of consistent and exceptional support for the applications on the part of Haughey as Taoiseach, an unvarying association with both Dr O'Connell and Fustok in respect of all the applications, and a payment of £50,000 made in approximately the middle of that period of years by Fustok to Haughey in a manner that could on no appraisal be viewed as transparent.

The report added, 'Many of these applications were granted in unsatisfactory circumstances, and in the teeth of robust departmental advices to the contrary.' The explanation advanced by Haughey for the payment – that it was a payment for a horse – was described by Moriarty as 'highly unconvincing and improbable'.

The second controversy came in December 1990. Passports were granted to eight Saudi Arabians and three Pakistanis for a promised investment of £20 million sterling. The recipients were Sheikh Khalid bin Mahfouz – owner of Saudi Arabia's only private bank and one of the world's richest men – and his family and friends.

In a highly unorthodox procedure, then Minister for Justice Ray Burke personally authorised the naturalisation certificates at his home in Swords, County Dublin, late on Saturday 8 December 1990. The normal practice was to pass the matter to a senior official, usually an assistant secretary with the delegated authority of the minister.

The passports were handed over personally by Haughey to the Mahfouz party the following day, apparently over lunch at the Shelbourne Hotel.

The story had begun in August 1990 when an English firm of solicitors had written directly to Burke at the Department of Justice with a tantalising proposal that 'an extremely wealthy Arab gentleman of Royal connections ... could make an immediate investment in the country of £100m sterling'. In a follow-up letter three days later, the solicitors identified their client as Sheikh Khalid:

> We have indicated to you that the Sheikh is extremely interested in rapidly ascertaining whether or not a waiver of the normal rules governing an application for citizenship can be applied in his case ... We believe that it is maybe in your country's interest in this case to grant special treatment because of the financial investment that this gentleman could make in your country.

Burke refused to meet representatives of Sheikh Khalid, but he did arrange for them to be put in contact with the IDA, the state agency responsible for attracting inward investment, as was standard practice.

In every other respect, however, much to the consternation of some officials in the Departments of Justice and of Foreign Affairs, the proposal appeared to be granted very special treatment.

In a clear breach of the statutory regulations, the passports were issued for the applicants (six adults and five minors) on Friday 7 December 1990, the day before the naturalisation certificates were signed. The passports' date of issue was given as 8 December, even though they were written up in the Department of Foreign Affairs on the previous day.

Other standard procedures, including the need to swear fidelity to the state, the payments of fees and the requirement that the applicants should have been resident in Ireland for about 60 days, were also put to one side.

It was more resonant of a tin-pot dictatorship than a modern, democratic republic. The new Irish citizens did not even need to swear an oath of fidelity to their new country and their passports were personally delivered by the Irish Prime Minister.

The promised investment of £100 million sterling had been scaled down by the day the passports were issued. A letter to the department from Haughey Boland – Haughey's old accountancy firm but by now part of Deloitte Touche – and signed by Sheikh Mahfouz confirmed the availability of £20 million sterling for suitable commercial concerns in Ireland. This in itself was unusual, since the government generally required that the investment should be in situ before the passports were given.

The granting of the hurriedly arranged passports did not appear in *Iris Oifigiúil* – the official state gazette – until almost two years later.

* * *

Questions were first raised about the granting of passports to Sheikh Khalid in 1994 when he became embroiled in the BCCI banking scandal. He paid $225 million to settle charges of fraud relating to the bank's collapse.

In the autumn of 1994 Gay Mitchell of Fine Gael put down a Dáil question about the circumstances in which the passports were granted. By then Haughey had been succeeded by Albert Reynolds and Burke was on the backbenches. Although the question was not reached, Minister for Justice Máire Geoghegan-Quinn, having considered the file, requested an assistant secretary in her department to review the case.

Some months later, Reynolds' Fianna Fáil/Labour government had fallen. As she prepared to leave the Department of Justice, Geoghegan-Quinn lodged a pretty stark memo on the file. 'I have read the file very carefully,' her observations began, 'and I have to say I am very concerned and alarmed about its contents.' She went on to describe the case as 'highly unusual to say the least' and noted that details about the promised investment were 'extraordinarily scanty by any standards'.

Her consideration of the file led her to conclude, 'I have some very serious concerns about the granting of naturalisation to the 11 persons in this case. If full, thorough and satisfactory answers to these concerns are not available, I am of the view that the certificates of naturalisation should, if possible, be revoked in each of the 11 cases.'

It is known that Bertie Ahern reviewed this file when he set about selecting a cabinet in November 1994 (when it looked for a few days as if he was going to be able to head up a new Fianna Fáil/Labour alliance) and again in 1997 when he did eventually become Taoiseach and made Burke his Foreign Minister.

In January 1995 the assistant secretary requested by Geoghegan-Quinn to investigate the affair reported his findings to her successor, Nora Owen of Fine Gael. The report found that Burke's decision to sign the naturalisation orders ran contrary to standard procedures in the department.

'It is the invariable practice, except in the case of honorary citizenship or a celebrity figure, for certificates to be signed at official level,' it noted. The inquiry also found that it had been possible to account through the IDA for only £3 million sterling of the promised £20 million (however, it would emerge some years later that at least some of the remaining £17 million was invested in various companies around the country, although some of this was repaid).

The report detailed how the then Secretary of the Department stated that he 'did obtain from the Department of Foreign Affairs passports for the 11 individuals on 7 December 1990 i.e. the day before the naturalisation certificates were signed'.

It also confirmed how statutory procedures governing the payment of fees, the swearing of fidelity to the state and clear evidence of connections with Ireland were not respected. It noted that the 'only evidence on the Department of Foreign Affairs file that these people are Irish citizens is a handwritten note on five of the applications that the applicants were to be naturalised'. It also identified a number of 'errors and discrepancies' in the manner in which the applications were made.

* * *

A month after the 9/11 terrorist attacks in the United States in September 2001, Mahfouz's name came up in the Dáil, with opposition TDs raising media allegations concerning the financing of al-Qaeda. The Foreign Affairs Minister Brian

Cowen confirmed the Mahfouz family passports had expired in 2000 and the question of revoking them had not arisen.

A Junior Minister at the Department of Justice, Mary Wallace, also told the Dáil that the basis of 'support for the revocation of the citizenship of Sheikh Khalid bin Mahfouz and his family would appear to be based on speculative reports in the media which are based simply on a family connection'.

Mahfouz, who died in 2009, successfully sued any publication that dared air allegations that he had funnelled money to al-Qaeda. He was often erroneously referred to as Osama bin Laden's brother-in-law – including in the Dáil.

He was a close friend of bin Laden's eldest brother, Salem, and admitted that in 1988 Salem asked him to fund the jihad against the Soviet Union in Afghanistan. 'In line with many other prominent Saudi Arabians and in accordance with US government foreign policy at the time, Khalid recalls making a donation of approximately $270,000,' stated a website set up to refute claims that he had sponsored terrorism.

* * *

The issuing of passports was also a major issue for Reynolds during his tenure as Taoiseach. In June 1994 it emerged that the Reynolds family firm, C & D Pet Foods, had benefited from a £1.1 million investment made under the passports for sale scheme. The money came from a wealthy Saudi family called Masri, and in return they had been granted Irish citizenship.

It was only then that the scheme really came to public prominence (the Department of Justice never specifically published the names of investors who had been granted passports under this scheme, instead including them in *Iris Oifigiúil* in the lists of foreign nationals who have been naturalised, although names obviously leaked out over the years).

Reynolds said he had 'no hand, act or part' in the affair. Labour Party leader, Tánaiste and Minister for Foreign Affairs, Dick Spring, declared there was nothing unethical about the deal but announced that tough new legislation would be put in place to cover the scheme.

Later in 1994, Geoghegan-Quinn announced the setting up of a new advisory group, with representatives from a number of government departments and state agencies. The group would vet investment suggestions and make recommendations to the Justice Minister.

Geoghegan-Quinn also announced that the new minimum investment would be £1 million per person to be naturalised and that the new citizen had to reside in Ireland for a minimum of 60 days in the two years after naturalisation. The new guidelines also said that state agency Forfás would monitor the investment made. She also committed to putting the scheme on a statutory basis.

This promise to introduce legislation was repeated by her successor, Nora Owen, in the new Fine Gael/Labour/Democratic Left Rainbow coalition in January 1995, when there was controversy over the granting of citizenship to two US billionaires, Kenneth and Robert Dart, heirs to the US foam cup fortune.

Approval to draft legislation was given at cabinet, but a specific legislative basis for the scheme was never put in place. And despite the commitment of the Rainbow coalition to further review the guidelines introduced after the story broke about the granting of the Masri passports, Viktor Kozeny was awarded a passport on its watch.

The Rainbow government also gave consideration in 1996

to extending the scheme to cover tourism projects. Minister for Tourism and Trade, Enda Kenny, said his department was looking at a proposal to allow wealthy foreign individuals to invest in tourism projects in return for Irish passports.

In the autumn of that year, the cabinet decided that while the processing of existing applications could continue, no new applications should be accepted pending the introduction of specific legislation to put the sale of passports on a statutory footing.

In March 1997 the Rainbow government decided that in the 19 cases on hand the previous autumn, commitments had been made, but another 50 cases were to be deferred until legislation was in place. Despite this, two months later and just before the general election, the policy was reversed and additional applications were accepted in respect of three companies based in Tralee, Ballina and Dublin. The decision was justified on the basis that it saved 500 jobs in the firms, which needed investment to stay in business. It had, of course, nothing to do with the imminent general election.

On the day before it left office in late June 1997, having lost the election, the Rainbow cabinet decided that a further application should be accepted in respect of a fourth company in the outgoing Taoiseach's constituency of Meath. It approved the substitution of an application for investment in a particular company where the original investor had withdrawn.

This was an extraordinarily relaxed approach, even if the investment was vital for the company in question. It ran contrary to civil service advice that each applicant should be treated as new and that names could not be substituted. The application was also submitted after the cut-off date of September 1996, which should have rendered it invalid.

* * *

Some years later it emerged that three members of the hugely wealthy Getty family had procured passports in 1999. Two other members of the Getty family received passports under the scheme in 1995. It is known that Irish citizenship confers significant tax advantages on US residents.

It was clear that public unease was growing and the scheme was drawing to a close. Shortly after taking office, the new Fianna Fáil/PD government announced a review of the 'passports for investment' programme and said that all applications should be deferred pending the submission of this report.

When the report was complete, Justice Minister John O'Donoghue told the Dáil that it had found that 'by and large, the main elements of the statement of intent were complied with'. However, the report revealed a number of breaches in the guidelines for the operation of the scheme set out in a statement of intent in 1989, particularly relating to the requirements on residency and evidence of good character.

The requirement of 60 days residency in the state prior to application for a passport was not complied with in 56 cases. It was adhered to in just ten. The commitment to reside in the state after naturalisation was adhered to in 17 cases and ignored in 49. The evidence of 'good character' was established in 17 cases and not in 49 others. 'By and large', it all pointed to a pretty lax regime of monitoring these new Irish citizens.

Over the period 1989 to 1994, according to the report, the range of investments made under the scheme widened from industrial development to include, for example, some property and forestry development and the shipping sector. In this period, 66 investors, plus 39 spouses and children, were naturalised.

After the new guidelines were introduced in 1994, 29

investors, plus nine spouses and children, had been naturalised. In general, the provisions of the terms of reference had been complied with, the report said.

The report revealed that the scheme brought in investment in excess of £90 million. 'It is difficult to say precisely how many jobs have been created/preserved but the information suggests that the figure is in the thousands,' it said.

It also set out the various difficulties in regulating such schemes – verifying character references for persons who have never lived in Ireland; checking whether the persons concerned have, in fact, honoured the undertaking to spend 60 days in Ireland in the two years after naturalisation; and the inability to take effective action against persons who might not honour their commitments regarding residence. It should not have taken a special report to reach those conclusions.

What was also telling was the report's investigation into which other countries gave citizenship in return for investment or direct payments to governments. In so far as the Department of Justice could tell, they were Christopher & Nevis, Tonga, Belize and Pamana. O'Donoghue, to his credit, was clearly of the view that the scheme, as constituted, should not be re-established and it was formally abolished in April 1998, although any applications that were in the system at the time were processed. Of course, it was still open for investors to seek permission to reside in the state and then later apply for naturalisation.

In Ireland, the decision to abolish the scheme was not a universally popular one. Business figures told the media that 'politicians have contaminated the scheme with the Masri and Mahfouz controversies ... It is the politicians who have damaged the scheme, not the investors. Now they are talking of knocking it on the head. That's crazy.'

Most factories concerned were in locations where the chances of finding replacement industries would be 'zilch', one non-political source who had worked on administering the scheme told a newspaper. The investors could be encouraged to make 'risky' investments.

Another source said the scheme had been 'squeaky clean' since the creation of the interdepartmental advisory committee in 1994. 'I argued very strongly early on for making it simple and transparent. If we end up scrapping it then that's stupid. Other countries have similar schemes. In my view it is a useful scheme.'

Of course, such arguments were not entirely without merit. But the counter argument is that a viable business will be able to secure investment from traditional means – a point emphasised by the fact that some of the businesses that did receive investment under the scheme closed a few years later.

And then there is the more important point about putting a price on or soliciting offers for an Irish passport, one of the essential symbols of citizenship and sovereignty.

At the time the government was considering abolishing the scheme, one London immigration service, as well as describing Irish passports as 'one of the best travel documents in the world', noted that 'as Ireland is the only EU country to offer such rapid nationalisation, this programme is usually the first choice for those that can afford it'.

If the scheme made so much sense, why was no other EU country operating a similar one? The answer is obvious. They were not willing to put a price on citizenship and sovereignty.

The fact that some of those who obtained Irish citizenship under the passports for sale scheme then brought Ireland into disrepute by their actions only emphasises how wrong the scheme was in the first place. Des O'Malley has estimated that up to half of the naturalisations were given to 'unsuitable and improper people' who had not 'fulfilled the necessary conditions'.

It was another PD leader who finally closed off any potential for reintroducing a similar passports for investment scheme. After the referendum of 2004, which ended the automatic entitlement to Irish citizenship of children born in Ireland to non-Irish parents, Justice Minister Michael McDowell brought forward the Irish Nationality and Citizenship Bill to give legal effect to the changes proposed in the referendum. A section of that bill specifically outlawed investment-based naturalisation. McDowell told the Dáil:

> The investment-based naturalisation scheme was a product of another time, when the economic climate was quite different and when there were genuinely held concerns in government and on nearly all sides of the House about the future prospects of companies and enterprises experiencing real difficulties. I do not doubt the sincerity with which the devisers of the scheme put it in place, but my reservations, in principle, about it are long held and a matter of public record. There is widespread agreement that the scheme was abused in some instances.

Citizenship, he continued, was a:

> ... complex of rights and obligations shared by people of a common nationality and a symbol of the sovereign nature of the nation state. Governments have a duty therefore to safeguard the institution of citizenship to ensure that it continues to fulfil the requirements of its role as a manifestation of a nation where membership of that nation has an intrinsic value, not just a price.

And the unavoidable conclusion is that the 'institution of citizenship' McDowell referred to was at times abused and at other times devalued by a scheme that put a price, rather than a value, on membership of the Irish nation.

* * *

We know what Viktor Kozeny paid to secure an Irish passport. What we cannot quantify is the damage that giving him an Irish passport has done to Ireland's reputation abroad.

The main argument that was put up to defend the passports for sale scheme was the protection of jobs. While no doubt genuine, this is the same argument that was put forward years earlier to defend the Irish Sweep (see Chapter 2) and years later to defend lighter regulation (see Chapter 10). Until the Irish nation starts to adopt as its starting position the belief that it is not just the rule of law, but the spirit of the law that is paramount, the same arguments will continue to be put forward and the same mistakes will continue to be made.